MW00815273

Chosen

Chosen

From the Alien Hybrid Program to the Fate of the Planet

by

Yvonne R. Smith C.Ht.
&
James P. Lough

Chosen
Third Edition
© 2023 Yvonne R. Smith C.Ht.

LEDGE MEDIA
WHERE THE LEADING MEET THE EDGE

Published by:

LedgeMedia
P. O. Box 230054
Encinitas, CA 92023
info@LedgeMedia.net
(800) 939-5311

ISBN 13: 978-1-944891-73-2

CHOSEN (1st edition) contained startling transcripts of subjects' recollections of alien abductions, which hypnotherapist Yvonne Smith unblocked via regressive hypnotherapy. The updated and expanded 2nd edition added surprising new evidence of a change in ET interactions and how they affect humanity. In this third edition, the dialogue and images remain identical with only minor changes to formatting and grammar, which has been edited to improve readability.

******

Have you ever wondered what is in your Subconscious?
Really, really wondered?

As an internationally recognized expert, Certified Hypnotherapist Yvonne Smith probes deep into her subjects' subconscious which "CHOSEN" dramatically reveals with the subjects' unedited transcripts, as Smith seeks the cause of their unexplained stress, to release them from the trauma many had needlessly suffered.

Comparing the similarities of unblocked suppressed secrets reveals why some individuals wonder…were they "CHOSEN?"

This candid exposure of their unlocked memories will rock the very core of your own reality!

Endorsements Of "*Chosen*" (2008)

Yvonne Smith's "CHOSEN" gives the reader a unique glimpse into the complexities of their lives, and Yvonne's role in facilitating their acceptance and understanding of their most unusual experiences. Abductees in "CHOSEN" give us insight, through their regressive hypnotherapy recollections revealed in actual transcripts, how they have come to confront and accept their fate.

-Kathleen Marden, Researcher, Author
Coauthor of Captured! The Betty and Barney Hill UFO Experience

******

Yvonne Smith provides invaluable assistance to abduction experiencers with her skillful use of hypnosis and her compassionate understanding and support. Her book "CHOSEN" will help others move through the pain and confusion of abduction issues and come to a place of peace and integration. She has a remarkable way of explaining the use of hypnosis in the abduction experience and showing how it deepens and opens memories within each individual. Yvonne's expertise is greatly appreciated by the Board of OPUS.

-June Steiner, President
Organization for Paranormal Understanding and Support (OPUS)

******

How does one even begin to comprehend and discuss the UFO subject? The bold answer to this question is to read "CHOSEN" by world acclaimed abduction researcher and Certified Hypnotherapist, Yvonne Smith. She has climbed the highest mountain in her presentation of alien abduction cases, capturing the complete realm of human emotions. With her vast experience, Yvonne Smith skillfully demonstrates her knowledge in bringing life to the hidden memories of abductees. "CHOSEN" is truly a testament to the world of alien abduction.

-Roger K. Leir, D.P.M.
Alien Implant Researcher

******

Yvonne Smith deftly explores abductees' fears and confusion about their extraordinary events, "CHOSEN" is about the dynamic that exists between researcher and abductee and the healing process that Yvonne Smith can provide them.

-David M. Jacobs, Ph.D., Temple University
Abduction Researcher, Author, Lecturer

Dedication

I dedicate this book to:

My mother Rose and Father Hector who have both crossed over and in spirit, as in life, continue to guide and support me.

My sister Zaquesh, who encouraged me through the writing of this book and who lovingly took care of my beautiful Maine Coon, Briana and our precious "rescue" dog, Bradley while I was engrossed in my research and travel to complete this book.

To my sons, Brandon and Brent who have been my strength, supporting me in my work for over two decades in this very difficult and complex field. I love you both...you are my gift from God.

To my writing partner, James Lough, Esq. who has selflessly devoted hundreds of hours of personal time and energy to support me, CERO and CERO International and whose courage I admire.

Budd Hopkins, whose support and friendship enabled me to use my hypnotherapy tools to assist so many victims of post-traumatic stress disorder from "close encounters." He is greatly missed.

Most of all to those CERO members who by permitting the use of their experiences may educate and assist others. And to all of the CERO members, past and present, thank you for your faithful support of my efforts to not only assist you, but your support and encouragement of others who now find themselves wrestling with the difficulties of recovered memories.

Yvonne Smith
June 2017

To Martha and Donna Lough

James P. Lough
June 2017

Preface To *"Chosen"* (2008)
By Don Schmitt, co-author *"Witness to Roswell"*

The very last time I had dinner with J. Allen Hynek was at one of his favorite restaurants in Evanston, Illinois. Hynek, the consummate astronomer that he always was, wrestled often with the vast distances between star systems and how inconceivable it was to physically travel from point A to B.

Which is why his surprising remark stays with me to this day. "Don, it's smacking more and more of nuts and bolts," Hynek had truly completed his life's mission: From the chief debunker at the Air Force Project Blue Book, which led him to an unapologetic acceptance of the UFO phenomenon, and lastly, accepting all of his colleagues he damned, that some UFOs may indeed represent someone else's physical hardware.

The question remains: what would cause a highly respected academic so deeply rooted in methodology to think beyond his rigid box. More directly, as an "old man in a hurry" as he often lamented, Hynek realized that the "how" no longer applied. The reality of the situation left him with no other conclusion-near-impossible distances withstanding. A physical phenomenon was interacting with our planet and its inhabitants.

I am sure three of the areas of research that led to Hynek's epiphany were the physical trace landing cases, report of recovery of actual hardware, and more relevant to this time, reports of UFO witnesses claiming to be abducted. It was through Dr. Hynek that I was introduced to the late Stanley V. Mitchell for assisting us in this area of UFO investigation. At that time, Mitchell was the president of the American Hypnosis Society and was credited with developing battlefield medicinal hypnosis which was implemented during the Korean War. Hynek had placed me in the most competent hand and what impressed me was Mitchell didn't allow his personal skepticism to jade his professional expectations and placed a higher stake beyond theory in the advancement of both medicine and science. To quote Professor Jacob Barnhardt in the classic movie, *The Day the Earth Stood Still*, "It isn't faith that makes good sense, it's curiosity."

Budd Hopkins once described to me the most eye-opening level of despair and helplessness in a revelation from an abductee. When asked to put into words the innermost feelings at the very time of the encounter, Hopkins was startled by the gentleman's observation, "Imagine floating out in deep space and your tether line is cut, the vacuous isolation, the absence of anything familiar, of anything earthly." For the very first time, I came to realize this may indeed represent a specter none of us had ever anticipated. The elusive phantom known as UFOs was staring us in the eye and it wasn't pretty. And no medical journal or scientific thesis provided the answers.

Even Freud, who believed traumatic events can be repressed into the inner sanctum of the mind, never envisioned that researchers such as Hynek, Mitchell, Hopkins, David Jacobs, John Mack and Yvonne Smith would open a door beyond the breath of human existence. Call it the beaconing of the stars if you will.

If there is anything I have learned by investigating what many would consider the biggest story of the millennium, by that I am referring to the Roswell Incident, by proving to myself that an actual UFO crashed in New Mexico in 1947. This seminal event makes everything else possible. If Roswell happened as I have become convinced that it did, then some abduction cases have to be real, physical experiences. The latter is simply an extension of the former.

The same hypothesis would apply to those proactive in work with abductees. My position remains steadfast: Whosoever proves the reality of the UFO phenomenon, we all win!

In reading through the personal accounts in "CHOSEN', I found myself perusing familiar territory. The patterns and commonalities are the one constant that connect so many of these searching individuals whose journey fortunately leads them to one as experienced and qualified as Yvonne Smith.

Having known Yvonne for over twenty years, I have witnessed time and time again how she puts these "victims" before her own well-being and personal health. Their pursuit for the truth becomes hers and together they explore the inner chambers of the UFO abduction experience which at times has robbed them of their earthly security blanket. Their situations are reminiscent of my own case studies with "black widow spiders in bedroom windows" which turn out to be eyes and the work crew up ahead on the road "who were all too short."

For many, the initiation is different. Sadly, the final outcome is all too predictable. Thankfully, these "chosen" have a respite with Yvonne. Observing her professionalism seasoned with a selfless concern for administering to this rare selection of people who may indeed have touched the very cold of space itself.

Even though Yvonne would probably remark that her foremost interest is the raw data, I have seen otherwise. She strives to enable these earthbound "space travelers" to rediscover their inner peace. To take back that which was snatched from their very psyche and proceed into the future-enlightened yes, but more importantly, secured by the touch of a caring hand and comforting word. Clearly, all of those entrusted to Yvonne Smith's counsel not only have found a friend for life, but more importantly, someone who is not afraid to pull back the curtain and say "boo" to the boogeymen.

Foreword By Grant Cameron

A couple of years back I received a message from prominent UFO experiencer, Chris Bledsoe. He told me that the aliens he had encountered, who he refers to as "The Guardians," told him to contact me. They told him to tell me that "the message is in the music" and that I should begin by looking at a couple of songs.

The Guardians must have known that I was a musical idiot who did not even listen to music, because in their message was a hook that ended up dragging me down the rabbit hole. The hook was that one of the songs they mentioned as containing a message was "*After the Gold Rush,*" by singer-songwriter, musician, producer, director and screenwriter, Neil Young, who had grown up in the city of Winnipeg, the same Canadian city where I grew up and still reside. Had it not been for this synchronicity, which the aliens obviously knew about, I may have never taken the bait.

A quick review of the lyrics to Young's song presented a haunting and surreal message about Mother Nature being "on the run." The lyrics appear to warn of a future environmental apocalypse caused by our treating the natural world like a gold rush and when the gold is all gone, the Earth will become a ghost town. At that point, flying saucers will arrive to take people to another planet.

The final lines of the song (written in 1970 when the only publicly known abduction case was Betty and Barney Hill) completely parallel the message given to 37% of UFO experiencers who participated in a massive survey conducted by the Foundation for Research into Extraterrestrial Encounters ("FREE"). These experiencers claim that the beings they dealt with warned them of natural catastrophe or depopulation of humanity in the future.[1]

More hauntingly, the final lines of the song also parallel statements by many experiencers that there will be some sort of dramatic event and that they will play a role during these events. Almost 85% of experiencers in the FREE survey stated that they believed they had a "mission or important task to do but not necessarily knowing where the compulsion comes from."[2] That may be why at least a half dozen major musicians, who

---

[1] "COMPLETE Phase 2, Questions 1-257 (Anonymous) - FREE Survey," http://etletstalk.com/members/wp-content/uploads/2015/12/Phase-2-English-Summary-Data-No-Emails-No-Names-PDF-Pie-Charts-December-9-2015-CutOff-Date.pdf

[2] *Ibid.*

appear to be experiencers, almost like a moth to the flame, have also recorded versions of Neil Young's *"After the Gold Rush."*

Of all the words in the musical message in Neil Young's song given to me by Bledsoe's Guardians, one jumped out at me. That word was "*chosen.*" I immediately remembered that Yvonne Smith had written a book about "Experiencers" called *Chosen.* Yvonne Smith has always been ahead of the game in her understanding of the UFO experience, because those who have encountered the intelligence behind the UFO phenomena are indeed chosen. We now know that UFO abduction is not a random event. It is something that starts in early childhood and doesn't appear to cease. Whatever the nature of the events, experiencers are lifers.

There are two schools of thought on being chosen. One is the male left-brain, rational, analytical, competition-oriented paradigm, which has many supporters. In this model, researchers see the experiencer as a victim of an extraterrestrial race with self-serving motives. In this model, the experiencer plays no participatory role. The other is the female right-brain, creative and existential view, which is much more focused on the experiencer than the aliens. Yvonne Smith is the pioneer in a wave of women who have begun to research alien abduction. The research has led to a more right-brained holistic, intuitive, and compassionate reframing of what experiencers are reporting.

Yvonne Smith understands that if we are ever to get an answer to the UFO mystery, it will come through the accounts of the experiencers themselves. This is where Yvonne has invested her research efforts.

It will not come from watching lights in the sky, but by listening carefully to experiencers who are interacting with the intelligence behind the phenomenon, and helping them access memories and messages that have been placed in their subconscious minds.

This idea has recently been reinforced by James Semivan, a former CIA briefer to the President of the United States, who with his wife encountered beings in their bedroom in the 1990s. He talked about how his personal experience with the beings had shattered his understanding of reality, when he stated, "The measured and linear approach is arguably laughable. How do you make sense of any of it when there does not appear to be any apparent 'there' there?" As Yvonne has pointed out many times, the phenomenon is much more complex than aliens flying around in tin cans.

Yvonne realizes that if an answer is to be found, the experiencers have it, and since 1991 she has hosted experiencer support groups for the chosen. Based on her model, I set up an experiencer support group in Canada which now has organizations in two cities to support experiencers, and we help them explore and search for answers to what has happened to them.

It was while attending one huge experiencer support group, which Yvonne was leading, at the UFO Congress in Phoenix, Arizona, that I realized the importance of the work Yvonne was doing. People came from all over the country to sit in a back room of the conference center and tell their stories, much like closeted gays of the 1960s did, taking their first steps into the light.

During one session in a very crowded room, one woman began with what sounded like a victim statement. She mentioned how she believed the people at the conference really didn't care about the experiencers in the back room. She spoke about the loneliness and lack of support Experiencers receive from the UFO community.

Having had my own experiences, and after four decades trying to understand what I first saw in 1975, I shared with the woman and the rest of the group an idea which came to me and was so meaningful that I sometimes think it came from somewhere else. I told the group that there is no doubt the UFO story, when it is fully understood, will be the greatest story in human history—the SuperBowl of all stories.

I reminded the group that no matter how difficult their experience was, they were chosen to be in the stadium where the SuperBowl plays out. They could have been picked to be untouchables in the streets of Calcutta, India, and spend their days in the junk yard looking for something valuable enough to sell, so they could have food for tomorrow, but they were not chosen for that.

Experiencers, I reminded them, have been picked to play in the SuperBowl of all stories. They may not know whether they are the quarterback or the waterboy, but they are in the stadium playing in the big game. Playing in the most important game on Earth makes experiencers perhaps the most important people in the world to listen to. In 500 years, they will be the lucky ones who got to walk with Jesus, or be involved in the signing of the United States Constitution.

The stories in this updated *Chosen* are the reports from experiencers detailing, as best they can, their role in the big game. The FREE survey shows that 75% of experiencers believe they were given "telepathic or thought transference, or direct knowing," given to them by an ET; 37% claim that at one point in their experience they knew the answer to everything in the universe. This indicates that all the answers we seek may be stored somewhere in their minds. This knowledge may be available to us if people like Yvonne can find the password to hack into what they were told.

Having carefully researched the U.S. government and the coming disclosure that we are not alone in the universe, I know that in the last year, the program is speeding up inside the government to get out the message. I am told from multiple sources that there are many teams, which appear to be operated by contractors connected to the CIA, racing to acclimatize the masses to the idea that we are not alone. I hear the same tone of "urgency" as Yvonne describes in Part Two of this book. Perhaps the government is being pushed by the same "shift in the alien program" detailed by Yvonne. After 42 years of research into UFOs, I can attest that there is a quickening.

Readers should digest every word in this updated version of *Chosen* with care, as these stories contain key clues in answer to the UFO mystery. Yvonne Smith is on the leading edge of this wonderful mystery and has been chosen to help broadcast the big game. She is in the stadium talking to the players and every observation she makes should be recorded for history.

I am proud to call Yvonne Smith a research colleague and a friend. The discoveries Yvonne details in this updated version of *Chosen* will become the basis of textbooks on the subject in the future when the truth of the UFO mystery is finally revealed. It is a must-read for people seeking answers to what is really going on.

Grant Cameron
Winnipeg, Canada
May 2017

Introduction To "*Chosen*" (2008)
"My Personal Journey"

At age 16, I was excited to have a studio contact me and ask me to participate on the popular television program, *The Dating Game*. Me? On television? Of course, I was eager to accept a seemingly once in a lifetime opportunity to appear on television. At that time, it was far beyond the wildest of imaginations that I would eventually become a hypnotherapist, have hundreds of clients suffering trauma from close encounters, that such a subject would become so popular and of great interest that I would be called upon to discuss this subject on several television talk shows and weekly programs.

I was born in Los Angeles, California and grew up in a comfortable loving home with a typical daily routine. Dad would go to work with a lunch bag Mom had prepared. Mom would then hand lunch bags for my sister, Zaquesh and me, walk us to the school bus stop and wait for the bus to take us to the Catholic school we attended. Mom would then clean the house and do the family laundry. Then at 3:00 p.m., Zaquesh and I would return home from school, have an after-school snack and do our piles of homework. Of course, with a Catholic upbringing there was no meat to be eaten on Friday and we attended mass every Sunday.

I enjoyed my carefree childhood, my family and activities and assumed that the next stage of my life would involve marriage, parenting and homemaking. Such a life was taken for granted at that time. Little did I know what unusual and dramatic involvements lay ahead.

When I attended John Marshall High School, some of my friends were members of the sports teams or cheerleaders. I was the school mascot! A barrister! Upon graduation from high school, several of my friends and I thought it would be a good idea to obtain jobs with an airline so we could take advantage of the travel benefits. However, that never happened for me. I was hired by the Los Angeles Superior Court system where I spent the next 10 years as a supervisor for prospective jurors. While there, I met my husband who was an attorney practicing in Los Angeles. We had two sons, Brandon and Brent and my anticipated career as a mother and homemaker began.

During this early family life, I found a book that my mother had given me before I married, but activities with my young sons kept me from reading. The book was UFO investigator Ann Druffel's "*The Tujunga Canyon Contacts*". Her book discussed the use of hypnosis to unravel two women's terrifying story of a UFO visitation and their abduction. I finally read it and the experiences recounted by the two women impressed me.

While the book's subject matter involved abduction by aliens, at that time, I was more impressed by the discussion of using hypnotherapy to assist people suffering from post-traumatic stress experiences. Until that time, I was not familiar with the concept of "post-traumatic stress disorder" (PTSD). Furthermore, I had never understood that hypnosis had a legitimate medical use and was not simply a tool used by entertainers to make people bark like a dog or quack like a duck!

Following up with some research about hypnosis, I found that the American Medical Association and several highly respected medical schools had accepted its medical use and its benefits for many years. I was surprised to also find cases in which hypnosis was used in place of anesthesia during surgery.

This new information about hypnotherapy, combined with programs I saw on television described the trauma suffered by victims in post-traumatic stress situations. It gave me a new interest: while my boys were attending school, why don't I take hypnosis classes? I researched hypnosis schools and luckily found the only accredited hypnotherapy college in the United States, The Hypnosis Motivation Institute...only thirty minutes from home. So, I enrolled. After dozens of classes and hundreds of clinically supervised internship hours, I excitedly attended graduation with my proud family to observe. I received my Certificate of Hypnotherapy diploma!

Soon after graduation, I received a phone call from my mom asking if I would accompany her to a *Whole Life Expo* event scheduled in nearby Pasadena, California. The *Expo* included presentations not only by health experts, which mom believed I would enjoy due to my interest in hypnotherapy, but also included presentations of the paranormal. In fact, one lecturer was none other than pioneer abduction researcher, Budd Hopkins!

We attended the Expo and in the exhibition hall, my mom suddenly grabbed my arm and exclaimed under her breath... "That's him...that's Budd Hopkins!" He was walking directly toward us! Not being the shy type, my mother called to him, "Mr. Hopkins!" He immediately stopped and turned to her with a pleasant smile at being recognized. My mom told him how much she enjoyed his book, *Missing Time* and how much she respected and accepted his ufological theories. The polite and gracious demeanor of this handsome gentleman so impressed me that I was eager to hear his presentation. Little did I know at that time; Budd Hopkins would play a very important role in my future career.

We attended his lecture and my mom and I were struck by how many of his clients involved UFO abductions. The abduction aspect of his presentation was very dramatic, but at that time, my greater interest was his description of hypnotherapy used to relieve his subjects of the trauma they attributed to "*close encounters.*" During my post-graduation days, I continued working at the clinic of HMI while I built my own practice. At the clinic, my hypnotherapy knowledge was used primarily for weight loss, smoking cessation, individuals who continued to be traumatized by childhood abuse as well as cancer patients.

As I developed my private clientele, I continued my involvement with the smoking and weight loss therapy as well as relieving my cancer patients of their fear and anxiety. Local medical doctors, psychiatrists and psychologists began referring patients to me who continued to suffer from trauma without improvement. They felt their patients would benefit from hypnotherapy. As I worked more and more with PTSD victims, I noted that many of them attributed their trauma to a possible UFO encounter. It amazed me that their recollection of details described during our sessions were remarkably similar as they formed a pattern...and these clients have never met.

I considered it meaningful that these clients who were referred to me had been "pre-screened" by their doctors...their tests results in the "normal" range, displaying no signs of "psychosis" or "fantasy prone" tendencies as well as sincere in their experience descriptions. I was equally impressed by their sincerity and precise description of details while under hypnosis. Further, I became more and more concerned with their traumatized emotional state which manifested itself during hypnotherapy with uncontrollable crying, shaking, anger and sometimes profane language. There were moments they exhibited extreme fear and though hypnotized, attempted to jump from the couch and run away from the event they were reliving.

I realized that once my clients left my office, they felt isolated. Who do they talk to? Many were not able to confide in a spouse, significant other or a family member. It was then that I founded "Close Encounter Research Organization" (*CERO*) for the purpose of providing continued personal attention and a safe environment for clients to safely express themselves during the monthly support group meetings.

The more I became involved in my practice in working with "Experiencers/Abductees," I began to receive invitations for lectures, panel discussions as well as television and radio interviews along with many of my CERO members. These brave souls wanted to reach out to those who might be watching to let them know there is help and they are not alone...the way they once felt.

In *CHOSEN*, I am providing the public with excerpts of actual transcripts of emotional, dramatic and traumatic recollections of encounters described by my clients during hypnotic regression. Read these startling and unedited transcripts taken from actual hypnotic regression sessions. People from all walks of life, socioeconomic and ethnic backgrounds. They could be your co-workers, family members, your doctor, dentist, teacher, lawyer, etc., etc., etc. People who have no reason to make up such stories and in fact, would have more to lose than gain to perpetrate such a situation.

Read their stories and their transcripts carefully...then you decide.

INTRODUCTION

In 2008, I published my first book, *Chosen*. It focused on the challenges faced by nine people who were dealing with the trauma of abduction experiences. Of those whom I saw around this time, some were referred by mental health professionals who were incapable of dealing with this unique type of trauma. My practice had begun helping people lose weight and quit smoking. However, over time, my openness to see people that, at the time, were having unheard of experiences began to snowball.

Since I knew of no one around who was dealing with these issues at the time, I sought out other persons who were helping this ignored group of people. I wanted to collaborate on methods and procedures to both recover memories without influencing them and to help these people cope with the trauma in their daily lives. I began working with Dr. John Mack, Professor of Psychiatry at Harvard University; Budd Hopkins, artist and author of seminal books such as *Missing Time*; and Dr. David Jacobs, Assistant Professor of History at Temple University. With them, I took part in the first academic conference on the subject at Massachusetts Institute of Technology in 1992.

The Conference was a revelation. It helped me understand that I was not alone. While I had read about others in the field and had one-to-one contacts, it was the first time that I was able to work with these pioneers in a collaborative environment. The Conference also had brave Experiencers who stepped forward to tell about their experiences. They were experiencing the same phenomenon as my Close Encounter Research Organization (CERO) members back in California. I returned to my practice with newfound purpose.

The original edition of *Chosen* chronicled the life experiences of several CERO members, including two friends who were taken at the same time and separately recounted their experiences. Their experiences followed similar patterns that likely revolved around the "hybrid program" where cross breeding of our two-species seemed to be the goal. The incidents covered in the original *Chosen* mostly occurred in the 1990s to early 2000s. While my fellow researchers offer different explanations of the ultimate goals of the ET[3] hybrid program and their ultimate motives, I preferred to help the Experiencers cope with the trauma of their interactions and leave the

---

[3] We use the term "ET" to denote who is contacting the individual being discussed. ETs contacting humanity may all be working off the same Agenda or there may be variations between groups. This book refers to ET only in the context of interactions with non-human entities by the Experiencers discussed herein.

theorizing to others. In that sense, the original *Chosen* was a "nuts and bolts" view of the abduction phenomenon.[4]

Since the publication of *Chosen*, I continued to work with CERO members and others helping them cope with the trauma caused by their experiences. I published a second book, *Coronado* (2014) that took more than fifteen years to research and write. It was about the experiences of CERO members who were part of a mass abduction at a 1994 Conference in Coronado, California. It took a while to piece together the experiences of people who separately recounted their involvement in one of the largest mass abductions ever chronicled. Each recounted detail that corroborated the experiences relayed by others. Significantly, President Bill Clinton was staying next door at a private residence when the mass abduction occurred. Whether he or any of his Secret Service detail were witnesses or unwilling participants is a mystery to this day.

While *Coronado* analyzed a "mass abduction," the details of each person's experience fit the general pattern of abduction for medical/hybrid program purposes. The pattern, in many ways, mimicked that discussed in *Chosen*. The pattern, with some exceptions, has continued for most of the length of my practice. However, in about 2011, I noticed a momentous change in the pattern reported by Experiencers.

While most Experiencers were still seeking my help to unlock the causes of their trauma, an ever-increasing group of people were asking for my help to find out "what they were supposed to do." Each was either aware they were Experiencers through conscious recollection or, after going through my screening program, were likely to have had ET interactions. Each used almost the same phrases such as "I want to know what I am supposed to do" or "I need to do something." They came to seek my help to unravel this mystery in their lives. Besides new members, I was hearing the same refrain from long-time members who were sharing these "urges" with me. Many were getting "messages" of planetary destruction or other possible catastrophes. Some were anxious over their feelings that they are to play a role in future events but they are unsure about the events or what role they are to play.

In the past, some Experiencers have had these feelings. However, the number of these Experiencers who are coming forward with these intense feelings is far more frequent today than in the past. The changes in the numbers of experiencers coming forward with these messages was dramatic. At Experiencer Sessions at Conferences, it was and still is the most common trait shared among Experiencers. While my professional

---

[4] We use terms such as "abduction", "experience", "abductee", and "Experiencer" interchangeably. Yvonne's goal has been to help the person cope with the anxiety and trauma of their experiences and leave the labeling to them. Each person must deal with having been chosen in their own way.

colleagues around the world may disagree about the meaning of these changes, almost all agree that something is happening.

This updated version of the original *Chosen* has two purposes. The first part retells the stories of the experiencers that were the subject of the original *Chosen*. The retelling of their experiences will help illustrate the nature of the phenomenon as we have known it for the past six decades back to the seminal case of Betty and Barney Hill in the early 1960s.

The second part of this updated version will discuss the change in emphasis seen by many Experiencers since the publication of my last two books. Either conveyed through virtual reality screens on ships; through neural engagement by an ET staring into the eyes of an Experiencer; or through non-local "downloads," Experiencers are getting messages of some impending crisis that they are likely to play a role in assisting Earth's inhabitants. The first Chapter in Part Two is an introduction to the shift in emphasis I am seeing from many Experiencers. The Chapter also talks about similar findings from other investigators.

The remainder of Part Two highlights a few Experiencers and goes into depth about their "urgency" and how it came about. My co-author, James Lough, discusses his recent urgency "to do something" and the path he has taken because of these messages.[5] Another Chapter chronicles Debbie Archer and her "urgency" issues. She is one of those who have been experiencing interactions for decades but now is part of this "shift" in focus. Finally, we put together some concluding thoughts on what this all means. We offer some theories put forward by other researchers and experiencers. The theories about what is happening are as diverse as the phenomenon itself. Each postulate about what has been going on in the last several years and how it fits into the possible agenda of ET.

This updated version has been difficult to bring forward. Many of the messages put forward by Experiencers who feel this "urgency" are not pleasant. While the recent events in politics have been tumultuous, this book is based on the experiences of those who interact with ET more closely than any others. Their messages pre-date the recent political turmoil and are quite sobering. While many in the researcher community have developed their own theories about the ET Agenda, good, bad or indifferent. I have left these theories to others and worried about the people I try to help. However, I cannot see hiding what I and others have found in the urgent messages so many have been given. Knowledge is something that should not be hidden. Judge for yourself what it means.

---

[5] Each Chapter in Part Two will have a note indicating its authorship. Yvonne Smith wrote Part One, which includes most of the chapters from the original edition.

PART ONE

CHOSEN
For the
Hybrid Program

CHAPTER 1: Laci And Loretta

**"Planes are not supposed to fly that low!
That's not a ****ing plane!"**

A. Laci And Loretta Explore Shared "Missing Time"

In the early summer of 1993, I received a call from Alice Leavy, a Mutual UFO Network ("MUFON") investigator. She wanted help with a sighting report from two women who had experienced several hours of "missing time" following their sighting. "Missing time" is where a person has memory loss and cannot recall anything for a fixed period. Alice was aware of my hypnotherapy practice that mostly dealt with people who wished to break an unhealthy habit, like smoking. She thought that it might help with determining what happened to the witnesses during the simultaneous gap in their memory. Hypnotherapy is often useful in recovering memories and she thought that the two women might be able to gain insight into their missing memories through hypnotic regression. Based on my interest in the subject matter, I listened to Alice's request with interest. I agreed to schedule separate consultations with the two women to begin the process for possible hypnotic regression.

My initial interviews were set up to see if they were appropriate candidates for hypnotic regression. The process includes an interview about their general background to look for issues indicating whether that hypnotic regression may not be appropriate. At the interviews, each separately told me about themselves. Based on my review of their backgrounds and state of mind, they appeared to be normal adults who had just experienced something unusual.

Laci was born on a California army base. She was raised in a typical middle-class family with her older brother and sister. Considering her family's military background, I would have expected her to have a formal demeanor. However, when I met her she was casually dressed in jeans and T-shirt. This turned out to be typical of her down-to-earth nature. At the time, she was married with two sons and a daughter. She ran a home day care center. Laci impressed me as a happy person who had an active and loving home life. I found no "red flags" that would make me hesitant to recommend hypnotic regression.

The same was true of Loretta. She had a background that is typical of today's world. Loretta was born in Iowa and had an older brother and a younger sister. When she was five, her family moved to California where her parents divorced. Despite her parent's divorce, nothing in her background indicated anything out of the ordinary. When I met her,

2

Loretta was a single mother of three daughters. She was a college graduate and had been a graphic artist. Prior to our initial interview, she decided on a career change and enrolled in law school. When we met, she was attending law school part time, working and raising three children. Between raising her children, working and attending classes, Loretta's life was very full.

Laci and Loretta lived near each other in Southern California. They met when Laci began taking care of Loretta's three children in her daycare. They saw each other every day and developed a friendship. The two became lifelong friends.

Loretta had a limited interest in UFOs. She would read articles about MUFON meetings in her local paper. The local MUFON Chapter held meetings at a local library. She was curious about the UFO subject, but too embarrassed to attend a meeting alone. After all, "it's a meeting about UFOs!" she exclaimed to me. In November 1992 Loretta asked Laci if she would like to attend a meeting with her. Laci accepted. She was interested about going to "a UFO" meeting and it gave her an opportunity to get out of the house. A "girl's night out" was something she rarely did while raising young son and running an in-home daycare.

During the initial interviews, they both remembered arriving at the MUFON meeting at 7:30 p.m. and watching two 45-minute movies, which were followed by a 20-minute break. Following the break, the meeting organizers were about to present a third movie, however Laci and Loretta became concerned that they had each told their families they would be home no later than 10:00 p.m.

Loretta could not see the clock from where they were seated so she turned around and asked the lady sitting behind her for the time and was told it was 9:30 p.m. Meanwhile, Laci noticed that the gentleman next to her was wearing a digital watch so she asked him for the time. He also said it was 9:30 p.m. They both decided to leave the meeting to get home on time.

During their separate interviews, they both commented on how cold it was. It was the week before Thanksgiving, it was a crisp, clear and starlit night. They got into Loretta's car and began the 20-minute drive home. Loretta started driving north on Highway 101, one of Southern California's busiest freeways. After driving a very short distance, they both saw an intense light in the sky. They both recalled that because it struck them as very funny Laci had commented: "Oh, isn't that strange, we just leave a MUFON meeting and now we see this giant light in the sky!"

They each remembered that while approaching a freeway overpass, Loretta said to Laci, "It looks like a plane," and that Laci then became very upset saying that planes are not supposed to be flying that low.

3

Loretta said Laci commented that, since her father was a pilot in the military she grew up around airports, she knew planes are not supposed to fly so low over a populated area. They similarly commented that everything had happened so fast from the time they both saw the bright light above the overpass to when it descended underneath the overpass they were driving towards.

In separate pre-hypnosis interviews, they each described similar details of their sighting. After comparing notes and the audio tapes of their separate interviews, their collective memories of the object that flew under a freeway overpass were consistent throughout.

During my interview with Laci, she stated she emphatically told Loretta: "That is not a plane!" Laci remembered Loretta replying: "Then it must be a helicopter." In response, Laci relayed that she corrected Loretta: "Helicopters wouldn't go underneath the bridge (overpass) because of the propellers!"

Laci tried to make sense of what they were seeing. Both conveyed that they were confused that they could not see a shape but only a bright light, which illuminated the overpass. It appears that light was coming straight at them! Laci said she rolled down the window and screamed obscenities. Laci told Loretta: "I don't hear any sound, that's so strange. Oh God, we are going to crash!"

As she described the events, Laci was agitated. She said that it was a wide freeway with four lanes of traffic going in each direction. When Loretta moved to the fast lane, Laci commented to her that the light appeared to be pacing their car. As Laci explained to me, she said:

> "The freeway was wider than just two lanes. And, as we changed lanes going to the left. The light moved with us. Not after us and not before us…but in the same motion. I don't remember anything about that light after that." Laci did not remember the light going away. The next thing Laci remembers is exiting off the freeway. They took the exit several miles past the exit for their homes without knowing why they had driven past their regular exit. Laci said she asked Loretta to stop at a grocery store because she "had the munchies."

She described an unusual setting when she entered the store:

> "…what was really strange was the two people at the checkout stand. There's a bag boy and a…and a checkout girl. They're standing there like they have nothing to do, all

4

the time in the world. There's nobody in the store which is kind of weird, 'cause those are busy stores. It's maybe ten to ten. We get our stuff, check out. And as we're coming out the door we came in, there's a big clock over the door. The clock said a quarter to midnight! The time just shocked us. We looked at each other, saying, Oh My God, what happened! We gotta get home, we're late!"

Laci told me: "I didn't put two and two together." In her separate interview, Loretta told me Laci had excitedly commented about the bright light not passing them but, rather, that "...the light moved with us." Loretta also stated that Laci stopped screaming at the light as soon as it disappeared...and that, "...the last thing I remember (*of the bright light*) is this thing mirroring our car, equal distance with our car."

Loretta recalled next remembering that the window that had been down was now rolled up. Laci lit a cigarette and was sitting there really calm and Loretta sensed that it was as if Laci was confused but trying to understand what had happened. Realizing she had passed their off ramp, Loretta said she turned the car around and headed back home. After exiting the freeway, Loretta said Laci asked her to stop at a market, since she was craving some junk food. Loretta stopped at the grocery store and went into the store with Laci.

Once in the store Loretta said they looked around and noticed that they were the only people in the grocery store. Loretta said:

> "What was really strange, there was nobody in the parking lot and the checkers were standing around. And it was closing, that store doesn't close until midnight! There was nobody in the store and this was the Wednesday before Thanksgiving! There are always people shopping at 9:30 p.m. the night before a holiday!"

When Laci and Loretta arrived at their homes, both families were very concerned. It was after midnight when they got home. They had said they would be home by 10:00 p.m.

After that night, Laci and Loretta refused to talk about it, even with each other. They separately described being traumatized and having bouts of depression. Laci complained of crying fits for about a month following the incident. Loretta had panic attacks, heart palpitations, crying, screaming. Loretta had the feeling that she was going to die every time she approached a freeway overpass while driving.

5

Both women made appointments with their doctors and each were prescribed antidepressants. Loretta's doctor diagnosed her with post-traumatic stress disorder (*PTSD*). She told me that his diagnosis confused her, she could not figure out what traumatic event she could possibly be suffering from. The antidepressants did not help Loretta. But, why should it? After all, she had only seen a bright light.

Having received no benefit from doctor's visits, Laci and Loretta sought help from non-traditional sources. They contacted the local MUFON representative to learn about the experiences of other people who have had "missing time" episodes. Traditional medicine did not give them any answers so they looked to others who have evaluated these strange episodes that UFO researcher Budd Hopkins was doing pioneering research at the time. The MUFON representative recommended that they contact Yvonne Smith.

B. Laci's Recollections During Hypnosis

After Laci and Loretta had gone through the initial consultation process, both decided to separately undergo hypnotic regression to learn what had happened on November 20, 1992 during their "missing time" on the freeway. On August 24, 1993, Laci and Loretta, along with the two MUFON investigators arrived at my home office to begin hypnotic regression. Laci decided to go first. I provided refreshments for the others while they waited in my living room.

As Laci made herself comfortable on my couch as I began pre-hypnotic relaxation "mantra" which led her responsively into a hypnotic trance. I gently guided Laci's subconscious mind back to that very cold night of November 20, 1992. Laci first describes her conscious recollections of attending the meeting and leaving when she and Loretta became concerned about the time. The following is her recollections under hypnosis about leaving the MUFON meeting:

> Laci: It's 9:30 p.m., back to the car. So cold and clear. Which way did we come? Oh, we have to go to the left, this is the ramp. Loretta's just talking about her kids.

After a long pause.

> Laci: Ah! It's a huge light!
> Yvonne Smith ("YS"): Where do you see the light?
> Laci: It's over the freeway, I can't see…it's too bright, so bright! Loretta should move, change lanes!

At this point, Laci begins to bring forward memories from her subconscious that she did not "consciously" remember.

> Laci: It's like we're going so slow, like she's not even pushing on the gas. It's like everything stopped. NO! NO!

Laci began to become very agitated and began to cry.

> YS: Remember, now you're safe, you're just exploring now. And whatever happened, you came out of it. Now take a deep breath and just tell me what you're feeling.
> Laci: Somebody's trying to open the door and I'm trying to hold the door closed! I can't control this, I don't see anyone open the door! OH! Loretta's door is open! She's not in the car anymore!

Laci's body tensed, and she struggled for words to describe what she "saw," indicating she was having great difficulty with the memories that were coming forward. This was a painstaking session, but I knew that I had to guide Laci through what may have happened to her that night, even if the memories were frightening.

> YS: Where did Loretta go?
> Laci: I don't know! The dash lights are on, her door is open!

YS: Do you see Loretta anywhere?
Laci: The light is so bright I can't see outside.
YS: Where is the light?
Laci: In front of me (*crying*).
YS: You're doing fine, when you verbalize it, you're going to feel much relief. Just tell me what happens.
Laci: Standing in front of the car, Loretta's standing next to me (*crying*).
YS: Loretta's next to you? Just tell me what's happening, Laci, you're doing fine."
Laci: I don't know how to explain it! I don't know where we are!
YS: You're not standing in front of the car anymore?
Laci: NO! (*crying*)
YS: Can you describe your surroundings?
Laci: It's cold, I wanna go home! (*crying*)

At this point during her session Laci kept screaming that she wanted to go home. I continued to calm Laci down by using verbal directions, instructing her to focus on my voice. Slowly during this session, Laci began to break through her blocked memory.

Laci: Something's holding my head down! (*she was crying, not wanting to open her eyes*)
YS: OK, I'm going to count to three, and when I do, you are going to be able to just take a quick look and describe where you are, and then, you can close your eyes again. One, two, and three, Laci, what do you see around you?
Laci: Oh, no! No! No! No! No! No! No!

Laci just about jumped off my couch, crying and screaming that she wanted to go home. When my clients begin to relive the trauma, I always tell them that I am going to touch their hand or arm, for instance, to help relieve some of the fear. So, I laid my hand on her shoulder.

YS: Tell me what's happening, I'm touching your arm, tell me what's happening.
Laci: I don't know! I've never seen anything like that!
YS: Just describe it.
Laci: It's cold! God, he looks like a spider! Let me go! (*crying and hysterical*)

8

I began telling Laci to take deep breaths and informed her that she will be able to describe everything without experiencing the fear.

> Laci: It's huge, this thing, this huge head!

Then, Laci just about stopped in mid-sentence, as if in amazement:

> Laci: There's Loretta.
> YS: Where's Loretta?
> Laci: She's standing on a bridge, she's on this bridge…inside this room, …and she's watching me and they have her against the wall, and she can't move! She's crying.

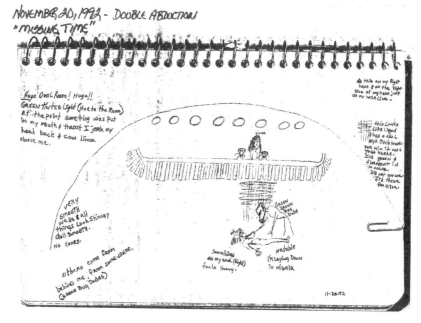

At this point, Laci reported that she was back in the car.

> Laci: (*crying again*) They said they would come back. I don't know why they're gonna come back! I don't know why!

I suspected that when Laci told me that she was back in the car, she was not ready to continue exploring. She had been in hypnosis for about an hour, so I decided to bring Laci back to the present time, so she can relax and reflect on what came forward. When I brought Laci out of hypnosis, she was still crying, and with her great sense of humor, she chuckled through her tears, saying "I think the main line busted."

I enjoyed a laugh with her, which released the tension for both of us. During the debriefing, I asked Laci how she was doing. Laci told me that she felt "good," but that she was "surprised at the emotion level." "I was so...I was so emotional. I'm remembering things that I don't even know what they were...how do you articulate something if you don't know it?" With that said, Laci went outside for, according to her, "a well-deserved smoke."

C. Loretta's Recollections During Hypnosis

When I asked Loretta if she was ready for her first session, she said she was very nervous but, at the same time, was very anxious to explore the hidden memories she believed had been causing her so much anxiety. Because Loretta was apprehensive, I sat down with her and began the session by explaining the benefits of hypnosis and dispelling the myths. After I wrote down a few details about the night in question, I began the process of hypnotic regression.

Once she was in a hypnotic trance, Loretta began to relive the night she and Laci attended the MUFON meeting, and, as Laci had expressed in her first session, Loretta became concerned about the late hour since she had also told her family that she would return home no later than 10:00 p.m. She described that when she and Loretta left the meeting at 9:30 p.m. They got into her car and headed for the freeway.

> Loretta: It's beautiful outside, cold, lots of stars. It's 9:30 and we have to go to Von's (*grocery store*) first, have to buy one thing at Von's. I have to be home by 10:00. I'm getting on the freeway.

She pauses as if trying to analyze what she is seeing.

> Loretta: I see this star looking at us. Gets real big, real fast, coming at us. Then I hear Laci say, Oh My God! This can't be happening! We're laughing, right after our first MUFON meeting!

Loretta pauses again, and very quiet, almost in a whisper:

> Loretta: Nobody else is on the freeway. Why is nobody on the freeway? Laci is screaming. I tell her it's just a

plane. Laci screams, it's no f....ing plane, what the hell is it? Laci rolls down the window, screaming and yelling that it is not making any noise! We're going to crash! Why are there no cars? Got to get out of the way, switch lanes. I'm in the fast lane. Oh, my God!

As though Loretta was thinking out loud, as she relived the experience, she verbalized each step and action that she was going to take. Throughout the entire ordeal she was very calm, unlike Laci who was hysterical. At one point, Loretta commented how they were 'total opposites.'"

Loretta: The whole time this is going on, she's cussing, swearing and screaming at the light "mirroring" our car, "going equal distance with our car."

Loretta remained quiet for a while, and then I asked her:

YS: Can you verbalize what you are experiencing? Just describe what is happening around you.

In a very soft voice:

Loretta: Huge wheel beside me, no windows, no doors, tiny windows, right there in front. Fat in the middle, pointy on the sides. The windows are geometric shape, not square.
YS: Do you see a color?
Loretta: (*speaking very calmly*) Light gray, no numbers, no letter, no logos, no stripes.
YS: Where do you see this?
Loretta: Right there, in front of me, just sits there, (*whispering*) so huge, it's flying, but slow.

As if trying to convince herself, Loretta kept repeating in a whispered tone:

Loretta: Must have been an airplane, must be an airplane.

Loretta described exiting the freeway saying that she had to go to Von's. As with Laci's first session, I knew that this was her subconscious coming into play, protecting her. Loretta was not ready to continue. But in my many years working with these cases, I know that once I break through the block, what occurred in these periods of lost time will begin to flood forward, and ultimately the abductee will begin to feel much relief. I gently pushed Loretta to back up a little in memory time to the point where she could begin to describe the "Object."

> Loretta: I'm afraid. Laci and I don't have to say anything or look at each other. We're both afraid. "They" know. Everything has a reason.
> YS: Who are "They?"
> Loretta: The 'Whites'… they can't be fooled. They've caught us. No way we can go. I'm afraid, been watching us the whole time. Waiting. "He's" not real.

I asked Loretta who "he" is, but she did not give me a direct answer.

> Loretta: Not supposed to care, just don't care, doesn't make sense. Looking at us… in front of us. I hate that light, made those cars go away. Nobody will ever know.
> YS: Are you still driving?
> Loretta: I think the car is still moving, it's supposed to be moving.

At this point, Laci's and Loretta's recollection of the events differ. Loretta continued in her consistently quiet tone:

> Loretta: Half of Laci's body is out of the window.
> YS: You see Laci's body going out of the window?
> Loretta: I'm not supposed to ask questions or tell anything.
> YS: Where's Laci?
> Loretta: She's gone. Pulled her up out of the window, up in the air. Not supposed to know anything… don't ask questions… agree to everything!
> YS: Did "they" do something to you?
> Loretta: Not supposed to question that.
> YS: Loretta, did something happen to you?
> Loretta: (*whispers*) Maybe.

Loretta could not get past this point in this first session. The next thing that she recalled was exiting the freeway and going to Von's, where both women discovered that they were two hours late. I suspected that due to the extreme trauma that Loretta endured due to this puzzling experience, she was not ready to move forward to unblock her subconscious memory.

Loretta seemed to have implanted instructions in her subconscious to not say anything or tell anybody about this incident.

After this first session, Loretta called and told me that while she was washing dishes, she had a "flashback" memory, one which she had not recalled consciously or during her first hypnosis session. I always caution my clients with the fact that because we are accessing and opening the subconscious mind, spontaneous memories may suddenly come forward during the course of a normal day.

Loretta's flashback:

> Loretta: While I was washing dishes, I suddenly remembered that it was a small star, then it got bigger and bigger, and then tiny lights came off of it in different colors. But I didn't remember that before. There's these little baby lights, kind of like fireworks, shooting off of it. It started out as a small star that got bigger and bigger, then all of a sudden, it was a big light and I thought it was a plane!

It's interesting to note that in these first hypnosis sessions Loretta recalled an object, while Laci recalled seeing a bright light.

D. Laci's Second Session

Laci scheduled her second session for October 23, 1993. Once again, I regressed her back to the night of November 20, 1992. I returned her to the moment when she looked over and saw that Loretta was no longer in the car.

> YS: Are you sitting in the car, Laci?
> Laci: No, I'm standing up under this light. Don't know what it is, I'm under something and there's lights and what the hell is going on?
> YS: Tell me what you're feeling. You're standing up, under something? How does your body feel?
> Laci: It's like it's not there, I...I don't know.
> YS: Just tell me what's happening. Is Loretta with you?
> Laci: No! It's big! I wanna go home! I don't know how I got here! (*starting to cry*)
> YS: Can you describe your surroundings? Are you by yourself?

13

> Laci: (*crying*) I'm laying down… feels like I'm laying
> down. I wanna go home!

Laci's body shook, or rather convulsed, as though going through uncomfortable trauma as these buried memories began to come forward. I used positive instructions to allow her to remember without continuing the trauma. As the session progressed, Laci described pressure on her arms.

> YS: What kind of pressure do you feel?
> Laci: I don't wanna do this anymore! I don't know who
> "they" are!
> YS: Are they right there with you?
> Laci: They move and I don't…I…I can't see them walk,
> they just move! They shouldn't do this. They don't even
> care!

I asked Laci what "they" were doing. She answered, crying: "They're doing what they always do!"

When Laci blurted this out, I realized that unbeknownst to Laci she has had these experiences earlier in her life. During her initial interview and the subsequent conversations, Laci never mentioned any childhood memories that might be indicators that she had been taken before. She did, however, share with me a 1952 sighting when her Mother and her Grandmother saw a silver disc hovering over the Air Force base where her Father was stationed and where her family lived. When I asked her how her Mother and Grandmother reacted to the sighting, Laci laughed and said, "They just turned around, went back in the house and never talked about it!" As odd as this may sound, I have heard this from many multiple witnesses, usually families, when they discuss a significant sighting years later.

During this session, Laci's movements indicated pain and pressure in her ear. While "they" were performing a procedure on her ear, she expressed a great deal of anger because "they" were not listening to her. She screamed and cried out that she saw Loretta standing on the bridge, as she did during her first session. After spotting Loretta, Laci said that "they" moved her (*Laci*) to a different room. I then asked her to describe this new room and what she was experiencing.

> Laci: They put something in my hand and it's holding me
> down, pushing on my hand. Oh! There's no windows, no
> doors, there's nothin'! Oh! It's tubes and marks on the
> walls and the tubes!

YS: OK, you're going to feel me tap your forehead and when I do, you're going to focus on the marks on the walls, they are going to be in your memory now, you're going to be able to describe what they look like and you will be able to draw everything that you see in this room.
Laci: (*calmer*) I'm just standing and turning and looking, and there's so much. Squares and, uh, marks. Tubes, and, uh, everything's the same color. This is a nightmare. It's not a color...metal...it's cold.
YS: I'm going to touch your forehead, now focus on those marks on the walls, embedded in your memory. Now describe them.
Laci: Ok, like an "L" shaped like a beak. And a, uh, a line goes like this. (*Moving her hands, and arms, Laci attempts to draw what she is describing in the air*) Circles with stuff inside the circle. And uh, funny lookin' things.

I asked her if she was by herself.

Laci: No, there's a hundred of these things, I don't know what they are. And now they're doing that to Loretta.
YS: What are they doing to Loretta?
Laci: I don't understand what's going on. They're telling her stuff. They don't got mouths! They make sure her eyes are closed, she's laying down, and now they're telling her something, I don't know what they're telling her.

Suddenly, Laci was startled and became very agitated. She opened her eyes during her session screaming that she wanted to go home and started to jump off my couch. Once I calmed her down enough where she could once again focus on my voice, I directed her to go to her "favorite place". This is a predetermined place of nature that I ask my clients to choose as a safe place when initiating a hypnosis session. I gently counted Laci out, she awoke, and we began the debriefing, post-hypnosis discussion.

YS: Do you remember what startled you so much?
Laci: (*taking deep breaths and sighing*) A face... a face in my face... and they know my name!
YS: Do you feel this has happened to you before this incident?
Laci: (*long pause and almost in a whisper*) Yeah. I had bloody noses as a child quite often.

As the revelations of the session began to sink in, Laci began crying. Different events throughout her life began to make sense to her. On this day, Laci got the confirmation she hoped for, but at the same time dreaded. It became all too real.

Laci felt pain in her ear. The body retains memories, and when she described the coldness and pressure in her ear, her body retained the physical discomfort even after I brought her out of hypnosis.

The "missing time" event that Laci experienced with Loretta had also produced some physical evidence. After that event, Laci noticed a triangular shaped layer of skin which appeared on her "right" hand. When I examined her right hand under the light, I could still make out an indentation; the indentation of missing tissue in the shape of a triangle. This is the same hand that Laci described something or someone holding or pushing down on during her hypnosis session.

I asked Laci to describe what was on her hand. However, at that point, she became distracted by the recollections produced during hypnotherapy concerning the room with no doors or windows, so did not respond. I asked her during the debriefing about what she saw on the walls in that room, she replied: "Like writing, something like that...everywhere. It's just everywhere and everything!"

Laci sat and cried as she tried to articulate and make sense of the conscious recollections produced by the hypnosis session. I realized her case would require much work.

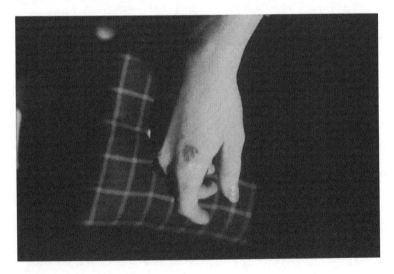

E. Loretta's Second Session

On October 23, 1993, Loretta prepared herself for another trip back in time. When Loretta was deep in hypnosis, I once again took her back to that fateful night. Loretta breathed heavily, as though hesitating to again confront those memories. Then she allowed herself to once again explore and, after a very long pause, she spoke:

> Loretta: There's this face, looking at me. I'm no longer driving. I'm standing here...someone's standing right here.
> YS: Who is with you, Loretta?
> Loretta: Looks like a black shadow. It's my 'guard.'
> YS: Are you still in your car?
> Loretta: Don't remember pulling over, stopping. I'm standing here. I feel sick. Laci's standing next to me. I feel sick, nauseous.
> YS: Did you stop the car?
> Loretta: No, stopped by itself. Don't see the car.
> YS: Where are you standing?
> Loretta: On the freeway, everything's stopped.
> YS: Just tell me the next thing that happens, you are remembering everything very clearly now.
> Loretta: I don't remember anything...not supposed to. That's all I remember... the guard. (*Loretta pauses, as though making a visual search of her surroundings.*)
> YS: Try to analyze anything, just describe what you're experiencing.
> Loretta: (*very slowly*) See his back and profile, he's skinny, 4-5 feet tall and no clothing. I wanna go home, don't wanna be here.
> YS: Just allow yourself to remember.
> Loretta: We're standing under the light and Laci's gone.
> YS: Where is Laci?
> Loretta: Laci went to the light.
> YS: Do you follow Laci?
> Loretta: No.

Then Loretta said they were back in the car, and she described Laci sitting quietly smoking. It was apparent to me that Loretta was blocking a substantial part of her experience, particularly at the point when she saw the "guard." At times, she would divert my questions by repeating that the light must have been

17

a plane… or by reverting to an irrelevant conversation she and Laci had while leaving the MUFON meeting.

During the debriefing Loretta said that she kept seeing images of the bright light and someone standing very close to her… the one she called "the guard." She saw Laci going out the window before she saw the guard.

Loretta also remembered that the time really did not register with her until she arrived home when her mother was upset. Loretta remembered something that she wanted to share with me which occurred a few years before this missing time experience. When she was married, she had a dream that she heard a low-grade hum. In this dream, she saw clear cylinders on a wall with liquid inside each of them…a "pinkish" colored liquid. She sensed that she was not supposed to be in this room.

She also recalled that as a teenager she would often wake up with twigs and leaves in her bed, and as a very young child she would tell her parents that she had not caused them to be there. The following is an October 20, 1993 excerpt from Loretta's journal:

> "I remember being about 5 years old, sitting on my tricycle in the backyard. Late one afternoon/early evening, right before sunset, I sat looking up at the sky…sitting and looking. I voiced out to my mother… 'I know you are not my real mother…I know you are not my real parents. I know I really come from somewhere else. It's ok.' I knew in totality, that my parents were 'limited beings,' and at that moment I had an 'unlimited thought,' nothing mattered except that I just 'was.' I knew I had a purpose and everything was fine: I was supposed to be 5 years old at the very time that I was 5 years old. I felt very old and wise. In retrospect, I was wiser than I am now."

Once the Experiencer breaks through and recovers a partial memory of an incident, other memories begin to emerge. Loretta could consciously recall a related childhood memory.

F. Laci's Third Session: Other Missing Time

To retrieve additional details on the missing time experience of the previous session I did with Laci. I regressed Laci back to the point where she had found herself in a different environment:

> YS: As you are now in a safe place, describe what is happening, Laci, you are going to be fine.

Laci: I'm laying. I'm laying down, uh, I don't feel like I'm laying on anything.

YS: Can you feel underneath you?

Laci: I can't move my arms...I...I'm trying to move my arms and, uh, I'm trying to uh, uh, scream...I know I'm screaming, I can hear it in my head, and nothing's coming out! Something standing at the end of my feet.

YS: Now focus on your feet, you're safe, you're exploring, now look down at your feet.

Laci: Huge! Thing.... head is huge!

YS: Just look at him, you are doing fine.

Laci: He looks smooth, and he's r-r-r-real lanky, uh, real long arms and...!

YS: What is he doing? Just look down there and tell me what he is doing.

Laci: (*with a very strained voice*) Staring at me. Uh, he thinks that he knows me...and I don't know!

YS: He is telling you that?

Laci: Yeah... but I don't know how he's telling me. He just says he...he knows me and I'm supposed to be here! Poor Loretta!

YS: Do you see Loretta?

Laci: They won't let her go, she's standing above me. She's standing here like...she's a mannequin.

YS: Who is with Loretta?

Laci: Uh, little guys... three...uh, they don't look like this big guy at all.

Laci is referring to the taller being that is standing by her feet. I asked her to describe the beings with Loretta.

Laci: They're small. Uh, they look transparent, almost transparent. They look unborn. They're shorter than Loretta.

She's nodding, like saying "me...ok." They're gone now, and Loretta's gone. When Laci saw that Loretta was no longer there, she became anxious; clenching her fists and moving her head from side to side; eyes still closed, but appearing to look for Loretta.

Laci: There's pressure, I don't know what it is...my head!

YS: Describe the pressure on your head.

Laci: It's up in my hairline and on my forehead. Like something's there, just In, oh! one place on the right side!

Artist Steve Neill

Laci described a dome shaped instrument with rivets on her head. I then asked her if she could feel somebody holding her head, she replied "no".

Laci: Oh! They're coming back!
YS: Who is coming back?
Laci: THEM! They're so fast, they move so fast! That big guy's with them...he's taking that thing off my head....and then he said. (*Laci starts crying*)
YS: Just tell me what's happening.
Laci: (*crying*) They've known me a long time! And that...he's not gonna hurt me, (*tearfully, but trying to talk through her tears*) and that I'm doing this because they need...because they need me! He...keeps telling me I...know him...and that he...he has to do this because I...I'm a part of this...I'm a part of this!? Can't be a part of something like this!

Laci became so hysterical, she could barely speak. After some deep breathing exercises and calming suggestions, I asked Laci if she wanted to continue, she nodded a "yes."

> YS: Now as you are feeling very calm and nothing can harm you. Just tell me if he is still talking to you.
> Laci: No! He, uh…He wants to, uh… (*starts to cry*) wants to show me something! And I…I…I don't wanna go, I just wanna go home!
> YS: Remember, Laci, you did go home, but now you are exploring and you are safe.
> Laci: He wants to show me, uh, my past! (*Very upset, she begins to cough.*)

Again, using calming techniques I relieved Laci from her anxiety. When she was ready, Laci said the tall being who was standing very close to her, leaning over her, was telling her that her past experiences are meaningful to her life, that she is taking it the wrong way, and that this was a "job."

She described images from when she was twelve years old. The being told her that they were sorry that she can no longer reproduce because, she was told, that she had been reproducing through them since age twelve.

Laci also began describing an age fourteen experience. Quite often, the hypnotic subject spontaneously regresses to another time in their lives, another memory which is significant to that person. Laci recalled vacationing on Catalina Island with her family, scuba diving on the other side of the island by herself.

> Laci: "I'm always alone, I, uh, I don't have any friends or nothing. There's all these bushes, and uh, little…little guys are in these bushes by the sheep and goats. And they're calling my name. And the goats…they're just standing there." (*very upset and begins to cry*)
> YS: "Just tell me what happens, Laci, you are in a safe place now."
> Laci: They're calling my name…and, uh, they said I had to come with them…and I don't want to! I- I can't move now. They just have me. I don't wanna go!
> YS: You're just exploring, just tell me what is happening.
> Laci: (*hysterically crying*) And they take me…and they said they just wanna take something from me and that it belongs to them! I don't have nothing that belongs to them!

Laci described being taken into a craft as she kept repeating, "it's a clear day, how come nobody's around"? Laci is placed on a table.

21

Laci: It's cold! They don't get what the wetsuit is! They think it's my skin and they want to know what happened to me!

It was interesting to note that the beings were confused about her wetsuit, mistaking it for her skin. This was reminiscent of the 1961 Betty and Barney Hill case, the first documented missing time case at which time, during Barney's examination by the beings, they discovered that his teeth were removable. The "leader," as Betty called him, came into her examination room very confused and asked Betty: "Why do Barney's teeth come out and yours do not?" It seems that, from time to time, we humans are capable of confusing even the most advanced intelligences!

As the session continued…

Laci: It's cold. It's…it feels like it's pulling! And then…then they just take something out! I don't know what it is….I don't know what it is…I can't…I can't look anymore!

Laci was so hysterical at this point in her session that it was an emotional struggle for her to get through this unbelievable memory when she was a young teenager.

Several cases of my young abductee clients who were at the onset of their periods described having something either placed in their bodies or something being removed. This, of course, continues throughout their lives when a woman has her tubes tied or has a hysterectomy is of no consequence to the alien agenda.

YS: Take deep breaths, Laci, and at the count of three, you are going to describe very calmly what they are taking from you. One, take another deep breath; two, get ready to look; and three.
Laci: I don't know what it is! It's just like a blob! I…I hurt, I…hurt! And they don't care!

When this procedure was over, and the beings told Laci that she could go, something very unexpected happened. Laci started screaming…

Laci: I forgot! I forgot my…my…ring! A turquoise ring that my dad gave me! I don't know where it is…maybe I left it on the beach! My mom's gonna notice it's gone!

When I brought Laci out of her age fourteen experience, she told me that she forgot about her missing ring. She never did find it on the beach or in her parent's boat. Many years later, when Laci became a young woman and a wife, she told me that the ring which she lost during her abduction from Catalina Island when she was a teenager, suddenly just "appeared out of nowhere" on her dresser in her bedroom room! Laci did not remember seeing it in that place previously. It was just there. Laci gave me the ring at her next session, which I prize to this day.

I advanced in time her session regarding her missing time experience:

> Laci: I'm scared! I, uh, go into…a…another room. And …and, uh, this really creepy guy, uh, shows me a map…my mind…they remind me of the past…and they want me to know…about my future. (*very upset*) I…I don't know where Loretta is! They won't tell me where she is…this is all my fault! (*crying*)
> YS: Release that negative thought, Laci. This is not your fault.
> Laci: He said, 'I am going to tell you that Loretta's fine. We're telling her some things and she will be fine.' And…I don't believe him!
> YS: Just tell me what happens next.
> Laci: (*exhales, sounding relieved*) Oh, there's Loretta, oh…and they're showing her something on a…a…panel and a wall. And, uh, they're telling her something. I don't know what they're telling her. She's standing next to them and they're…they're little guys!
> YS: What's on that panel and wall?
> Laci: I think it's a window…it's black to me. And, uh, like a panel, like a desk. And they're showing her stuff. And, uh, I don't think she can, uh, move too good. I think she's supposed to stand there. She's looking out…I think it's a window…she's standing there with them, I can see her back.

Then Laci said that they were letting her go. Her next memory is of being in the car with Loretta and going home and again saying, "I gotta go to Von's." When I brought Laci completely out of hypnosis, she was feeling pain.

Very often, after reliving the traumatic memories, the body retains all of the memories. Depending on the severity, it may take a day or so for the body to release the trauma. One client felt the leg pain for several months after her regressive sessions, though, emotionally, her anxiety was relieved.

G. Thoughts About Laci And Loretta's Experience

Because they lived far from my office, these were my last sessions concerning the missing time experience that I did with Laci and Loretta. Interestingly, during their hypnosis sessions both Laci and Loretta felt nauseous. Both women had "weird" feelings about the month of November. The year (1994) after their "double abduction" sessions, both women returned to me for further private hypnotic regression exploration, wanting to then delve into other memories. Loretta was very curious about what else may have occurred during her childhood.

During the time Laci and Loretta were seeing me for hypnotherapy sessions, Alice and another MUFON investigator were discussing the progress of our investigation when another MUFON member overheard their conversation. He told the investigators that on one night on about the same date Laci and Loretta had their encounter experience, he too was driving home from a MUFON meeting and also spotted a very bright light while driving under a "bridge." And as he recalled, they almost "fell on the floor" when they heard this. The MUFON investigator Alice asked if he would agree to an audio taped interview, he did agree, and on September 25, 1993, the witness gave Alice his taped account of what he recalls that night in November:

> "I remember driving home from a MUFON meeting last year and I was startled by a bright light by a bridge. Let me start by saying that I am not sure about what month or the exact time. All I know is that it was something unusual...I remember after the meeting, late last year (1992) October/November, I was driving home on the freeway, I remember getting home at 12:15 a.m.
>
> According to my wife, it was around Thanksgiving. I remember it was about 11:15/11:30 p.m., as I was approaching a bridge, I saw out of the corner of my right eye, I saw a bright light streaking by from the right to the left, and I was going under the bridge, I lost sight of it. I thought it was probably an airplane, as I was near the airport.
>
> Several times, I went back to that area, but I have not been able to pinpoint the exact spot (where he first saw the bright light). It was just so odd...it was very low, went very fast and there was no noise.

I remember the drive home. It was a clear night and I felt an eerie feeling on the way home. I said to my wife, "strange things on the freeway!" I put it out of my mind, forgot all about it. Until about June/July 1993. I found out that somebody was abducted after the meeting in November, when I heard about it. I wondered if that thing…obviously, I didn't completely put it out of my mind. I wondered if there was a connection here.

I remember that the whole month of November was very active with sightings in the central part of the coast. Me, my wife, and several neighbors saw circulating light spheres in the clouds, I know they weren't searchlights. After about twenty minutes, I went back in the house, and I'm sorry that I did.

I periodically think about it (*the bright light on the freeway*)."

This witness's situation did not involve missing any time, since he arrived home just about the time his wife expected him, living approximately two hours from the location of the MUFON meeting. Because of this independent witness coming forward, Laci and Loretta received confirmation that there were, indeed, strange lights in the sky the night of their abduction.

When I begin an investigation on a case, one of my requests of my clients is to keep a journal to document any spontaneous memory, vivid dreams and/or possible unexplained body marks that may appear overnight.

During her hypnosis sessions, Loretta kept repeating the fact that she is not supposed to tell anyone what happened to her. Even though Loretta would occasionally be "blocked" from verbalizing during hypnosis what she was experiencing, she would then explain details when she "returned" from hypnosis. As a diligent person, Loretta began keeping a journal after her initial interview and first hypnosis session with me.

When she gave me her journal to read, it was apparent that Loretta's life was changed forever after their abduction experience. An excerpt from Loretta's journal dated October 20, 1993 reads:

"December 1992…I'll mention the acknowledgement-zoom-star later. I was Christmas- shopping for food. Holiday food and wrapping paper, misc., etc. When I came across the misc. kitchen aisle and found the shelf paper section. In a nutshell, in a frenzy I emptied the cart of groceries and replaced it with 12- 20 rolls of shelf paper. I later went back for the remainder of what they had in stock.

It was no ordinary shelf paper. This one was different. I stayed up 'til 2:00 a.m. I redecorated my whole refrigerator. My whole refrigerator looks like a 3-dimensional doorway into outer space! My kitchen has a Victorian theme with antique pictures and tin advertisements, roses and brass, look to it. Except...for the refrigerator.

When Loretta gave me a copy of her journal with the above passage, she also gave me a sample of the wall paper that she was so compelled to purchase and which she used to decorate her refrigerator...a wallpaper with a Star System design! This seemed to be startling confirmation of what Loretta had seen when Laci described under hypnosis that the "beings" were showing Loretta something and "...she's looking out, I think it's a window"...and Loretta's subconscious seemed to spark her reaction of familiarity causing her the irresistible impulse to purchase the wallpaper.

Loretta was a very strong, independent woman and proud mother. And even though the night of November 20, 1992, deeply disturbed her, Loretta had a continuing compulsion to delve into her many fragmented memories, hoping that all the pieces of her puzzle would someday make sense. On October 20, 1993, Loretta expressed her continuing trauma by adding to her journal:

> It gives me great pain to even begin to describe the confusion and anxiety I feel when I go back to November 20, 1992. Almost a year has gone by and that night...I will never forget. I am disappointed (extremely) in my behavior or lack, pertaining to certain incidents that happened (that night).
>
> My passivity and non-emotional, sober, mechanical responses reminded me of a 'Stepford Wife' personality. It is so unlike me to lack in dramatic, animated compassion or to be drained of adrenaline when faced with a near head-on collision.
>
> I know how I'm supposed to feel and I voice that...that is the way I feel...but I have no feelings. I have no response. I have no feelings. I have no interest. I feel I should submit...no questions asked. Just do it without thinking twice. Don't worry. Don't judge. Don't think. Don't analyze. Don't calculate. Don't fear. Don't cry. Don't fight. Don't disobey. Don't argue. Don't resist. Don't ask questions. Don't remember. Don't respond. Don't do anything. Oh well.
>
> I have an 'oh well...whatever' attitude. This is the part that gives me great pain, confusion and anxiety. I'm a vocal, animated, feisty, sometimes boisterous person. My passenger was/is even more so than I. Together, we're fun to be around with, but something about that night, something so disturbing, so irrational, so illogical, so impractical, so rack-my-head against-the-wall-for-the-millionth-time crazy.
>
> Is this what it is like to be human? My perception of being human...is to experience in totality... 'the human experience,' to feel feelings, to experience experiences, to

think thoughts to live every moment to the fullest, if it means to be sad, happy, scared, mad, jealous, silly or excited...then, I accept that.

I would rather feel sad than not feel anything at all. Something happened...that denied me 2 ½ hours of a 'human experience'...denied or robbed. I'm trying to find a word to describe what was taken from me. I was manipulated somehow and I feel cheated. There is a void now. I cannot explain what it is exactly, but, I'm in mourning for it...I feel that perhaps I died. Perhaps, I died, just 'a little bit,' but not completely.

I mourn for a part of me that will never come back. A part of my 'humanness' is gone. I don't know what it is or where it went. But I know, like I know the back of my hand. There is a void. Whether the void is inside me or outside this solar system...is irrelevant.

There is a void and maybe, just maybe I've been there...as once a human.

Loretta passed away in 1999 after a lengthy illness. But I remain grateful to Loretta for her trust and faith in me as her hypnotherapist to guide her through these very intimate, personal and traumatically frightening memories.

CHAPTER 2: The Case Of Mary

"The clock doesn't come on, nothing's working, and the car won't start!"

A: Sleeping In Her Car

Mary felt distressed, worried about her sanity. She convinced herself that her memories were made up or an exaggeration of an actual event. However, Mary would experience subsequent events that would trigger new memories that further confused her and left her feeling alone and unable to share her feelings with anyone. This was especially difficult for a forty year PhD. in Psychology with a successful counseling practice.

I first met Mary in 1993 when I was lecturing at the Whole Life Expo conference held in the Los Angeles area. Sitting in the audience, Mary was startled by the similarity of her memories to the case studies in my presentation. After a post-lecture question-and-answer period, Mary approached me privately to share her suspicions about herself and her brother having possible abduction experiences since childhood. After our discussion, Mary and I scheduled an initial interview.

On June 29, 1993, Mary drove up from San Diego for the initial interview in my Los Angeles area office. Mary arrived wearing a gray suit with a white blouse accented with a pearl necklace. She was dressed as you would expect from a successful professional woman. She appeared distressed and explained how she would often awaken in the middle of the night with a sense of someone in her room, feeling a tugging on her ankles or wrists, and hearing a buzzing sound, "…like the ocean sound in a conch." Sometimes she saw a mass of small blue lights in her room. She recalled some similar childhood memories and said that for many years has dreamt about UFOs. She spoke in a professional manner and expressed what she hoped to achieve from hypnotherapy:

> "Missing and partial memory is very distressing to me. Resolving once and for all, whether my family and I went through this experience and what exactly happened, if anything. Resolving the fears and phobias these issues raise, whatever their origin. I want to free up energy for my professional and personal life."

From our initial interview, Mary came across as a highly intelligent, independent, yet sensitive woman. It was easy to see why she was well respected by her colleagues. She had accomplished many of the goals she set for herself as a young girl. She expressed that coming home to peaceful surroundings, including two cats, was a peaceful haven from her many responsibilities and often demanding career. Her memories of multiple unexplainable incidents at home deprived her of this refuge.

Her professional training did little to prepare her for a world she never knew existed. Little did she know that her world, as she knew it, was about to shatter, thrusting Mary into a world of unanticipated experiences, but one she could no longer ignore.

During her interview, Mary told me a story about the time she and her mother were browsing in a local bookstore. As she was browsing through numerous titles, a very unusual book cover caught her attention: *Communion* by Whitley Strieber. In that book, Strieber describes personal accounts of his experiences with non-human entities beginning when he was a young child. For some odd reason Mary could not explain, she became mesmerized by the unusual face on the cover, a beige headshot of a stereotypical alien, with large, dark, almond shaped eyes staring back at her. An overwhelming feeling came over her as she continued staring at that face, an undeniable, she says, "instant recognition!" At that time, such alien imagery was not common.

She immediately grabbed the book, walked directly to the checkout line and purchased it. I chuckled when Mary said, "And I'm cheap, but not with this one." Mary told me that she was very confused about her mother's angry reaction, protesting Mary's purchase. Her mother knew Mary loved to buy books and was accustomed, in her mother's words, to Mary "blowing" her money on books...so her mother's behavior puzzled her. Why would she be so upset about her purchasing a copy of *Communion?*

As soon as Mary arrived home, she was anxious to begin reading her new book. While reading it, a memory flashed before Mary's eyes. Mary was seven years old and her brother Frank was five. The book reminded her of an incident when early one morning, her little brother was screaming that there were three bald men with big black scary eyes looking in his window at him. That early morning wakeup call had the entire household in an uproar!

She remembered that her parents rationalized her brother's outburst by saying that it must have been the three little Latin girls who lived around the corner. Mary remembers her brother being furious with their parents' explanation saying, "No girls got here!" It was an odd incident that the family never discussed again.

Mary closed the book and once again studied the cover of *"Communion."* She gasped in recognition as she was realizing that it was exactly what her brother described to their parents that early morning. Stunned by her childhood memory, Mary reopened the book, continued reading, and began to cry hysterically. This was out of character for a woman with a professional practice that required her to maintain her decorum always. Her reaction to Strieber's book was so out of character for her because, as she stated, "I tend to be emotionally over-controlled; I have a problem not crying at funerals!"

During her interview, Mary went on to tell me that she had a number of "out of body" experiences ever since childhood, as well as hearing high pitched sounds which she believed might be connected with the abduction phenomenon. Discussing her numerous recollections of "out of body" experiences picturing her "physical" body floating above her bed, she described specifically one such experience:

> "The first one I remember is when I was eleven years old. I woke up to a feeling like my nose hitting something. And I looked up and, um, there was what I thought was a wall. And I rolled over and I was in the air above my bed!"

31

Describing another vivid memory, she pictured herself lying on her back with her hands on her thighs:

> "And what woke me up was I felt that same funny feeling on the skin of my thighs that I had felt. And um, I felt myself come up out of the bed like this, but I was conscious of my body and I could feel the blankets down over my feet. It was the oddest thing. My legs, my body were up at about a 45-degree angle. And then I felt something grab my ankles in the air and it was like a physical pressure on my ankles, and that scared me, it was dark, I was scared."

Mary's memories brought up the possibility of "astral projection." However, during the abduction, the person is "physically" taken from their environment. We are not dealing with the "etheric" body as described in the definition of OBEs or Out of Body Experiences. One of the "symptoms" of abduction is the sensation of feeling "paralyzed" and being "lifted," which occurs during the onset of an abduction and "slammed awake" or "dropped in bed" once the abduction is over and the individual is brought back to their original location. Mary described being physically being lifted; these bodily sensations and partial memories were among many experiences which brought Mary to seek help and decide to undergo hypnotic regression. At the end of her interview, Mary looked at me and said,

> "This issue brings up two unpleasant alternatives. One is that it's real and that's not a pleasant prospect. And the other one is that I'm crazy. And I find myself alternating between the two hypotheses."

I assured Mary that she was not crazy. Her memories were very similar to other memories I have heard from persons who have sought my help. These types of memories are recalled both consciously and under hypnosis by many abductees. To Mary, they were outside of her traditional training and experiences with her patients. As a high functioning professional with no other "rational" explanations for these memories, she wanted to explore them further.

Mary scheduled her first hypnotherapy session for October 4, 1993, and subsequently underwent three further regressive hypnotherapy sessions involving this event. Mary described her background as very busy with a career, which took her to Northern California for a lucrative job, permitting her to buy a comfortable home for herself and her beloved cats. On weekends, she would often enjoy the scenic drive south along the coast to visit her many friends she left behind in Southern California.

On a Monday in the winter of 1991, she arrived home from her trip very tired around midnight, and looked forward to some much needed sleep before facing the new work week. . When she put her key in the front door and entered her home she felt that something was not quite right. She had what she called an "eerie" feeling... as if someone or something was in her home.

She began turning on every light in the house, though she made a point to tell me: "I don't like to waste power; PG&E is so damned expensive." She nervously checked her home, room by room, closet by closet, but found no intruders. Apprehensive, but at the same time feeling very tired from her long drive, Mary rushed around the house putting her clothes away and cared for her pets before she turned in for the night. She knew she had a full workday scheduled for the next day.

Suddenly, she told me in our pre-session discussion, all the lights went out. "I'm so scared, I've never been afraid of the dark before, I just feel so scared; this is absurd, I've lived alone for years." She stumbled around in the kitchen looking for candles she remembered putting in one of the drawers. She located a flashlight, lit a couple of candles, and rechecked every window and every door in the house to reassure herself that everything was securely locked.

She readied for bed, thinking to herself that she hoped the utility company would soon correct the problem. Then, as she adjusted her bedroom venetian blinds to allow the moonlight to come in, she was startled by a shadow passing by her bedroom window. Based on this background information, I placed her in a hypnotic state.

During this first hypnotic regression session, she described this very disturbing incident which she experienced on her return from Southern California.

> Mary: "God, there's someone out there. Oh, my God, I'm scared shitless. My heart is going like crazy. There's someone out there! I can't sleep in the house!"

Mary described being extremely frightened... too frightened to stay in her house. Because of the late hour, she was not sure if the whole neighborhood was without lights or just her house. She made a decision she later called "crazy," but at the time seemed very rational to her: "I'm gonna sleep in my car tonight. If there's somebody out there, at least I can take off."

Grabbing a pillow and sleeping bag, Mary slowly looked out the front door to make sure the coast was clear, and then made a rapid dash for her car. Locking all the car doors and reclining her driver's seat, Mary got as comfortable as possible. After a long pause, she commented on how bright it was outside. And her session continued:

> Yvonne: Is there a full moon?
> M: It's brighter than the moon. I know the moon isn't that bright. I don't know how long I've been asleep. It's not moonlight, it's like white light. I think I'm up on my elbow, I don't like this. I think I'm going to get out of here. I put the key in the ignition. I wonder what time it is... the clock doesn't come on... nothing's working, and the car won't start!
> YS: Are you able to look around outside of the car?

Mary's eyeballs seemed to be moving under her closed eyelids, searching:

> M: I don't see anything. Wait a minute! I can see the rose... but the roses are supposed to be in the way. I'm really confused. I see the countryside. I think I'm still in the car, but I shouldn't be able to see what I'm seeing.
> YS: What are you seeing, Mary?
> M: I can see my yard, but the roses are 5-6 feet tall. I am in the car and I'd like to roll up the window, but I can't. That's the trouble with electric things. I can feel the steering wheel, but I can't see anything at all. It's pitch black. Oh! I don't feel good!

B: Submerged In Breathable Liquid

> M: It's kind of green...like antifreeze...Oh, my god! He wants me to get into it...

Mary is trying to make sense of what she is recalling, and after a long pause, she whispers:

> M: The door opens. The driver's side... someone opened the door, and undid my seat belt. I was wearing a seat belt but what the hell was I wearing the seat belt for? And I step out of the car, and [hesitating pause] I seem more

34

relaxed. I'm in a real dark enclosed space. I don't see anything, but it's familiar.

YS: Is someone with you?

M: Yes.

YS: Can you see who is with you?

M: No, I just feel like I'm walking on a metal surface, like the way they make metal staircases, out of that kind of metal. But there's someone there... I think two... near me in the dark. Someone's touching my left arm. I'm not scared anymore, but my back hurts ...and my shoulders. (*sounding tense, she continued*) There's a kind of light ahead. I'm walking toward a big room. I left a really big room where the car is, like a parking structure. I'm walking down a hall. The light's getting brighter. I can see someone to my left who's still touching my wrist. He's wearing something black, like a black exercise outfit. I'm 5' 7" and he must be about 5'4" something like that. Oh, god! He turned and looked at me! He's one of those guys with the big eyes. I just see the one eye. God, those guys are ugly! I remember as a little kid, I liked bugs, and then all of a sudden... it was real sudden... I acquired the worst hatred of bugs. And this guy, his eyes, they look like a bug's eyes. Oh, he's showing me somewhere, and I'm being told to step into a room, big room, really light, real white light. I can't focus too well.

YS: What do you see in the room?

M: There's a lot of activity in the room. There are people like this guy, doing things; it's almost like a factory. There's equipment and it's moving across the floor. Everything is white in there. There are ladders, some sort of vehicle-like equipment going across the room. He's telling me to walk in. He sort of gestured me in there. I see some cases along the wall.

YS: What do the cases look like?

M: They're glass, a kind of scratched glass and where the panes come together is a white sort of frame. And there's like a mist in them, but I can't really see. For some reason, I don't like those! I think there's someone sitting in it!

YS: So they are big cases?

M: Yeah, taller than I am. They're at least six or seven feet tall. And they're... I don't know... maybe two feet or so out of the wall, sticking out of the wall.

YS: Can you see someone in there?

M: Yeah, I see a shape in there. I don't know. There's something about it I don't like. There are tubes or pipes. Maybe grayish, different colors. There are metal ones, grayish and whitish ones, they go into the cabinet. Yeah, I think there is someone sitting in there on a seat or a bench inside, like those kinds of showers that have a seat in them.

YS: Do they look human?

M: Yeah, looks like a black person with very, very dark skin sitting there facing the right side of the cabinet. They're very still. I don't think they're dead though.

YS: Does it look like an adult person?

M: Yes, adult woman, maybe 45-50. I can see her leg. I can see her head. There's mist there. Her hair is straight, but it's not like an Afro. She looks so tired, she's just sitting there. I don't think she's got any clothes on. I can't see for sure because of the fog in there. She looks tired, I'm very tired. I don't like this. (*Mary looks uncomfortable.*)

Mary's voice filled with compassion as she described the lady sitting in the tank, commenting on how sad, tired and sick she looked. Mary also described many other "cabinets" in that room. She described a wall, and a sub wall which separated the "cabinet" area from the "factory" area. She describes seeing one of the "buggers" in front of her, taller than the other "guys." The little "guy" is looking up at her and he's touching her left elbow with both of his fragile appearing little hands.

> M: Ugh, I hate it when they touch me. I start walking and he walks beside me. On the right side, I see other kinds of cabinets. These are horizontal, (one is) maybe 6 feet long and there's something green in it… kind of like antifreeze, and there's no lid on it so I can see that there is all liquid in there. And there's tubing going into it, I think I see three of these things.

M: (*highly agitated*) OH MY GOD! HE WANTS ME TO GET INTO THAT THING! He's pulling away! I have this orange sweatshirt on and it's being pulled off of me. I've got a t-shirt and underwear and, oh my God, I'm naked! There are others around now. I don't know where they came from and nobody is saying anything, but I get the idea I'm supposed to get into that tub. I can't really move…
M: (*Mary appears horrified.*) I'm in the water!
YS: Does it feel like water, Mary?
M: No…like antifreeze…is sort of slippery, it's green colored, I can open my eyes in it, I don't know why I do that.

Mary became very agitated while she was describing herself in the tank of liquid. During her session, her body was very tense; her face was flush red then became very pale.

YS: Mary, just describe what's happening.

M: Oh shit! I put my hand up, and there's a lid on it! Shit! I'm trying to get up to where the air space is…and there isn't any! They're gonna kill me. I'm trying to push at the glass, but I can't seem to move very much.

M: (*agitated*) I'm gonna drown!

At this point in the session Mary's face was very pale, especially her lips, as she described herself taking in the liquid. I directed Mary to focus on my voice, and gave suggestions to desensitize her from this situation which appeared to terrify her.

YS: Remember, Mary, you did not drown. You came out of it and you are fine now and you are safe. Just tell me what's happening.

M: Oh god!

YS: Okay, Mary, tell me what's happening.

During Mary's fear of drowning, trying to hold her breath and being trapped in this tank, suddenly indicating a revelation, her tone changed:

M: I had to breathe and I did!

YS: Are you still submerged?

M: I'm in it, yes. I can breathe this stuff! Oh, I'm real dizzy. Oh, my God! (*long pause*) I remember reading years ago about some dog that drowned in a lab and they brought him out and he was fine. (*Seemingly amazed she continued*) I can breathe this stuff. Oh, that's weird! I thought it would feel real heavy and horrible. Oh! I'm kind of dizzy!

I moved forward very close to her, watching Mary "reliving" being trapped in this tank of liquid. Her body began to slowly release the tension, and I watched as her skin tone began to regain some color.

YS: Do you still have your eyes open?

M: No, I'm kind of relaxed. I wonder if I'm drowning. I don't seem so scared anymore. Uh, it's kind of dark in here. Now I can sort of see. I can see a whole bunch of their legs, I can see three of four of their little legs. There's kind of a purplish tone in here, green, but there's like a purple tone to it too. I'm in here for a long time. I'm awake but I'm not awake. They never leave me.

I gently brought Mary out of her first hypnotic state and back to the present time after about an hour. During her debriefing, Mary's first reaction to what she consciously now recalled was, she said: "really bizarre." Mary thought she was going to die in that tank when the thick liquid, she compared to antifreeze, went into her lungs. Yet she found it surprisingly easy to breathe, "like air…to my utter shock, I could breathe this stuff. I felt oxygen returning to my blood and I could inhale and exhale this material as lightly as I could ordinary air."

Her recollections surfacing during hypnotherapy reminded Mary about a recurring dream that she had as a child. In her dream, Mary was swimming in the same type of "water" she described in her session. Moreover, in her dream she could breathe. It never previously occurred to her, when describing her somewhat similar dream experience, as "odd, that I'm swimming and breathing at the same time."

I can only speculate as to why Mary and others are put through this very frightening, disturbing "submerged in liquid" procedure. Do the captors intend to condition and train the human body to adjust to a yet unknown future experience to which those who are chosen will be subjected? Perhaps tremendous speeds of their advanced movement through space? …. or to the atmosphere of their place of origin? …or both?

While I was working with Mary in 1993, I took a short break to take my sons skiing in Lake Arrowhead. One night while relaxing in our rented condo, I watched James Cameron's movie *The Abyss*. I was intrigued by the story about a group of Navy Seals dispatched along with the crew of an under the sea drilling rig to retrieve a sunken U.S. nuclear submarine. The exciting "Hollywood" plot suddenly hit home when actor, Ed Harris, was given a liquid breathing deep diving suit! In amazement, I watched his helmet fill with liquid and, after a moment of panic and dizziness, the character "Bud" began "breathing" in the liquid!

Prior to leaving for vacation, I had conducted a second session in which Mary again described how she was placed in a tank and forced to breathe liquid, which felt heavier than water. And now I was watching this process on the screen! How could this be? I had no idea that in 1993 our Navy had such a thing! It reinforced my belief that the abductees, who had been describing this procedure under hypnosis, had not been making this up. Why would anyone contrive such a horrifying scenario? Or, I wondered, was *The Abyss* director depicting a personal abduction experience?

Continuing my research, I discovered that in the 1960s, experiments had been performed with liquid or fluid breathing. Dr. J Kylstra who was a physiologist at the State University of New York at Buffalo found that salt solutions could be saturated with oxygen at high pressures. Dr. Kylstra experimented with mice in a U.S. Navy compression chamber where he kept them alive for no more than 18 hours. In 1966, Dr. Leland Clark developed a technique where a mouse survived for over 20 hours breathing fluid.

In the early 1990s, the technique of fluid breathing was improved. Scientists kept dogs alive in perfluorocarbon for two hours. Once the dogs were removed, they were slightly hypoxic, but after a few days, they returned to normal. These tests were now ready for human subjects. The U.S. Navy has been using oxygenated perfluorocarbon for liquid breathing, one would imagine for the purposes of submarine escape and under the ocean oxygen support facilities.

I also read colleague Dr. Bruce Maccabee's brilliant *"Acceleration"* abstract in which he states, "Visual and photographic sightings of UFOs carrying out impossible high-speed maneuvers are presented for study. For the first time, we are able to quantify the amazing acceleration of these craft." In his 35-page article, Bruce uses several eyewitness examples of "acceleration," including a 1947 sighting of his own grandmother. What caught my eye toward the end of Bruce's article was a parenthetical note:

> "Note: A UFOnaut or abductee inside a UFO accelerating at 500 Gs would be pushed by the wall of the craft with a force that would make him seem to weigh almost 500 times his normal weight on earth. A human body might be crushed at that acceleration, and the skin might be pulled off the bones, unless the human were suspended in a liquid and the lungs and other body cavities were filled with liquid."

During her debriefing, Mary was still in disbelief: "To my utter shock, I could breathe this stuff. I felt oxygen returning to my blood and I could inhale and exhale this material as lightly as I could ordinary air." Abduction experiences individuals describe as being escorted into a room where there are other humans and a large container of water which resembles a "pool" are not rare.

In Mary's second session on November 22, 1993, we continued from the point in time of her first session when she "clambered" out of the tank after it was drained of the liquid. Three "little putty looking bug-like things" again escorted Mary down the narrow hall past the big hallway and an exit that she recognized as where she previously walked.

> M: There's something else, I see a pink area like a pink light.
> YS: Where do you see this area?

M: It's beyond that exit along the corridor. It's on my right side.

YS: Can you see what's in that room?

M: A pink purple light. There's a room in there.

YS: Can you describe the room, Mary?

M: There's like a little entrance to the right. There's other people in there.

YS: What are these people doing?

M: They're in a big tub…like, I mean a spa or swimming pool and they really look relaxed.

YS: How many people do you see in there?

M: Let's see. There's a woman to my left and a couple of kids. There's a guy sitting on the opposite side with his feet dangling in the water. There are two kids…skinny little kids, boys. They're standing in the pool; the kids are real subdued. A couple look my way, but they don't see me. This is absurd!

YS: Describe the pool.

M: Uh, it's round…it's, I don't know, maybe 20 feet in diameter…oh…and the water is a pink, lavender color. But it's not the same thing that I was in before. Maybe it's just the light…there are lights on top of it, and it's warm in there. Well, I'll be damned! I'm stepping in it too. This is silly!

I asked Mary to compare the water in the "pool" with the liquid she was able to breathe in the tank.

M: It feels like regular water…it's warm though, it's nice and warm. I think it's supposed to wash that chemical off. I think that's why I'm here. I think there's a lot of it in my hair…I don't like that. There's a bunch of lights up above the thing and they're in a straight line over the pool…and they give off a pinkish light. This is bizarre!

When I brought Mary out of hypnosis, she expressed how "weird" she thought that experience was with the other people in the pool area. She could not get over the "ludicrousness" of the situation, but she had a strong impression that she was taken to that room to wash off the chemical that lingered on her body after being submerged in the tank.

C: Mary Discusses Her Conscious New Recollections

Several months after her session on November 22, 1993, Mary wrote me a letter about what she remembered consciously from this abduction experience in 1991. Mary recalled standing in another room which she described as oval or round with a sunken area in the center. There was a "raised dais" on all sides made of white metal. In this room, Mary described a conference table, "very plain and modern, with rather smoothly rounded edges." Beyond the conference table, she described three more beings who were taller than her smaller escorts. These beings seemed more substantial to her with larger heads, wearing long white robes with raised cowl-like collars and wide sleeves, "one of them was wearing a sash from his right shoulder to the left hip, this one moved from the group behind the table toward the edge of the dais, so he was quite close to me.

Mary begins to describe her impressions from her conscious memory. I believe what Mary says is too important to paraphrase, so I am presenting her writing to you in its entirety:

> I had the feeling I'd been in 'conversation' with them. There was no sound. I looked at them and thought about questions I had for them and the emotions these questions posed for me. It almost seems like this was a question and answer session I was being allowed for some reason. I remember thinking that I probably would not be able to think of the things I most wanted to know. I did think about who they were and where they came from.
>
> I got a flood of fleeting images in my mind and faint emotions. These beings do have emotions but they are not as intense or as personalized as ours are.
>
> I sensed fear, anger and sadness from them and frustration and admiration (*of our Earth*). But these sensations were not very intense. The images and the feelings I can sort of represent as words in what follows, but they were not verbal at all and I'm sure there have to be distortions in my interpretation of what I felt and saw.
>
> The feeling I got was that these beings had originally come from somewhere else, a place that no longer exists. They claimed to have been here 'long enough to be naturalized citizens of Earth.' The feeling I got was of dozens of thousands of years. They live here, though they are capable of extraterrestrial travel.

43

I had the feeling they had looked long and hard for a place they could survive, and Earth partly filled the bill. I had a wistful and cautionary sensation from them about how escaping our planet was not a real solution for our problems. Our bodies have evolved here on Earth, and we are very finely tuned to the nuances of this planet. Incoming solar radiation fits a particular section of the electromagnetic spectrum, peaking at not quite 0.5 microns in wavelength. Existing day in and day out in a radiative spectrum different than that is stressful on the human body, and living in space means we would face this stress permanently.

Our bodies have circadian rhythms suited fairly closely to a planet with a 24-hour rotation-emigrating permanently would amount to permanent jet lag. Similarly, our bodies are adapted to a particular magnetic field with a particular range of strength and orientation and would be profoundly disturbed by permanent exile from it. Again, our bodies have evolved to cope with a particular tight gravitational range, and absence from it even for short sojourns in space is known to damage astronauts' and cosmonauts' skeletons.

The human species, through great epidemics through history and prehistory, has evolved to cope with a great variety of the resident microbes. And on it goes, leaving Earth will exert extreme stresses on permanent emigrant populations, stresses that in such a slowly reproducing species as ours could result in extinction of these populations. High death rates will certainly exert selective pressures and evolution, but small populations are vulnerable to inbreeding error and random loss of genetic diversity (the founder effect and gene drift).

The point of this is that these creatures feel that we take too cavalier an attitude toward the only environment in which we can truly be comfortable on a very deep level. They see us doing something that they witnessed their own species doing long ago on whichever system they came from, something that grew imperceptibly, incrementally, until it reached a threshold and then produced complete, sudden, and qualitative change to conditions in which they could not continue.

The reason they care about our behavior is that it will affect them, too. They live here but not well and not comfortably. I get the impression that they don't even exist on a day to day level in the same dimension on this planet with us. They rotate into our world as needed and out into their own dimension here, in which they are barely hanging on. I get the feeling they can't endure our sunshine, our gravity, our geomagnetic fields, our high-octane emotions for long. They've managed some kind of half-existence here. Whatever we're doing that will have systemic, global impacts on us and the economies on which we depend will make their tenuous existence even less tenable, even impossible.

On another issue, I get the feeling that they are trying to manipulate our genetic material to create bodies fully adapted to our planet but which can also house their own kind of consciousness, their souls, if you will. They are trying to create a body into which both species can incarnate and express their own styles of consciousness. They're having a helluva time of it, though, above and beyond the technical difficulties of micro-manipulating the extraordinarily complex DNA of Earth creatures. Even as our bodies are not adapted to life on other worlds or permanent residence in spacecraft, their consciousness is not adapted to life in our stormy bodies and brains. And, if we're moving as fast as they fear to alter irrevocably the conditions of life on Earth (theirs and ours), they may not have much time left to create a life form adapted to this world, a world which may ironically change out of their design parameters. (*emphasis added*)

Mary's impressions focus on the hybrid breeding program. The highlighted text gives some insight into the apparent purpose of this ET species choice of Earth and the reason for the hybrid program. Her feelings about their environmental concerns relate to their choice of this planet and desire to keep it at least manageable for their needs.

During the 1990s when Mary's abductions were taking place, there was much debate among researchers as to the intent of the ET group that operates the "hybrid breeding program." Was it for good or evil? The primary protagonists at the time fell into two camps. The "Evil ET" faction, for lack of a better term, was made up by Budd Hopkins and Dr. David Jacobs. Dr. John Mack, the Harvard Professor of Psychiatry, believed that, despite the trauma, the ET interactions were positive for human beings.

Mary's opinions fall somewhere in between these opposing camps. This ET group is using our species for its own purposes in a clandestine program. Mary believes they have been doing this for thousands of years. Those chosen are mostly unaware, on a conscious level, that they are participants. These aspects suggest a one-sided relationship that, if disclosed to the world at large, would likely generate a fear-based response.

On the other hand, people are returned home safe and sound with, for most participants, little or no disruption to their daily lives. Mary believes that the ET group behind the hybrid breeding program is concerned about the way we treat a planet that is perfectly suited for us. Yet they do not appear to be deflecting us from our choices to treat the planet so shabbily. This indicates that our "free will" to carve our own path is not being inhibited. This ET group may co-habit this planet, but they are not taking active measures to supplant us as the dominant force on Planet Earth.

The Hybrid Breeding Program, at least from the perspective of Mary, has many elements that do not fall into the "evil alien" perspective. The motives of this ET Group, from one chosen person's perspective, does not neatly fit into a "good or bad" cubby hole. Based on a recent survey of others who are chosen, Mary's view seems to be the current predominant view of Experiencers. More about this will be discussed in Part Two. Mary's observations seem to fit the "mostly positive" view most Experiencers have about the ET Agenda.

D: Andreasson Case Similarity

The adaption-to-a-different-environment aspect of Mary's case reminded me of the "The Andreasson Affair" case study by Raymond Fowler.[6] That situation concerned Betty Andreasson who was seated in a strange, transparent plastic chair. Once seated, Betty described a clear "plastic" encasement that fit perfectly over both her and the chair. Like Mary, Betty described hoses going into the enclosure; with three hoses connected to her nostrils and mouth.

When the beings told Andreasson that they were going to put liquid in with her, she also became hysterical, telling her captors that she was going to drown! As the liquid filled the enclosure, she was also amazed she could

---

[6] Fowler, *"The Andreasson Affair"* (1994) Wildflower Press (Newbery, OR). Original publication date, 1978.

breathe in the liquid. However, unlike Mary, Betty was breathing the strange liquid through those connected tubes.

When Ray Fowler debriefed Andreasson, she told him that while she was immersed in this liquid, she felt that she was being transported. She speculated that the strange "tank-like apparatus" somehow protected her while *en* route.

Considering the tremendous movement or great speed experienced by Betty Andreasson and others while immersed in liquid, could it be that the indescribable fear Mary experienced while similarly submerged in, as Mary put it, a "viscous, oil but not an oil" liquid, distracted her from a similar movement occurring at the same time?

Mary's impression about the beings manipulating our genetic material to create bodies to become fully adaptable to live and survive on planet Earth particularly struck me, because after years of study, abduction research is taking those of us who are eyeball deep into this phenomenon into a direction that we are not quite sure we are ready to accept.

Mary graciously agreed to share her story to let other people who are just beginning to deal with their own experiences, know that healing is possible and so can be a satisfying life after abduction. She wants people to know that life is not defined by the abduction experience, and even though the experiences will most likely continue:

> "...facing this issue will allow you to choose how to respond to it and will thereby, let you somehow integrate it into your life. I have come to terms with the possibility that I have some sort of narrow-gauge mental illness and the even more unnerving possibility that these really are truly alien encounters. But, I am confident that I can live my life and find satisfaction in it and not be overwhelmed by these questions and fears and the experiences themselves. Indeed, I am somewhat less paralyzed with terror when I sense the experiences starting over the last few years."

I have a profound respect and admiration for Mary's great sense of humor over the many years I have known her, as well as her bravery in her continuing quest for answers and her acceptance of her situation.

CHAPTER 3: The Case Of John[7]

"They're telling me to...to have feelings for this baby. That it's mine!"

A. John Describes A "Missing Time" Experience

When I started accepting clients that had possibly extraterrestrial experiences, I did not advertise this new area of my hypnotherapy practice. Even though I was not reaching out for this new type of client, they began to find a way to my doorstep. While I was unaware of it, word began to spread that I would see clients with unusual stories without preconceived notions about what was "wrong" with them. This seemingly ordinary group of people seemed to have one thing in common. They each had a story to tell that they could not understand or explain through conventional means. They came from all occupations and were well adjusted but lived under varying levels of stress from an unexplainable source.

One such referral came through a radio program. Without my knowledge, I was one of the subjects of discussion on a then popular Los Angeles area radio program hosted by Dr. David Viscott. His guest was Dr. David Jacobs, Temple University History Professor, who had written extensively about the UFO abduction. Dr. Jacobs mentioned my willingness to see clients who wish to explore the sources for unusual consciously remembered experiences. In each instance, the client had memories of unusual occurrences with blank spots that were very stressful and needed to be explored.

John was one of these persons. He listened to the program and recognized similarities between what Dr. Jacobs was discussing and his own fragmentary memories. When my name was mentioned, John decided to see if I was available to help him explore his own experiences. He found my number and called me. After a brief discussion, we arranged an appointment at my office.

On November 15, 1992, John walked into my office for his scheduled initial interview. He began by explaining he felt a need to talk to someone who would be knowledgeable and hopefully sympathetic to what he saw in the sky, December 31, 1980.

John, a young, unmarried, native Californian, was a hard-working independent contractor installing new roofs on homes and apartment buildings. He kept a very busy schedule. At the time, he was building his own home.

---

[7] An update on John's interactions with ET is found in Part 2.

For the last twelve years, John described experiencing crying bouts whenever he attempted to talk about some time lost (*"missing time"*) following his sighting of a UFO. He contacted me hoping hypnotherapy would relieve his anxiety from that experience. As he stated, he wanted "...to find what happened to make my life better with the understanding of what happened."

Having lost his Father to a heart attack when John was 33 years old, he kept very close to his Mother, visiting her often and attending to her needs. Because of this closeness to his Mother and having a fairly good relationship with his siblings, he told me that he felt confident with his family about discussing what he saw on the night in question. When John finally told his family what he remembered, he was relieved that his family offered their support and felt very happy that he had made the right decision about sharing this strange event with them.

During John's pre-hypnosis interview, he explained that on New Year's Eve 1980, he planned a driving trip to Northern California to bring in the New Year with his girlfriend. He packed his 1977 Ford pickup truck and began a long journey on Interstate 5. As he drove alongside the usual holiday traffic, he noticed two cars traveling beside him, keeping a pretty good pace with his truck.

At close to 10:00 P.M., approximately 80 miles south of his girlfriend's place in Sacramento, he recalled while approaching a bridge, he noticed some lights ahead of him. He spotted a large, dark object, which reminded him of a "sting ray" with lights emanating from the bottom. The object was flying very low and moving slowly above him, from his left to his right, heading towards his car. John passed the object, looked behind him, but could no longer see it as he crossed the bridge. He was so amazed by this strange flying craft that he felt he had to take a closer look. "I have to see what this is."

John was struggling as he tried to be as accurate as possible to convey to me the events of that night and the hours that he cannot account for. Throughout the interview, he was visibly shaken, trying to hold back his tears, struggling to release and verbalize a troubling memory that he held inside of him for twelve years.

He decided to pull over and take a look at the object. However, he did not actually remember pulling over. The next thing he remembered was his truck "acting funny," with the engine sputtering. He felt as if he had just awakened from sleep, feeling "groggy," with both hands on the steering wheel. As he slowly looked around, he noticed there was no traffic on this busy freeway, and the two cars that were pacing him throughout the trip were nowhere in sight.[8] From his perspective, only a few minutes had passed. Yet there was "no one else was around" on a normally busy freeway.

It wasn't until he stopped at a phone booth, to call his girlfriend that he began to realize that something was just not right. His girlfriend was angry at him for missing New Year's Eve. It was 1:00 a.m. Since only a few minutes had passed in his mind, he thought it was around 10:00 p.m.

John could not put this phone call out of his mind. He thought he had called around 10:00 p.m., but it was 1:00 a.m. Three hours had passed, but he had no recollection of what happened during that time. How could that be? He had no definitive answer and could only be truthful with his girlfriend about his sighting when he finally arrived at her house at 3:00 a.m.

At the end of the interview, John looked at me, his eyes red from tears, anxious for answers, twelve years was long enough. Before John left that day, he made perhaps one of the most important decisions of his life. He booked his first hypnotic regression session.

B. John's Hypnotic Regression To 1980

November 17, 1992, John arrived for his session and, although he was nervous, he resolved that there was no turning back. Once under hypnosis, I guided John back to New Year's Eve 1980. Segments of his hypnosis recollections are described in the following session transcripts:

> JS: It's afternoon, I'm in the truck driving, holding my hand on the gearshift. There's traffic, it's a long, bouncy trip, driving… driving, it's a long way. I see a lot of open land, fields…just keep going, it's getting dark.
> YS: Ok, just keep describing what you are doing.
> JS: (*sighing*) I'm still going, still driving, highway 5, driving north. Yes, there's traffic around me…I'm driving…yes, I can see the bridge…I know I'm coming up to it…I see the on-ramp.
> YS: Ok.
> JS: It's dark. And I'm on the bridge, I…I can see, it's dark, a dark object over the bridge. It's going…it's going from west to east. It's not very high above the bridge.

---

[8] John exhibited the earmarks of a "missing time" episode. The abductee is not aware of a break in time. Suddenly, they find themselves in another place and time. Significant amounts of time pass without any awareness by the person experiencing the event.

YS: Can you describe the dark object?

JS: It's going slow (*sighs*) it's going really, very slow, unusual slow. (*whispers*) What is it? I'm wondering what it is. I can't make it out completely. And I see it going east, following the road, coming towards me, turning... I know it's...nothing I've seen before. (*crying*) I can't stop looking at it. It's off to my right...above me. (*whispering*) I know it's above me...I know I have to pull over... I pass it by, I don't see it, I'm past it.

YS: Just look around, John, do you see the object?

JS: I look behind me, I don't see anything, no, I don't see it." (*whispering*) Where is it? I know I have to pull over and look at it.

YS: Do you pull over John?

JS: I don't remember pulling over. Why don't I remember? (*long pause*) Don't wanna remember.

YS: All right, do you see it behind you?

JS: No.

YS: Do you know where it is now?

JS: No, I don't. I don't.

YS: Now, you can't see the object, so you continue driving?
JS: (*whispering and crying*) I feel like I just woke up. I just felt like I'm put back in my truck, I don't know, it's just a feeling.

I told John that I was going to touch his shoulder and as I do, I asked him to take a deep cleansing breath, as he will go into a deeper sleep.

YS: Ok, John, I'm right here and you're safe, we are going to back up just a little bit in this memory, now let's go to the point where you are looking at the object and you tell yourself that you want to pull over to look at it.

52

JS: (*breathes deeply*) I'm in my pickup truck, I'm just past the bridge (*whispering and crying*) and I don't see it. I know I'm gonna pull over. (*whispers*) I know I'm gonna pull over.

YS: Ok, just allow yourself to remember.

JS: Now it's turning. Turning motion, so slow...coming towards me. I know it's nothing I've seen before. (*crying and whispering*) I can't stop looking at it. It's off to my right, above me. (*whispering*) I know it's above me...I know I have to pull over...

YS: OK, you tell yourself to pull over. Are there any other cars around you?

JS: Everything seems, (*hesitates*), bright, bright light. It's all around me, inside the cab, just white, white. (*crying*) I feel like I'm being...floating. I can't move, nobody can float like that, why, how is this happening?

YS: John, you're doing fine, whatever happened, you came out of it and now you are just exploring. Allow yourself to remember now, you're going to feel much relief.

JS: I can't move, I have absolutely no control over this (*whispering*) rising higher and higher...I feel like I'm sitting, like I'm sitting in my truck, but I'm not. (*whispering*) I have no control. I can't move, I can't move.

Artist Steve Neill

Once John managed to break through his blocked memory, he began crying uncontrollably. He could not accept what he was experiencing and was "afraid" to tell me as he continued crying out, "It's not happening. It's not happening!" John found himself surrounded by "these little things, little people."

JS: (crying) I don't wanna look, I don't wanna see them.

To ease John's anxiety and direct his attention away from the "little people", I asked him to describe his surroundings.

JS: (*long pause, trying to compose himself*) So sanitary, so perfect, so clean. It's a big room: desk, counter top like around the room, maybe three feet from the floor area. Screens, dividers between certain areas...open areas. Right now, I can't, I can't be comfortable right now. (*crying*) I'm sorry.

After about an hour and a half, I slowly brought John out of hypnosis. During the debriefing, John told me that he did not know that he could be hypnotized because he considered himself such a "control type" person. I explained to John that he was finally ready to explore and he consciously made the decision to trust me to guide him back through that momentous time in his life.

Before John left that day, I asked him to draw everything that he remembered while he was in hypnosis. I also asked him to keep a journal in order to begin documenting spontaneous memory, vivid dreams, unexplained body marks or any personal thoughts or feelings about what came forward in his first session.

At the end of each session, I remind my client that drawing and writing frequently comes from the subconscious mind. During regression work, the subconscious mind is opened, and more often than not, forgotten or buried memories may suddenly float to the surface when it is least expected. Keeping a journal will assist in the road to recovery as each memory is addressed.

C. John Has Recollection Of Lights

On December 3, 1992, John came in for his second session. I began John's induction into hypnosis and directed him back to 1980. During this session, John was once again having a tough time, visibly quite upset and while lying on my couch, his body began to shake uncontrollably.

54

JS: (*beginning to cry*) I wanted to do this. The whole inside of my body is just shaking, I can't stop it...nervous.

I encouraged John; giving him positive suggestions; and asking him to take some deep, cleansing breaths. I was hoping to relieve the tension in his body. As much as John wanted to get through his second session, he told me that he was just too nervous and could not "go there" this time.

John was crying as I gently counted him out. During the debriefing, he told me that he suspected that the reason he could not get back to that night is because of what came forward during his first session. He was still processing the fact that memories were coming forward that he never dreamed of which were disturbing and difficult to understand. John felt that his first session was actually easier, "Cuz before I didn't know."

John's third session would prove to be very different...

D. Traumatic Recollections Are Unblocked

By this time, I was getting to know John, as a sensitive, quiet, sometimes shy person with a heart of gold. I admired his bravery and his determination to get to the truth: "I want to find out if this thing really happened, will it happen again and has it happened before."

On December 15, 1992, John allowed himself to relax enough to go into a deep state of hypnosis. He described driving north on Highway 5, approaching the bridge as he spotted the object flying very low overhead and "very slow, unusual slow."

JS: I know I keep telling myself, "pull over and look at it". (*sighs*) I know I wasn't shaking then, but I'm shaking now. I can...and I know it's above me. (*whispering*) I don't remember pulling over, I don't.
YS: You're doing fine, John.
JS: Why? Why did I stop remembering? What happened?
YS: You're safe now, John.
JS: (*whispering*) I know why I stopped remembering. (*crying*) I want to stop being nervous and shaking, I just don't...I don't want to be afraid of this anymore.
YS: You don't have to be afraid, John, just go on and tell me what happened.
JS: I want to stop shaking.
YS: Deep, deep breath, John.
JS: I want to go through this to feel better. I want to remember. I want to go through it, it just seems I have no

55

control. I want to stop shaking. (*crying*) I don't want to fear this anymore!

YS: Remember, John, you have been controlled by this fear for a very long time. Allow yourself now to be in control, now, taking a deep cleansing breath, release the fear, just breathe, you will be released of the fear, you will be free of the fear.

JS: (*breathing deeply*) Ok, alright, I'm not going to fear this.

YS: Ok, John, you are in your truck, and you think about pulling over.

JS: (*whispering*) I didn't pull over, I don't remember pulling over.

YS: Just verbalize what you are feeling, what you are sensing.

JS: There's light all around me, white light. I can't move my head, I can't move my body, it's got a hold of me.

YS: What has a hold of you?

JS: The light, bright white light. I can't move my body, I feel like I'm in a sitting position, and I'm going higher! How can this be happening? It's got me. I have no control over what's happening!

YS: Just keep verbalizing, John, you are doing fine, you are safe.

JS: (*breathing heavily*) Oh my God!

YS: Just tell me what's happening.

JS: I want to…I know it's…Oh my God! I'm standing in a room!

John was becoming very agitated, crying and almost falling off my couch. I took some time to talk to him, calm him down, always reminding him that he is in a safe place. I also knew at this point that it would be beneficial to John to continue guiding him to recover whatever hidden memories were yet to be discovered.

YS: Ok, John, take a look around you and try to describe your surroundings.

JS: (*taking a deep breath*) Everything's so perfect, so clean. Oh, I'm looking around, I want to stop shaking. I'm seeing lights.

YS: Where do you see these lights?

JS: On a desk, around, going around to the con…contour of the room. It's going around. And above part of it, I think I see a round window above a screen. There's a

window, not very big, (*whispering to himself*) stop
shaking please.
YS: Is there anyone with you, are you alone?
JS: I don't want to see anybody with me, (*crying*), I don't
want to see people.

John was beginning to block again, but he finally described five
"people" standing with him and described them as having "shiny tight
skin". He described "the little people" to be "maybe 4 feet,
disproportionate arms, seem kind of, long arms, not too long, but maybe
just unnaturally."
The session slowly progressed with my questioning John about his
surroundings and how the "little people" were standing around him. John
kept telling me that he felt that he was in a "trance" standing there.

JS: I'm standing there, I don't want to go past this point,
why is this so difficult?
YS: You're doing fine, John, just go with it, just tell me
what happens next.
JS: (Crying) They take me by the hand, and I have no
control, they seem to have all the control, and I don't like
it, I don't like it!
YS: (*touching John's shoulder*) I am going to touch your
shoulder, breathe deeply, you will be able to tell me
everything that is happening without the fear... now
describe where they take you.
JS: They take me…they take me to the room through the
door. It's a dark room. It seems to be dark.
YS: Ok, go on, John.
JS: It's dark with lights in it…(whispering) I just keep
thinking, I don't want to believe this is happening.
YS: You're going to be fine.
JS: Oh…they lead me into this room. I know it…I know it.
It's dark, and it seems to be a smaller room… (*crying*) And
they're showing me things…they want me to look…I don't
want to look!
YS: Just keep verbalizing, John, you are going to find
much relief.
JS: They're showing me things. (Crying) They want me
to look and I don't want…I don't want to look!
YS: What are they showing you, John?

JS: (*crying*) I don't know, I don't wanna know…Oh, God! Showing me tanks?

YS: Tanks? What do the tanks look like? Describe the tanks.

JS: (*taking a deep breath*) Yes, they're above my head, maybe five, six feet above me. Uh, they're set into a wall, a round wall, kind of concave. Set with just glass.

YS: Ok, go ahead, John.

JS: Fluid in the tanks. Bubbles coming from the bottom. I don't know why they want me to look at these tanks.

YS: Just take a good look now, John, just tell me what you see.

As a therapist, I had to emotionally block myself from such heart wrenching testimony as I experienced with John that day.

JS: (*crying*) I don't want to see it, I don't want to be here, I don't want to be here!

YS: Just verbalize what you are seeing.

JS: I don't know what I'm looking at! Oh, it's not water, it's not water in the tank, it's heavier, looks like gelatin type, bubbles running through it.

YS: You're doing fine, John…do they tell you what the tanks are for?

JS: Yes, they're telling me something. (*crying*)

YS: What are they telling you, you're doing fine now, just verbalize it.

JS: (*crying*) Telling me that's my…

YS: Telling you what?

JS: (*crying*) That's my child in that tank! I don't want to see anything, I don't see it!

YS: I am going to touch your hand, John, just describe what you are seeing.

JS: (*crying*)

YS: Do you want to tell me what you see in the tank?

JS: I don't want to look. They are making me look, oh…they're making me look.

YS: John, I am going to count to three, you are going to take a peak and you are going to be able to describe what you see. Starting with one, it doesn't have to be long, two, you're going to get ready to look, and three, tell me what you see.

JS: (*crying*) I see a baby, Oh…with an umbilical cord. Sitting, but not quite sitting, in a laying back position.
YS: You're doing fine, John.
JS: They're telling me to…to have feelings for this baby. That it's mine. (*crying*) I don't know if it's mine, they're telling me to love it. They're telling me to feel love for that baby.
YS: How do you feel about the baby?
JS: Ah…I feel love for it, it's just a baby.
YS: John, do you want to stop, or do you want to go on?
JS: (*crying*) Please, I don't want to go on.

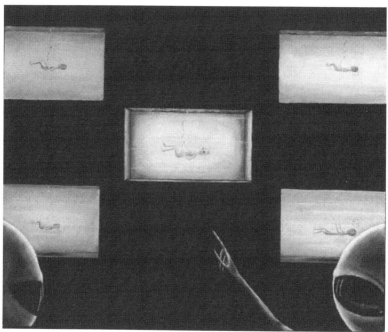

Artist Steve Neill

I slowly brought John out of hypnosis. He finally consciously realized why he had blocked these disturbing memories for so long. John did not have any children here on earth. This parenthood revelation was just too overwhelming for John. I believed he would finally find peace in his life, especially with the continued help of a support group like CERO.

E. John Faces Early Missing Time

John also wanted to explore a strange incident when he was eight years old. Since he began his exploration through hypnosis, he was anxious to find out exactly how long this has been happening to him. We did two regression sessions on this childhood memory. Once again, I recorded the account from John's conscious memory.

John and his brother were living with their parents in a home in Highland Park, California. On this night, his brother woke up and discovered that John was not in his bed. Alarmed, he woke their parents who looked everywhere for John. After frantically searching all through the house including the kitchen, John suddenly appeared in the kitchen which puzzled his family!

The following are excerpts from the Transcript of a hypnotic regression on February 17, 1993, exploring his *"missing time"* incident at age seven:

> JS: I just remember standing there and hearing my mom call out my name. I just remember standing right in the kitchen looking out into the living room. I remember seeing her coming out of the hall and saying: 'Here I am.' I don't know what happened...I don't want to see it. Ohhh, I'm not supposed to remember...I don't know why...I was told.
>
> YS: OK, just try to go back now, you are in your bedroom, everything is very calm, you begin to sleep very soundly. Now allow yourself to go back to before you found yourself in the kitchen.
>
> JS: Ohhh...Ohhh...yes, I remember laying there, turning over and waking up. I remember seeing these little things. They're small, there's like three of them. They are telling me to be quiet, they come to play with me. They seem tall as I am or a little taller, they come to play with me, they're going to take me somewhere. I feel like I'm floating, floating with them. They're holding me and I'm just floating up. I remember looking up through the ceiling seeing this thing with blue and white lights rotating above the roof of my house. Round thing going through the center of it, looking down, seeing my street, seeing my house. (*crying*) I can't believe this is happening.
>
> YS: OK, you are safe now, you can allow yourself to remember.

JS: They tell me that this is where we're going to play. 'We're going to do some things to see how you react, it's going to be fun.' Ohhh...I don't know what I'm supposed to do. I feel so strange in this place."

YS: Can you describe your surroundings?

JS: It's big, got a table in it, kind of clean, stainless white thing. It's so immaculate, so clean. They say, "this is where we live, we're going to play." I see some lights, a counter top, different lights, a little screen. I don't see anybody else, just me and these little guys.

YS: How many are with you?

JS: There's more than three, I think four or five. They're telling me that I have to lie on the table, that they're going to test me to see what I want to play with, what games. I shouldn't be here. They say, 'it's fine, you're alright.' I remember them putting something on my head.

YS: How does it feel?

JS: Snug, but doesn't hurt. They tell me that's so they can know what I'd like to play, kind of games, for later. They are doing something on the inside of my legs, I know they're touching me, but I don't know what they are doing.

YS: Do you feel like they are touching you with their hands?

JS: No. Kind of with an instrument, some kind of thing.

YS: Can you describe what that instrument looks like?

JS: I'm not sure, it looks like a little ice cream scooper, kind of, real small. Feels like they're scraping or something. This isn't right, they shouldn't be doing this to me.

YS: Take a quick look at the ones by your legs and tell me what they look like? Are they the same as the "little things?"

JS: No. He's got like a cape on, some kind of cape, just a large flowing cape, it seems to go down from the shoulders to the ground. (*crying*) They're saying if I tell you, they don't want to play. They lied to me.

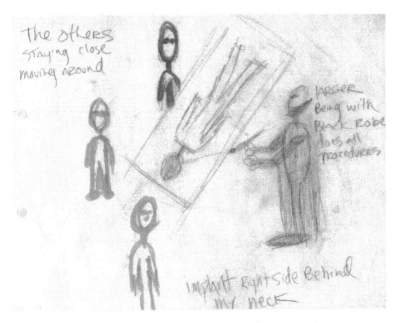

John asked to stop. He was too upset to continue. I gently brought him out with positive suggestions. Now, John had to deal with the fact that these experiences have been happening all his life. Armed with this knowledge, John was determined to find out as much as possible about his experiences. During the next several months, John scheduled more hypnotic regression appointments.

On December 3, 1992, John had another session to explore his *"missing time"* experience of New Year's Eve 1980. Because of what came forward in his first session, John was apprehensive during this session. While he was in hypnosis, his whole body was shaking which he could not control and no matter how many suggestions for safety and comfort that I gave him, he continued suffering from this nervous anxiety. I eventually brought him out of hypnosis. Although John had great difficulty with this last session, he was determined to keep searching for the truth in regard with his experience. He booked another session for December 15, 1992 to revisit his experiences on New Year's Eve 1980:

> JS: I know I keep telling myself, 'pull over and look at it'. I know I wasn't shaking then, but I'm shaking now. I want to relax right now and remember. And I know it's above me. I don't remember pulling over, I don't. Why did I stop remembering? What happened? I know now why I stopped remembering. I'm in the light, I can't move

my head. I can't move my body. I have no control over what's happening. Oh my God. I'm standing in a room. With lights, everything's so clean!

YS: Is it a big room?

JS: Yes, I maybe see 30 feet across. Everything's so perfect, so clean. Oh, I'm looking around, I want to stop shaking, I'm seeing lights.

YS: Where do you see lights?

JS: On a desk, around, at the edge of the room. Going around the contour of the room, I see a partition, dividing some of the instruments and panels and the lights, just various light, different colored lights in the seating area type of thing.

YS: Is there anyone with you?

JS: I don't want to see anybody with me. I see a door to the left.

YS: Are there people there?

JS: Yes. (*crying*)

YS: How many people do you see, John?

JS: Five, they're small, maybe 4 feet. Disproportionate arms, seem long kind of, long arms, unnaturally. I don't want to see this.

YS: You are doing just fine, John. Just go with it, tell me the next thing that happens.

JS: Ah, I want to, they're leading me somewhere, they take me by the hand. And I have no control, they seem to have all the control where I go and I don't like it.

YS: Now where are they taking you, John? Just describe where they're going.

JS: They take me to the room through the door. It's dark with lights in it...I just keep thinking, "I don't want to believe this is happening". They lead me into this room, I know it, I know it, it's dark and it seems to be a smaller room. And they're showing me things. They want me to look and I don't want to look. (*crying*)

YS: What are they showing you, John?

JS: I don't know, I don't know, oh, God! Showing me tanks!

YS: Tanks?

JS: Yes, like they're maybe above my head, they may be five. Six feet above me.

YS: What do the tanks look like? Describe the tanks.

63

JS: They're set into a wall, a round wall, kind of concave. And set with…just want me to look at these tanks.

YS: Is there something inside the tanks, John?

JS: I don't want to see it, I don't want to be here. (*crying*) I don't know what I'm looking at, I don't know what I'm seeing. It's not water in the tank. It's heavier, fluid heavier. Looks like a gelatin type, bubbles running through it, lots of bubbles.

YS: You're doing fine, John…Do they tell you what the tanks are for?

JS: Yes, they're telling me something. I don't want to listen.

YS: What are they telling you, John? Just tell me. Don't hold back.

JS: (*crying*) Telling me that's my—that's my child in that tank.

YS: That's your child? You see a child in the tank, John?

JS: I don't want to see anything. I don't want to see it. They are making me look, they're telling me to look.

YS: Just take a real fast peak, John. At the count of three, you're going to take a peak and you are going to be able to describe what you see. Starting with one, does not have to be long, two, you're going to get ready to look, and three, tell me what you see.

JS: I see a baby, a small developing baby. Oh, with an umbilical cord, sort of sitting there, floating…like sitting, not quite, kind of sitting, laying back position.

YS: What does this baby look like, John, does it look normal?

JS: (*deep breath*) Yes it does, except for the head is a little large. I think it, it looks skin-color to me. They're saying I'm here for a reason, there are a number of "them" telling me it's my child, to love it, to feel love for that baby. I need to connect, they tell me, to this baby…it will help the baby feel part of something.

YS: Do you feel love for it?

JS: Yes. It looks like a human baby…yes…I think it could be mine, maybe, so I do. (*deep breath*)

This very long session was extremely difficult and emotional for John. He does not have any earth born children and could not understand how this "baby" could possibly be his, but "they" assured him that it is. If this were the first account of "babies" being presented during an abduction experience, I would have seriously questioned John's sanity, as well as my own for devoting my life to this work. But, there have been hundreds of cases of people who have had encounter experiences such as John described. Children who, they were told, were theirs, and the experiencer thinks, "how could this be possible, I must be having a nightmare", except for the fact that their DNA was taken from them, ova and sperm and very disturbing strange and missing pregnancies. As a seasoned abduction researcher, these continuously reported accounts remain very disturbing. But, they exist, they are real and the ultimate question is, what are to become of these children?

The implications are chilling, but as you delve deeper into this book, you as the reader, will learn the truth from the many accounts of various "alien medical" procedures, all with a definite purpose, many only recollected through the cautious use of regressive hypnosis.

On August 8, 2007, John made an appointment to update me on how he has been doing since his last regression:

> JS: I was very apprehensive about doing the hypnosis, but I needed help and I trusted you, so that made a difference. The first sessions were difficult, but I found relief in each session, though they weren't always easy. The results usually from a session, I felt relief and better, questions were answered for me. It took a while for the process and the sessions to figure out exactly what was happening and through the hypnosis and meeting the other members of CERO, continued to help me in a positive way, so I kept continuing the sessions. It made a big difference in a lot of ways, in my personal life. Emotionally, it made a big difference, because finally, some of my questions were answered. The hypnosis made a big difference in figuring out stuff, I really had no idea what was going on. I knew a lot, but I was still missing stuff that I didn't want to deal with and in a way, being treated in such a caring manner and in a way, I felt comfortable in the sessions made a big difference in finding out a lot of stuff. Today, I would be having a lot of problems if I didn't figure this out, a lot of stuff that was going on. Today I'm doing much better, I've become accustomed to really what was going on since the age of 8, knowing that this is part of the design and still difficult at times (*John becomes emotional*).
>
> YS: What makes it difficult at times now, John?

JS: Difficulty comes with a lot of things, um, I've gotten way past the trauma and feeling like a victim, and that was difficult to get through, but now for me the difficulty is knowing that I am part of them and they are of me. There's something there that needs to be explored, why it's happening to people. The difficulty right now again is also, in another aspect, society in the United States is not open, some segments of society and the government isn't divulging what is happening to its citizens and the ridicule.

The answers are there, of course, they are not going to come forward, because it's a big, big story, it involves national security, people's lives, and that is very difficult to deal with because I feel I'm on the outside and ostracized and in a way unaccepted because this isn't acknowledged as a day to day activity with some people and that's part of the difficulty now for me. Before, it was feeling like a victim and um, feeling like I was kidnapped and experimented on which I was. I have transcended past that, which I am very grateful to you and the group (*CERO*) and the sessions with helping transcend that part, but there's always difficulties in this situation, it's a big thing and right now the difficulty lies in the acknowledgement of society and government officials that this is truly a situation.

YS: Besides being able to confide in your fellow CERO members over the years, are you still having difficulty talking about this with your family or co-workers?

JS: Well as far as family, I'm a very lucky person because my family knows the history and they remember the events that happened to me and they were part of it because I used to talk about certain situations, so they have a lot of understanding and also too, it has made a lot of clarity for them what was happening to me, because I would have events, missing time on trips or at home. You know, it made a lot of clarity for me. And people around me at work, I get ridiculed and then, I get more on a personal level, somebody will come up to me and say this or that happened to them, but for the most part, it's still a subject that is not discussed on a daily basis because of, it's too much for most people to consider and they go along with their daily lives, which I can understand, unless this has happened to somebody, I would feel the same as them that say 'well, this is not happening or this doesn't really impact me, so, it doesn't really matter.' I can understand that. I used to be angry at those people, but that's part of the therapy that helped me. I'm no longer angry at people like that when I get either, "the look," or "the ridicule," or um, the blatant I'm seeing things or it's evil. I have had that.

YS: Are you still trying to talk to people at work about it recently?

JS: Recently, if I'm approached, mostly, I still don't say anything because work is work and it's difficult enough. But recently, I had a gentleman who lives in Boyle Heights, a really nice kid only 28, he's had some experiences. This young guy had an experience with a bunch of his friends at 2:30 in the morning and they were nauseous afterward. All he remembers is the light, big bright light, they didn't see anything other than the huge bright light. Friends of his, blocks away, came running to the park they were at because it was something they had never seen either. And that was recently, this week! And from time to time, I'll have somebody open up a little bit and then the subject will go from there which is comforting and some of them, uh, they need answers too. I am really grateful that I have a lot of my answers through regression, it has made a big difference in my life. (*John begins to cry*) I feel more of a whole person, where I never did before. (*crying*) I'm sorry.

YS: Oh, John, I am just glad that over the years, me and CERO, were able to be there for you. Do you feel, John, because you have had these experiences just about all of your life, it has made you a better person, a stronger person...have you thought about that?

JS: Yes, absolutely, the impact and repercussions of the activity goes on such levels, major profound levels, it has made me a more aware person, a better person, I understand much more of realities and energy, I know that there is much more to this physical third dimension. It's led into other things that have allowed me to go beyond the everyday, to a better understanding of things that are to be and that do happen. But it has taken a while, it's a long road, the therapy has helped me throughout become aware of all these things that now I do understand. Because before, just being trapped as a victim, I stayed there, and there was a purpose, I needed to get that out. And through therapy, it helped get beyond, I know there is more to the experience than just the experiments. There is a higher purpose, not to say that I'm anything special, but there is a higher purpose, and I'm involved (*John's voice begins to quiver*).

YS: John you say, from the beginning you realize now that you are part of them and they are part of you…how did you come to that conclusion?

JS: Part of it was through the experiences themselves that I don't want to say conditioning, but them helping me acknowledge and be aware that we are all connected and I am part of them and they are part of me and it was major solidified when, which was a hard therapy to get through, when they showed me a baby they said was mine and I denied it, I said that I didn't have babies but, they assured me it was mine and to feel love for the child, and which I did, and that extends the line of us all onto another reality, not just me and so, in that way it's been a major difference.

A lot of things that went on with trips, experiencing missing time, I fully remember was events that are so ingrained and etched into my mind, they were so difficult to deal with and I had no reference so, I put them in the back of my mind and went on, but the experiences kept happening until I could no longer put them on the back shelf, and that was the time for me and I'm grateful that I found the resources in you, to help me muddle through the situation. Anything that's hard work and difficult, sometimes there's a grand reward at the end.

YS: Do you know, or do you remember or are aware of any experiences, within the last five to ten years?

JS: Absolutely, a major experience I had, I am grateful I was with a friend. We were coming out of the Sequoias, it was ten o'clock at night, we were coming back the same way we went up, it was a massive, big orb in the sky, I call it, I thought it looked like embers, a fire that died down, that's what it looked like to me.

YS: This was in the sky?

JS: It was in the sky in front of us, a massive, big, huge orb, it blinked out, went to the left, blinked on again, saw it, it was behind us. Me and a friend had major missing time then too. But I was grateful that somebody was there with me that time. She was kind of in shock, it was traumatic for her, but, the thing is that we saw an object and that stopped at that. We did have missing time, but she never went into the regression of figuring out what happened and I never did either. That is one of the major big experiences I would like to look into, unfortunately, my friend who was with me passed away. That experience really is the last one I want to figure out. I remember the events before and after, it's just the time in between. This one I need to know.

YS: Since you started doing regressions on your 1980 and other experiences, all these years, have your brother or sister mentioned anything, do they remember anything?

JS: You know, I just saw my sister last week and she remembers distinctly, I was living with her and a friend at the time. Upon coming back from that trip, they asked me what happened and because the person I was supposed to meet up there, she called my family because I was late and they were very nervous about what was going on. My sister recalled the conversation we had when I got back. She said that I told her the events up to seeing the light moving real slow, wasn't a helicopter, no noise, and wanting to see what was going on, she said I was getting emotional, so she stopped right there.

YS: So your sister remembers you coming back and talking about it.

JS: Yes, yes, she remembers. And after so many years, she told me that she remembers with the light outside her bedroom, her room was next to mine. Which was a surprise to me, we never had that conversation before. She said that she was afraid of the lights, but she knew that they weren't there for her. She finally divulged that, which I was very surprised, but I was absolutely happy that it's another conversation for me through this healing process.

YS: So, this is the time when you were about eight years old, you were missing from your bed.

JS: Yes, my brother woke up and I was nowhere to be found, it was a small house. My family said they looked for me everywhere for about a half an hour. I remember at some point, standing in the kitchen, my mother coming around the corner, screaming hysterically, 'where were you!' I didn't say anything, I didn't know at the time, I thought I was hiding or something. The next night, I peed in that area and I had problems with that after that night. I had already resolved that before, but when that experience happened, I started urinating in bed and in that corner.

YS: So this is the experience your sister remembers. In your conversation with her, did she remember anything happening to her?

JS: She says no. But we have had mutual experiences, we are very close. I remember five years ago when my mother got hurt, I was in major distress. My sister lives in Texas, I needed her, I wanted her to come, but I wouldn't ask her. At that time, she was having activity, orbs around the house and flashes of light out of the corner of her eyes, which she had never seen before and it was happening to me, so we were having similar experiences and the same with the clocks. She said that she was having problems with her clocks and I was having the same thing with my clocks. Mine was doing 2:22, 3:33, 2:34, 4:56. Not that I was doing anything consciously, but I needed help and I guess my anxiety and the pressure of that was creating some type of activity on her end. This experience doesn't stop, the abductions or the sightings, it goes on to different areas and different genres that I had no idea. Not that I was trying to make this happen, but I think through stress, um some sort of activity was happening between us. That was another strange little thing, I don't know if that's tied to the experience or not. But I think once a person goes through the experiences, the lessons which are taught go beyond just the abductions, about energy and time and manipulating things.

YS: Manipulating what sort of things, John?

JS: Um, things, clocks, lights, energy, stuff like that, not always on will, I can't psycho-kinetically move a pencil across a table, but other things will happen, I can't say, I can make it happen, but they will happen through sometimes stress.

YS: I know we have discussed this during a CERO meeting. But because of your experiences or because of your experiences, do you think that your psychic abilities have been enhanced?

JS: Well, of course that's part of it, that's the way they communicate. It's part of the learning process, communication and activity through the brain radiates past our physical being and that sort of thing what they do. It can be transferred and brought to this area, though it is heavy here, there's a way to figure out and it's a muscle and an ability that can be worked on. Some of it I do, some of it I don't want to, a lot of it, I don't want to know the future.

YS: Do you feel that you have seen future events?

JS: On a personal level, yes, I don't get into and I do not...I put the brakes on all that other stuff as seeing events, world events or city events...I never have worked on that because I think that's something that's gonna be a problem for me in a way that it's, um, it's distracting, I want to get back to my everyday life. Sometimes I know things about people, but for me, I refuse to divulge information because the bigger picture, day to day lives for people, I don't want to disrupt and it's nothing I want to get "the look" or "the ridicule" about so...there's a bigger plan and a bigger scheme and most of us don't know what's going to happen minute to minute. So for me to give somebody information that I might know...I'm just not ready for that and most other people are not and I'm not sure what people want to know certain things or not want to know certain things so that's another distraction for me that I refuse to get into. I just need to go about my life and try to work on me...my stuff. For the most part, yes, I have certain abilities to know certain things, but, on the psychic level, I never wanted to work on that area, I just don't need to know.

YS: It's been a lot for you and many other people to just deal with your experiences and try to make sense and incorporate them into your life.

JS: I know there are certain things that I need to do through what I have been taught, there's another level I need to go to at the moment...when I'm ready, it might be soon and I think it is soon.

YS: Is this something that has been told to you by the beings that you were with?

JS: It's a knowing thing for me, not so much what I've been told, it's a development thing and it just seems like

71

the next stage, the next development, the next experiment or exercise for me. I just know that it is part of what I should be doing, it's part of the program…my program, I need to continue the development. I know part of it is going to be really scary and disturbing for me, but it's something that I need to do, it's another part of the healing, as the hypnosis wasn't always easy, but going through the events and seeing the personal activity, the interaction but always on the other end of the therapy, I always felt better, it's always been a weight lifted off of me and I felt more of a whole person (*becomes emotional*). And this is the next level for me.

YS: It seems that the major experience for you was the New Year's Eve 1980, missing time experience.

JS: Yes, it was a major experience, because people were expecting me, they knew what time I would be there, they knew what time I left, it just didn't involve me, it involved the person that was waiting, it involved my family, because they knew, and then when I came back and the story that I told them about the light with no noise. So that was a major big experience for me, but I have had three or four others similar to that and each one was just really profoundly, a rude awakening, in my face type of thing. But yes, that 1980 experience was major, because it didn't just involve me, it involved others.

YS: John, I know this was very difficult for you, we did a few sessions on this, but do you ever think about the baby that was shown to you and what became of that child?

JS: Well, I think, um, for me, I know I think it was not only just that one, there was one other child, but I do think about it, I do believe that I have experiences that they, um, put emotion through me to help the development of that child and some aspects of the bonding and the experience for me and also the development of that child, uh, helping them help that child develop through some stages for answers, as I think most sentient human beings want to know where they came from and are they loved. I think also, too, I believe I have had other experiences in the development of the child and um, which has helped me and I know helped the child develop, in a way, they're lacking certain abilities and so that was very important for them and the child and me.

72

YS: Is this something that you remember on a conscious level, helping them with the development of these children?

JS: The part about the tanks and when they first showed me the baby was so traumatic that that memory I retrieved through hypnosis, the other stuff about the development I know, as far as you ask about definite conscious recall, some of this stuff I know, it's just inside of me, these memories come in sort of a subtle way, it's not a physical type of I'm seeing a tree or house right now, but I know in my mind and in my heart that the continued process of the development was happening, I don't remember the exact events when I was taken, only hints like waking up not feeling so good or the top of my head hurt or my clock all of a sudden going out or other weird things, but it's just a knowing thing.

YS: Do you think that any of those experiences when you're helping them with the development of that child were done here and not in their environment?

JS: Well, for me, I think it is mostly done in their environment, um, I think for that child or now adult to transcend and come here physically, I don't think that was the plan of that child. Like the small grays, the drones that do the work, that is not the purpose of that being, to come here and interact with me. It's for me to go there and interact on that level.

YS: John, do you recall how you helped in the development of that baby?

JS: It's mostly emotional, an interacting thing. There's nothing I could teach this child as far as physics, uh, anything like that, it's mostly just the interaction, the day to day, to know who they are. Even people who are adopted, they always seek their parents out, or most kids do, there's something inside of them, they're driven to find their roots. It's the same thing here, it's part of the development, part of the growth and the interaction of knowing "where I came from and who is this person."

YS: One of our theories is that they, "the beings" don't seem to have the capability of our emotions and even with the fact that they are more technologically advanced than we are, they still need us for development.

JS: Oh, absolutely, I know people who are highly intelligent, but they lack "people skills."

YS: Last time you interacted with that child, do you get a sense of how old that child is?

JS: As far as knowing when the last interaction was, I'm thinking it was probably at the end of 2006, I had a strong sense that I had an interaction that I needed, the child, but now an adult. I'm feeling that this wasn't the last interaction, but it might not happen again, I believe it was kind of a "goodbye" type thing. Why, I don't know, but that was the sense that I get. It was sort of that phase was gone and it's time for something else.

YS: Do you have a picture in your mind of what the child looks like?

JS: Um, yes, of course I do. More of human features, still very thin, very meek, still with a purpose and a meaning to do something. It seems almost to be driven, it needed whatever information it needed from me. It seems like it's gone beyond that and it's time for the separation and for us to move on. I think in a way they might have told me that helping in my next phase is for me to seek them out rather than them coming to get me and bringing me to the situation. I think it's like holding something away from somebody that's dear to them (*John becomes extremely emotional*). And the person trying to get there, I think it's something that they're withholding from me.

YS: Something like your child?

JS: Yeah, the child/adult they're withholding.

YS: So that you go on to your next phase?

JS: Correct, so I can develop an interaction on my terms and my level and it's sort of they're not going to facilitate it anymore for me. It's up to me.

YS: So it seems that you and that child both have a purpose and it's now time to move forward into that next phase of whatever you both are supposed to accomplish.

JS: I think the withholding thing isn't a cruel thing, it's more of a helpful thing for me and it's the next level that I need to attain.

YS: I know we talked about this earlier, but is it something that you think the time is now?

JS: The time is now for me. Of course, I always have to be concerned about the day to day and paying bills, so I'm a little apprehensive, but the time is now and it's something that I have to do. I believe it's part of the development, part of the process, part of what I've been conditioned and brought up to do as far as they're concerned. They haven't left me, they're still there, it's just that they're leaving it more in my hands and it's up to me now to seek them out and facilitate a way to do that. I think I know, I do have a way to do it, it's just taking the time and the energy and the willingness to go to that level. It's scary in a way because I don't want to displace my life too much, I still have to go work and pay my bills.

YS: Which is our reality, right?

JS: (*Laughs*) Yeah.

YS: Is there anything else that you want or need to express

JS: It's been a long road and I'm still happy and thrilled that I'm here and have gone through it. There's a light at the end (*crying*) for me, there's nothing else, this takes priority, really for me and um, I'm absolutely thrilled and happy that I got to this point, that I can deal with it and be more accepting of what's going on through the hypnosis and you helping me. I am feeling more of a whole person, where I always felt scattered and tattered and torn and broken. I still remember all that, but that doesn't seem to affect me now because I feel more whole. The therapy has helped me put so many of the pieces of the puzzle together. There are continuing questions, because this is just so big and so strange that it's difficult to accept and even though the activity was there, it's that leap to say "yes, this is happening," and that I took with you and I trusted you to do that and it's made a big difference in my life, I feel, absolutely, that there's hope for me where I didn't before. (*crying*)

YS: I think when a person finally acknowledges the reality of their experiences, and I have seen it over the years, the person is then able to grow. And John, you briefly mentioned, another child?

JS: The whole awakening and becoming a whole person was done through the therapy, figuring out that this is part of my life. About the other child, it was more so, I think something happened and it didn't work out, it was there for a while then I mostly have the understanding that there's the initial one. But something didn't work out with that other child, I don't know exactly what, there was something wrong with the child through the development and it happened early on. I don't feel the presence of the second, later child, there was no interaction after a period of time. The initial one is a female.

YS: You have done good work, John; you have played an important role with CERO as new members come into the group

An interesting side note to this, John called to tell me that on Thursday, August 19, 2007, the day after John's session, he noticed a perfect triangle on his left hand. As John explained to me, he wears two layers of gloves to do his construction work and it was not until later that day, while showering, he noticed his fresh mark which was raised and tender. I asked him if the triangle appeared to be a bruise, needle points or a layer of skin. John told me that there were several layers of skin removed which formed the triangle shape. It took a week for the mark to finally disappear.

As a long-time client, John knows that when physical marks appear overnight, I urge the individual to take photographs, since these marks often disappear as fast as they appear.

John: I know you have told us a million times to be sure to take photos, but, this experience has become such a part of me that I am almost blasé. You know as it has happened in the past with our CERO members, sometimes, body marks come up after a meeting. It's when I talk to someone like you, in depth about 'them', it tunes them in when I'm talking about them. It's just their way of telling me that they are there and they are not going away.

CHAPTER 4: Alfonso Martinez

"I'm floating through that thing….
right through the bottom."

A. Alfonso Seeks Help For Unexplained Incidents

I met Alfonso Martinez early in 1993 when I was lecturing at the Los Angeles chapter of the Mutual UFO Network (MUFON). After the meeting, I speak to audience members who have questions about my presentation. Alfonso came up to me and asked for my business card. He told me he would like to book an appointment to discuss some incidents that had occurred throughout his life.

On May 10, 1993, Alfonso Martinez came into my office for his Initial Interview. During the interview, Alfonso spoke in great length about his very difficult childhood and how, as an adult, he has difficulty trusting people. Since childhood, Alfonso suffered from unexplained fears. The fear of being taken; recurrent dreams of having to decide whether to save himself or die with family; floating dreams; fear of heights; and being lifted against his will. As long as he can remember, he has felt the need to lock doors and windows due to the fear of someone or something coming to get him. Feelings of being watched; often awakened by bright lights outside his window. Unexplained bruises and body marks. Since reading about the phenomena of "missing time," Alfonso stated, "I want to find out about missing parts of incidents," that he experienced in childhood. He shared that:

> AM: See, the main reason why I came to you is because I saw you on TV a couple of times now. And I really never liked myself till about two years ago. Two years ago, when a co-worker casually revealed a similar incident in the same neighborhood, I started reaping the benefits. I started feeling good. And as that started coming up, I suddenly quit hiding myself. I was real reserved. I didn't want anyone to know anything about me, and now, I see that it works against me. I'm tired of hiding.
>
> Mainly, I'm curious about four incidents. I would consider bizarre things that happened to me would not seem that important, but for some reason, the emotional energy attached to them is not appropriate and I'm curious. I am open minded and I figure probably nothing happened, because of my upbringing, I know that you can

77

make abstract things out of it. And if so, that's fine, I don't care, but I'm curious, I'm curious because there is more than one incident.

Like countless others, Alfonso was bothered by partial memories, as far back as 6 years of age, where he was physically missing from his Grandmother's backyard. It was the summer of 1949. Alfonso remembers that one day, around twilight, he was playing in her backyard and climbing his favorite tree. He would just "hang in there and just rest and just feel real mellow, I used to just love that". The next thing he remembers is walking from the backyard to the front of the house, it was already dark, he was frightened and confused. he never played in the backyard after dark, "I'm afraid at night and I'm afraid to be back there, 'cause the trees and stuff look like monsters at night". But, this time, he found himself alone in the dark of night, he recalls moving very fast, almost running to the front yard.

Alfonso remembers his older sister yelling at him, asking him where he had been. Everyone else was in the house, she was looking for him. His sister told him about a bright light in the sky, the whole neighborhood saw it, everyone ran into their houses, the unusual light scared them. She continued yelling at Alfonso, frustrated as to why he didn't see the light. She could not understand how he did not see it. She accused him of lying and hiding from her. She told him that she went to the backyard to look for him, but he was nowhere in sight.

AM: She said there was no way I could have not seen the light and there was no way that I could not have heard her.

The memory of his sister yelling at him, telling him about the strange bright light that everyone in the neighborhood ran from, everyone saw it, but him.

During the remainder of the interview, Alfonso told me about three other incidents that he wanted to explore. Alfonso had three hypnotic regressions on the "Backyard" incident. The following is taken from transcripts of his sessions:

AM: It's daylight approaching dusk and I'm hanging around the trees just being by myself. I got a feeling I've got to get out of the tree and leave. I don't know why. I suddenly got the feeling I'm all alone in the world. "I oughta jump off that tree and get out of here.
AM: I want to move, but I can't. I have a feeling like soldiers or cops or something are coming up.

YS: Why do they seem to be soldiers or cops?

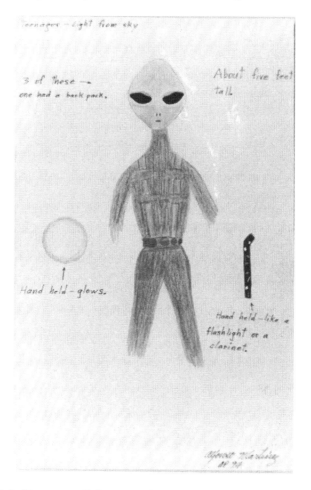

AM: Because of the way they move in unison, there's about three of them and they're wearing what looks like one piece leotard uniforms and there's something on the belts, some metallic thing on the belts. Their heads are bigger than normal, they look like eggs. They move real weird, that's it, they're floating, all smooth like.

AM: (*agitated*) They're pointing something at me, they point a long rod-like at me that controls me in the air, I'm floating like a balloon. (*crying*) I'm scared they're gonna kidnap me and take me away and I'm not gonna see my family no more.

YS: Remember, Alfonso, whatever happened to you, you came out of it and you are fine, strong and healthy. You are just allowing yourself to explore, now without any fear, just describe for me the next thing that happens.

AM: There's a big light, a big ball of some type, but the white light, it's bright, I thought it was the sun. The light's coming from the bottom of this big ball. I'm floating up through that thing...right through the bottom. It's real bright and somehow, I just float right through it.

YS: OK, you are doing fine, just keep describing what you are observing.

AM: I'm inside a room, and it's bright as hell, tremendously bright, but it doesn't seem to bother my eyes. There are some lights that are flashing going on or off, just like machines or something. I got a feeling I'm being watched.

YS: Alright now, taking a deep cleansing breath, look around you and describe what you see, hear or feel.

AM: There's one that's doing most of the talking...or is it by thought? It's hard to tell, but there's more than one...I'd say at least three more...the one that's trying to pacify me is a woman.

YS: Does she look like a woman?

AM: No...not like an earth woman...she has big eyes, but there's something real slender and graceful about her body. I can tell she's a woman.

YS: Do you get the feeling that they all look the same?

AM: They've got big heads...they're half solid, half energy like. They've got big eyes and they float. (*pause*) The lady wants to talk to me or something. It's hard to explain This...I know what I'm supposed to...like when they share feelings with me...I just know it. I pick up theirs too. I feel like I'm part of them somehow, but I don't look like them. She's reassuring me that I'm like them, but not the way I understand. (*long pause*) Something's gonna happen. I don't know what.

YS: Why do you feel that something's going to happen?

AM: Cause they talk when they're going to do something, I always know it. (*gasps*) There's a table or something in the middle of the room, there's a light being focused on that table, I got a feeling that I'm supposed to go to the table. (*crying*) I think I know why I feel funny. I'm naked. I feel ashamed to be naked. I don't know what I'm supposed to do, I can't get out of here!

YS: You're just exploring now, you came out of this and you are safe, just tell me what's happening.

AM: I just got this strong feeling. I got this feeling in my head that nobody wants to hurt me. I got a feeling that they're going to wait for me as long as it takes, and I'm going to go to that table like I'm supposed to. I'm thinking maybe I should go to that table. I start, half walking, half floating…as I keep approaching the table, the table keeps getting brighter. It looks like to me that the light's coming from somewhere else, but for some reason, the table lights up. This table is like molded or something, as I get next to it. It's getting lower. It's about two inches off the ground. I think I'm supposed to lay down on it. This stuff bothers me.

YS: You're doing fine, Alfonso, your mind is sharp and clear, just describe everything that you are experiencing.

AM: (*long pause*) Laying down on the table. There's something toward the ceiling. The ceiling is rising. (*almost in a whisper*) The thing is a gallery.

YS: Can you describe it?

AM: It's like an operating gallery. I look down at my hand, I can see my bones…the red of my blood, and there's a small red light flying around the room real fast. Things are coming out of the ceiling.

YS: What do you see coming out?

AM: Looks like globes…some are shaped like drums, they like point to me…they change colors and move back and forth…like they're sweeping my body.

YS: Do you see anybody in the gallery?

AM: I know they're up there. I got a feeling they don't want me to see them. This is confusing…'cause I know they're up there and I know those machines can read my mind. There's people up there all right. I got a feeling that they want to know me.

YS: Just take a deep breath, you are doing fine, Alfonso, describe the next thing that happens. Is there anyone standing around the table with you, do you sense anybody near you?

AM: No…that's weird, that table I'm on just pulled away, disconnected like.

YS: Tell me what happens next. You will be able to describe everything.

AM: Looks like desks coming out of the wall, a computer room, computer modules or something like black workbenches. Whatever instruments they have are real pretty. They look like jewels. They look like they are manuals or levers, they don't look like ours. There's a chair that comes from the floor, it is shaped like a pie, so that my legs can swing either way, it's comfortable and has arm rests. When I sat in it, it fit me, it moved me up to the console. The panel has like lenses in it, there's a light or something that sticks up on the right. When I put my hands over it, things happen on the screen.

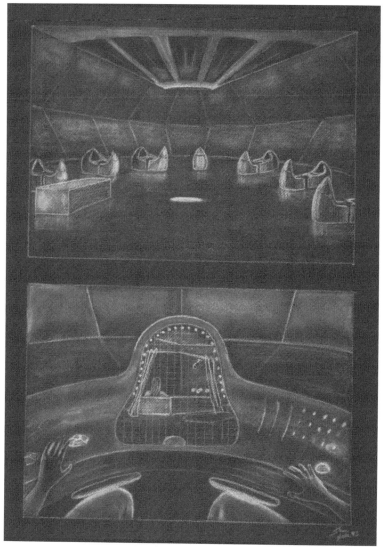

Artist Steve Neill

YS: "What do you see on the screen?

AM: I see my hand, the thing's acting like a camera, that's weird, I can see my hand on the screen. When I touch the big jewels on my left, like embedded in the panel, they give me energy or something. I feel dumb. I don't know what I'm supposed to do with this stuff. There's screens on the walls like television screens, they go all the way around. All the screens are showing different things happening everywhere.

YS: Can you describe what you see on the television screens?

AM: Pictures, but not like pictures we know...they're bigger, better than 3D. A bunch of balls and stuff moving. Maybe that's what they're showing...a small, I think they're showing me a miniature solar system that's perfect. They keep bringing up different scenes at different times, geometric shapes, prisms and weird stuff like that, and they watch my reaction...some kind of psychology test I guess? I can see my house, where that tree is or I was...see cars running on the road. Looks like...seems to me that there's something remotely in there somewhere...sending back all this information or something.

Alfonso found himself in another room, which he called "the second floor", he described being escorted in an "elevator" and into a room with "lounge chairs" that move around the room. He described stations with consoles and screens, which reminded him of "video game things" where beings with big "garlic heads" were working.

In this room, he described seeing a "human guy" wearing a "sparkly blue uniform" with black trim, "the trim isn't sparkly", though". As I questioned him about the "human," he said that he was wearing what reminded Alfonso of what astronauts wear on their heads, which was blue like his uniform.

AM: He looked at me and smiled, a regular white guy with blond hair... white hair, about six feet tall, normal build. To me, he looks like an athlete. Along with this "human" male, he also saw a "human female" with a sparkly gray uniform. The female was looking at a big screen while holding "...a clear, plastic, square thing with two concentric circles in the middle and a rod coming out of it...it all looks like it's clear plastic, but for some reason, it glows, she points, it hits those circles and things happen on the screen. She looks at me, like she's on guard duty or something.

As I listened to Alfonso describe these "human" looking beings, I remembered Travis Walton's account of entering a room and describing a human looking male wearing a blue uniform. In this room, Travis also described what he thought was either a map or a view of space filled with brilliant stars.

Alfonso described a very similar scene. At one point during Alfonso's experience, he described being in a room where he described a section of the wall which was "transparent, it goes from the bottom and then it follows the shape of the ship up. I can see the stars out there...I never see stars like this before. I mean they're beautiful...it's black and the stars are real bright, it's beautiful...I think I'm in heaven." (*tearfully*) "I feel real confused...will I get back to my own...my world...how am I going to make anybody believe me?"

B. Alfonso Receives Confirmation

After his session was over, Alfonso told me about something that happened at work. One day, he was talking to Ernest, one of his co-workers, the conversation led to the subject of UFOs, asking each other, "have you ever seen a UFO?" His friend began telling him about a light that he, his brother and several neighborhood kids saw when he was a kid. As he listened to Ernest's story, it occurred to Alfonso that he lived in that same area around the same time, why didn't he see the light? Then, like a bolt of lightning, Alfonso suddenly remembered the night his sister was frantically looking for him, yelling and telling him about all the neighborhood kids running into their homes frightened by a very bright light.

Shortly after Alfonso's session, I received a letter in the mail. The letter was from his co-worker, Ernest. For the sake of privacy, I have omitted his last name and address. The following is his letter in its entirety:

Ernest

Born May 29, 1946
East Los Angeles, California

At about the age of 6 or 7 years old, while playing in the street in front of my house (*address withheld*) with my friends. My older brother and his friend were also there on the street. We saw a light come down from the sky. I thought that my brother and his friend had broken the street light. So we all ran back to our houses.

But as I remembered, the light went back into the sky.

Before my brother died about seven years ago, I asked him if he remembered that night the light came down and went back up and he said "yes" he did.

And that is my story.

Signed,

Ernest
September 9, 1993

P.S. The light was about the size of a basketball, white in color. It came to about ten feet off the ground. When it went up, it went straight up.

The conversation and subsequent letter from Ernest was a turning point for Alfonso. Because of the abuse Alfonso and his siblings suffered growing up, Alfonso was filled with feelings of inadequacy and self-doubt. However, receiving this confirmation from a co-worker during what started out to be a casual conversation, led Alfonso on his path to self-realization, self-respect and his purpose in life.

C. Alfonso's Personal Progress Report

Since Alfonso's first session back in the summer of 1993, he continues to struggle with his experiences. Even though I have witnessed this emotional roller coaster, I have also seen a profound change in Alfonso, a spiritual transformation.

While writing Alfonso's chapter, I asked him how his experiences have influenced his life. On April 23, 2007, I received a letter from Alfonso, which he shared:

AM: I still don't know what happened to me. I believe that being abducted is only a part of my story. I should write my own book, but here is a very small taste of my views.

What I state here is a mixed bag of thoughts that are a mixture of some old and some newly evolved perceptions that I believe. The beings did not make it very clear to me what they wanted or more than likely I was in a higher state of consciousness. When I would return to my present reality, my more suppressed nature could not handle the other level of awareness. Therefore, don't blame the aliens if I got it all wrong.

I have partial memories of incidents that happened to me in reality. For example, as a child, I was playing outside with my younger brothers. I kept having a feeling of being watched, with intensity, from above. I thought that maybe God or some of his workers were observing me and judging me because I was a bad kid. I come from an abusive, disempowering, controlling and hostile family. I'm sixty-four and I'm still working on myself. Maybe in another hundred years, I'll be almost normal. I saw a small intensely bright red light. It fell from something that was hiding in the clouds. Just as it was about to hit me, I crossed my arms over my head and face. As I looked to see what happened, because I was not hit nor heard it land, I became aware that the shadows were long. A moment before, it had been a few hours before noon or noon, now, it was afternoon. I had already been called insane many times and now I had visual proof. I was overcome with abject fear. There is much that I'm leaving out, but I just want to give you an idea of what I have experienced.

As I struggle to accept myself, I wanted to know more about the missing parts of the incidents that I had experienced. But no matter what I tried, I could not remember. When I first became aware of the concept of missing time, I decided to find a hypnotist. I went to a few, but when I was interviewing them and I would mention that I might have had something related to flying saucers, their demeanor would change to something I didn't like. I needed someone that would listen, without prejudice and also be honest. If I was insane, tell me politely. I would then take my pills and live in la la land and would no longer be concerned about these memories. I was watching television and the program screened Yvonne Smith and she stated that she worked with abductees. I wasn't one, but I thought that at least she would be open-minded. I happened to see her at a MUFON meeting and I approached her. We set up a meeting and I went to have her attempt to hypnotize me. I did not think that I could be hypnotized, because I still don't trust people. When she put me under, I began to relate what had happened in the missing portions of my memories. I am ambivalent about the sessions. In some ways, some other incidents are clarified and yet, I still find it difficult to accept. Eventually, I was introduced to her abductee support group, (CERO). I'm the crazy one there.

The group mostly talked about their experiences, past and present. My main focus was denying I was one and then to what purpose? I am not special. I have lived a life of fear, distrust, denial and abuse. I am not a good example. In my attempts to understand my experiences, both other worldly and everyday reality, I have concluded that we are very quickly going to experience the beginning of the end. The saddest part of the whole thing is that it is not set in stone. We can choose another reality; all of us, but we are sheep. Many people are beginning to awaken to higher states of consciousness, but the majority still buy the same old dog and pony show. Science is showing us that reality is merely a perception. I believe that we are little seeds of God. But, we are gods nevertheless. We must live from our hearts and follow what our hearts inspire us to do.

I believe that we have been systematically misguided, ignored, brainwashed and exploited. I believe that the universe is much more majestic than we believe. I believe that we are much more divine than we allow ourselves to imagine. Our fellow humans, a few, have been doing this deliberately. I don't care why. I want us to wake up to our divine and awesome potential. I believe that we are seeds of creators.

With great difficulty, I have been ever so gradually, allowing myself to experience psychic endeavors. Mostly, I am an empath, I feel things. On very rare occasions, I have experienced a little future knowledge. My biggest obstacle is my own negative self-image. What my parents started on me, I perfected. Little by little, I have been acccpting myself and the world a little more. I try not to focus on the negative, because it gives it more power. I try to make the world a little better as best as someone like me can do. It is a struggle, but I believe that it is better to light a candle than to curse the darkness. If we will only try to allow ourselves to believe, we can make a paradise where we live. I suspect that some of us that are spiritually awake, may be harvested and integrated by other life forms. The majority will continue on the path to an unimaginable destruction. The ones that blossom later, will become seeds for the future generations. I will not be among the harvested, I'm still too biased, but you could.

Alfonso's experiences are similar to many "experiencers." Yet, like some, he still wishes that he had a mental condition or some other explanation so he can discount his memories and have a "normal" problem. You could take a pill, go to counseling and get better. First, his confirmation of his experiences by a co-worker who grew up in the same neighborhood helped him see that he was not alone in his experiences. While he chose hypnosis to explore his "missing time," he felt that he would be resistant because of his trust issues.

Even in a group therapy setting, he sees himself as separated from others while his experiences are remarkably similar to others. The type of procedure; types of aliens; and the setting all draw similar parallels with other experiencers. His predictions of the future of humanity are eerily similar to many of my clients, some who can remember consciously and others who recover these impressions through hypnosis. An increasing number of experiencers have conveyed the same thoughts about human destiny. Alfonso put it into words as follows:

> AM: I have concluded that we are very quickly going to experience the beginning of the end. The saddest part of the whole thing is that it is not set in stone. We can choose another reality; all of us, but we are sheep. Many people are beginning to awaken to higher states of consciousness, but the majority still buy the same old dog and pony show.

He sees humanity as on a path towards destruction. Most are going on with their lives as if nothing is wrong. A few are awakening to find that humanity must change the way it conducts itself or we are approaching "the beginning of the end". His sessions took place in 1993 and his letter to me on the urgent need to change the trajectory of humanity was written in 2007. As the reader will see in Part Two, these warnings from experiencers are increasing in both frequency and urgency.

Alphonso's "warnings" about the future of mankind in 2007 are an early indicator of the change in focus that I began seeing in those I was helping to cope with their experiences. This trend and what it may mean is discussed in more detail in Part Two.

CHAPTER 5: Double Abduction Of
John And Jesse

A. Jesse And John: Beginning Of A Long Relationship

A man named Jesse Long called me to inquire about my work as a certified hypnotherapist. He explained he had been treated by two psychologists and a chiropractor for some recurring emotional issues. The chiropractor used hypnosis in her practice, but Jesse wanted to go deeper into some disturbing memories. We decided to meet.

Jesse arrived at my office for an initial interview in July 1991. He appeared to be in his mid-30s. He had an athletic build but was very quiet and polite. He was a script supervisor for a film company that produced for major studios and television. He appeared to be nervous and troubled. Jesse stated he had been suffering from panic attacks, ranging in duration from five minutes to two hours. He claimed to have low self-esteem and to be lonely and depressed. For over thirty years, Jesse had been troubled by an incident that occurred while playing in the backyard with John, his brother, when Jesse was five years old. The first meeting in 1991 began our client/therapist relationship which has continued to the present day.

In 1957 John and Jesse's parents' backyard was lined with trees, flowers and covered with green grass which extended up a small hill behind their house. It was a typical backyard for the small town of Rogersville, Tennessee in the 1950s. There was a clothesline for the family to hang their laundry and a sandbox where Jesse and John would spend hours playing games and using their plastic buckets to build castles on the warm sunny days.

The day that continued to haunt Jesse began many years ago. He and John, who was a year younger, were playing happily in their sandbox, turning over their colorful buckets filled with sand as they surrounded themselves with their sandbox creations. For some unknown reason, Jesse's attention turned toward the hill, which he could see clearly from the sandbox. In our initial interview, he said he remembered seeing "a man standing holding what appeared to be an ax". He then described how "I took my brother's hand and we started up the hill" when Jesse saw the man "raise the ax."

At that point, Jesse's conscious memory came to a stop. As hard as he had tried in the decades since, he was unable to recover any further memory after the moment when he and John saw that "visitor" and they started walking up the hill. The memory continued to haunt him. Also, for as long as Jesse could remember, he always felt something on his left shin, directly under the skin. He told me he would have to roll down his sock so it would not rub his skin and cause additional discomfort.

Jesse had recovered some fragmentary memories of the episode while under hypnosis with the chiropractor/hypnotist two years before in 1989. But they only added to his confusion and increased his desire to know what happened that day.

He shared with me the transcripts from those earlier sessions, but the memories were indeed fragmentary. Jesse provided me with transcripts of his 1989 hypnosis sessions regarding his partial memories of 1957 to illustrate what he had recovered from the childhood incident so far. In one session, "DC" (the chiropractor/hypnotist) had regressed Jesse back to that time when he was 5 years old. As he once more looked up the hill, Jesse saw something he hadn't seen before...a house...but it was proving difficult for him.

> *DC:* Remember you told me you remembered what you thought was a house back there; just be able to see that and see it very clearly...be there. Let yourself experience it again...tell me what you see.
> *Jesse:* People working on a house.
> *DC:* And how many people do you see?
> *Jesse:* There's somebody over there.
> *DC:* Take a good look, just remember how many people do you see?
> *Jesse:* 8 or 6. One guy's just standing there with...just standing with a long thing...just standing there. The others are moving around and he's just standing there.
> *DC:* You said he was standing there holding something long?
> *Jesse:* Yes, like...like a big stick. It's very light in color.
> *DC:* What color would it be, Jesse?
> *Jesse:* White

During his hypnotic regression, Jesse described a house being built at the top of the hill with several people moving around and one person standing holding something in his hand. As the session progressed, Jesse described being in a prone position and that he would not feel his arms, hands or feet.

> Jesse: I don't feel my arms. (*Jesse turns white*) I thought I heard something.
> DC: Let's go to your legs, knees and thighs. Remember clearly, do they feel normal?
> Jesse: No, they're tingling.
> DC: What else do you feel, Jesse?
> Jesse: There's something on my chest...it's a box.
> DC: Does it cover your whole chest?
> Jesse: Yes, it's not thick, it feels longer than my body (*Jesse gasps*)
> DC: What's happening now, Jesse?
> Jesse: I better keep my eyes closed...there's somebody over there. (*Jesse taking quick breaths*) On my left...I better not look...I won't look!

DC suggested to Jesse who was feeling very anxious, to "take a quick peek" at who he saw standing on his left side.

> Jesse: I saw it...he is all light...white...he's looking at me... (*breathing quickly*) Looking at my chest...OH! My right arm hurts!
> DC: Jesse, I want you to move forward just a little now and tell me what happens next...the sequence of events...what is happening now?
> Jesse: I think they've gone.
> DC: What do you see now?
> Jesse: My eyes are still closed...the box is still on my chest.
> DC: Does the box seem supported by anything or is it just lying on top of your chest?
> Jesse: It comes out of that up there. It's like a long arm coming out of the ceiling.

DC asked a few more questions about Jesse's surroundings, but he jumped to another memory about being in his childhood bedroom. When I read this passage in Jesse's transcript, it was clear to me that Jesse was not ready to relive the details of what happened, at least not during that session.

Jesse returned to the chiropractor's office for a second 1989 hypnosis session to attempt to retrieve from his subconscious more details regarding what he experienced in his childhood home. He was again hypnotized:

DC: Are you lying down?
Jesse: Yes.
DC: Each cell has a memory...tell me what happens now.
Jesse: I don't feel my leg...my left leg. There's...like a circle with a triangle in it, it's over there to the left. My leg hurts! My body is tingling all over.
DC: Jesse, can you see your leg now?
Jesse: No, I won't look!

While Jesse described himself in a lying position, the chiropractor asked him several times if he was wearing clothes to which he responded, "can't feel any". He described a series of bright, flashing white lights, some diamond shaped. He also described seeing a door which kept opening, but he was too distracted by the series of lights to answer any further questions by the chiropractor if anyone was coming in or out of the room. Considering that Jesse was five years old, it would appear his captors were using this brilliant light show to deliberately divert his attention from whatever they were doing to him physically.

As Jesse kept describing the "flash", flash...flash" of light, he also felt the "box" on his chest:

Jesse: It's on my chest and it's dark when I see the flash, it's like dark. The flash is behind...over there by my feet. Oh...oh, I...a triangle of light with a little something moving back and forth. I don't know what it is. All I can see is the triangle.

The chiropractor suggested that Jesse move forward in time and once more Jesse found himself in the top bunk of his bed in his Rogersville home. Once again this suggested to me that Jesse was not ready to face what might have been the purpose of his abduction.

DC: Jesse, a while back you felt a sharp pain in your leg. Look at your l leg...she what you see.
Jesse: Yeah, there's a dot there.
DC: How large is the dot...the size of a dime, nickel, penny or smaller?

Jesse: Real small...like a...a...like a dot that you would draw with a pencil, it looks sorta dark red.
DC: Is the dot just on the surface of the skin?
Jesse: Yeah, but there's something there.
DC: Do you remember how that dot got there?
Jesse: It's always been there. There's something under there. It hurts to touch it...I'm not supposed to touch it.
DC: Why are you not supposed to touch it?
Jesse: Because it will hurt.
DC: Did someone tell you not to touch it?
Jesse: It will hurt if I touch it. Just forget about it!

When I interviewed Jesse in 1991 regarding his 1957 backyard incident, he told me that was approximately the time when he first noticed something in his left leg. While his mother was bathing him one day, she saw a "scrape" on his leg and asked if he had fallen. Jesse knew he did not fall, but he refused to discuss it with his mother. He told me, "I don't know how it got there...it's always been there...I won't let her see, I don't want her to see it...it will hurt if she touches it."

One of the post regression notes from the session with the chiropractor read: "he didn't mention it during the session, but he later stated he felt a tap from a point into his upper left arm, as if he was given a shot."

Jesse had x-rays taken of his leg in 1989 which clearly showed a foreign object directly under the skin. After living with leg discomfort and pain for over 32 years, Jesse made the decision to have the object surgically removed. The doctor who performed the surgery requested anonymity. Following are photos of the removed object:

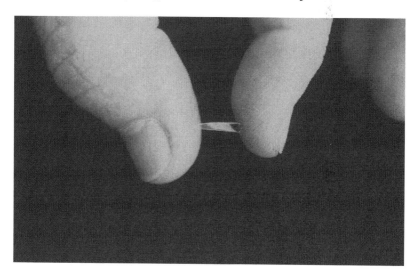

The triangular shaped object removed from Jesse's left leg had a glass-like appearance. A scientist conducted a preliminary analysis in November 1989. In his report, he stated that the "glass" or foreign object contained silicon, magnesium, calcium, phosphorus, and sulfur in unusual quantities. He calculated that the object was manufactured at 5,000 degrees Fahrenheit, which is significantly higher than the temperature used in making standard commercial glass, which is 2,000 degrees Fahrenheit. The scientist also observed that the object transmitted radio waves.

In July 1996, Jesse took the object to the Southwest Research Institute, a highly respected applied science and research organization in Austin,

Texas. Again, the findings were intriguing. The content of the implant was such which did not exist in the 1950s.

The Report reads in pertinent part:

Southwest Research Institute Materials and Structures Division

July 1, 1996

> *Summary of Analytical Results Performed on Jesse Long's Implant*
> *"The results of our various analyses of Jesse's implant have raised many intriguing questions and provoked equally intriguing speculations...*
> *I was astonished by the levels of calcium, phosphorous, and most surprising, sulfur in this specimen. No known glass or transparent ceramic was available in the 1950s with 6% phosphorus, 22% calcium and certainly not with sulfur at any measurable level, let alone 24.42%..."*

When Jesse began his 1991 private sessions with me, he was anxious to explore several other experiences that happened to him while on film shoots in Albuquerque, New Mexico and Gulf Breeze, Florida. He also hoped to uncover information about a "missing time" episode while driving on California's Interstate 10 as well as other unexplained incidents in his apartment in Burbank.

During hours upon hours of regression hypnotherapy, Jesse recovered startling memories of several "alien" medical procedures that he had undergone starting in childhood. As distressing as these revelations were, they explained the bruises, needle marks and rashes in very curious triangular shapes would appear on his body overnight.

One such episode took place in April 1994 after I had been working with Jesse for three years. It started with a frantic call from Jesse. He had awakened with a very strange mark on his body. Although he was aware of his experiences since childhood, this one was particularly disturbing to him. Jesse remembered going to bed around midnight. He was looking forward to some much needed rest as he had an early call on the movie set the next morning. He woke up at 4:00 a.m. As he stepped into the warm shower, Jesse felt a sharp stinging sensation. He stepped away from the force of the water and looked down in the direction of the pain. Jesse couldn't quite process what he was seeing. It appeared as if a layer of skin was removed from the top of his penis. It was in the shape of a triangle.

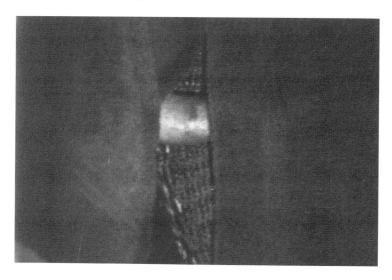

While investigating these cases, I also instruct my clients to not only keep a journal, but to take photographs of body marks that appear overnight. Most of these marks are not permanent and will often disappear as quickly as they appeared. Jesse grabbed his camera and asked his roommate to take a picture of the fresh mark.

We immediately scheduled a hypnosis session. Jesse arrived at my office for the session on April 21, 1994. He was clearly very nervous about the events that would have led to his strange body mark. As Jesse slowly drifted into a deep hypnotic sleep, I directed him back to that night...

> Jesse: There's a dark one at my feet, he's coming around to my left...I can't move!
> Yvonne: A dark one?
> Jesse: A dark being, a silhouette, he's coming around to my left...I see a big eyeball staring right into my face...I feel like I'm being pulled, oh, just pulled upward!

Jesse started to become agitated:

> Yvonne: Ok, Jesse, remember, this is not happening now; you will be able to describe without feeling the fear. Now take a look around you as you are feeling this pulling, are you in your bedroom?

His body tensed but his eyes moved under his closed eyelids.

> Jesse: No! I'm being pulled through this tunnel of light...pools of light... it's light then it gets dark.
> Yvonne: Is the dark one still with you?
> Jesse: Um...I think there's one on each arm...two of them. Oh, I see flashes of light all around.
> Yvonne: Are you still in the tunnel?
> Jesse: No...no, um...there's a ring of light right above me and it's spreading out over me, I think I'm inside. Ohhh, I'm feeling pressure on my eyes...they really hurt.
> Yvonne: Do you feel something touching your eyes?
> Jesse: Um...yeah, I think it feels like there's something uh, over my head to hold it down, but it's like pressure right on my eyeballs.
> Yvonne: Do you feel something over your entire head?
> Jesse: Uh...no...my right hand is numbed.
> Yvonne: Is something touching your right hand?
> Jesse: Um...no...it's just numb...there's the tall being to my left.
> Yvonne: Is this the same tall being?

A tall being had been a prominent figure in many of Jesse's experiences. I asked Jesse the question to clarify if this one was the same one.

> Jesse: Yeah...this big black thing came up over the left side of the table and it's leaning over me now, it's down on my chest, I think it's that restraining is...it's pretty big.
> Yvonne: You feel it over your chest?
> Jesse: Yeah, my chest is cold. There's this thing...what is it? Uh, this rod's coming down from the ceiling, it has a round ball on the end of it and there are four things sticking out of it...and it's like sparking from tip to tip. Light's being pushed out more really quickly. My right arm is tingling still. Just a lot of movement...the silhouettes are really moving around the table.
> Yvonne: Can you describe what these silhouettes look like?
> Jesse: Um...they can barely look up over the table, um, they're lit from behind, there's no lights on their face...And they have big heads and one is walking from the right side to my feet. And they're pressuring my eyes

100

again. The tall being is looking very, he's very close to my chest looking at me...leaning right down.

Yvonne: How many of the small ones do you see around you?

Jesse: Oh...um...they're not standing here right now...I was just rolled into this darker room. It's really cold in here.

Yvonne: Is this a smaller room?

Jesse: (taking deep breaths) Yeah...he's putting the tube on...over my penis.

Yvonne: Do you feel pain or discomfort?

Jesse: Um...my lower intestines really hurt.

Yvonne: Look down toward that area and tell me what's happening.

Jesse: There's a...oooh! It looks like sort of a half, like if you cut a ball in half and sit the top half on you and then there are spikes sticking out of it. Oh...it's really pressing down on my lower intestines. Just above the groin...uh, that hurts, it makes me feel like I have to go to the bathroom...just a lot of pressure.

It was clear that Jesse was in much distress as he described what he was physically experiencing.

Yvonne: Is that tube still on you?

Jesse: Oh, yeah...there they are...one on each side of me and one at my feet. And they're just down there working with the tube. It's hard to see exactly, because that...that black ball is sitting right on my intestines.

Jesse began to cry...

Yvonne: Ok, Jesse, take some deep breaths...look down toward your intestines and groin area and describe what is happening.

Jesse: Uh...there's two of them down there with that thing on my intestines, and, ok...they just lifted it off my intestines but, that thing's still around my penis and it...oh, they just took their sample.

Yvonne: Did you feel any pain?

Jesse: No, but I felt it, it's like once they took that thing off my intestines, there was no holding back.

The "sample" that Jesse described is the sperm sample procedure, which many male abductees report experiencing.

> Jesse: The one on my left, he reached over to the right and got something…he's got it in his hands. Oh…he just put something on my chest!
>
> Yvonne: Can you describe what he put on your chest?
>
> Jesse: Um, it's hard to see…um, they're really thin…they look like wires.
>
> Yvonne: Wires?
>
> Jesse: It looks like two, um, each one of the two splits off into two more…it's like a forked tongue.
>
> Yvonne: What do you feel as he put those wires on your chest?
>
> Jesse: (*breathing hard*) Right now, it's really cold, my feet are freezing. Oh, there's a rod to my left! Down at my legs…it's…it's pulsating light. One of them is looking at my groin area.
>
> Yvonne: Can you tell what he is doing?
>
> Jesse: He's doing something to the tube…oh, there's…it looks like a serrated knife…to my right.
>
> Yvonne: Can you feel what he is doing with the tube?
>
> Jesse: He has it over my penis.
>
> Yvonne: Can you describe the tube?
>
> Jesse: Well, um, it's real light in color…it's almost like it emits its own light somehow, maybe it's just reflecting light.

Experiencing the discomfort once again, Jesse's body tensed.

> Yvonne: Are you experiencing pain in your groin area?
>
> Jesse: Oh, I'm feeling pressure down there, they are pressuring down on my intestines area. It hurts so much and it's really cold…I'm cold all over.

He shivered as he became increasingly upset.

> Jesse: Light's pulsating right into my chest! My legs are going numb… they're tingling. The tall being is over to my left, he's to the left of my face, now he's at the top of my head…now he's over to my right and he's waking down to my feet, he's by my right foot…oh, my legs are really tingling.

Yvonne: Jesse, look down at your legs, can you tell what's making your legs tingle?
Jesse: Well, um...there's nothing there, except these wires still on my chest...oh, now, my whole body is starting to tingle, everything is tingling and my intestines are cramping up and they've still got that tube on me.
Yvonne: That light tube?
Jesse: Yeah, on my penis...it's still there, covering it. Lights are vibrating everywhere; my body is just vibrating really fast! Ow! Now there's this flash of light that hurts!

He cried out in great pain.

Yvonne: Take some deep breaths, Jesse, is the light hurting your eyes?
Jesse: Oh, it hurts my body, this place where the cables are coming out is flashing light...that tube is down there and flashes of light everywhere... OH, my whole body is vibrating...and...!
Yvonne: Ok, Jesse, you are doing fine, just tell me what's happening.

Crying from the pain, Jesse could barely verbalize what he was experiencing.

Jesse: Oh! That hurts! Well...they've...it feels like they've stimulated an ejaculation with electricity...and it hurts! That's really burning and it's like pressure right above...right above my penis, there at the base, like the tube is really...um...is really pulling hair on it. Oh, my goodness!

Very upset, crying and in obvious pain and discomfort.

Yvonne: I'm right here, Jesse, I'm going to touch your hand, you're doing fine, you're going to get through this.
Jesse: The door opened there, one of the silhouettes came around from my feet, he's over here to the left and he just removed the wires... and the tube just went up into the ceiling there, it's gone. The tall being is over to my left...he's looking right at me...right into my eyes.

When I brought Jesse out of hypnosis, he could not believe how excruciating the pain was he experienced during the electrical ejaculation. He was familiar with them taking his sperm from his previous regression sessions, but had never recalled this procedure.

Once Jesse began regression therapy, he had been trying to seek answers to why he has been targeted, why he has been put through so much physical pain and how their program involves him. It started with another unexplained mark on his body that had appeared from nowhere and was there years before.

Jesse was often out of state on location as a script supervisor. In 1990, he was driving through New Mexico on his way to a film shoot. This is how Jesse described to me what happened.

In September 1990 I was called to work in New Orleans on the film *The Awakening*. I decided to stop in Tennessee to see my family before I had to be on the set. I was driving my Camaro on Interstate 40, east of Albuquerque. I don't remember other cars on the highway, I was playing a tape to keep myself awake. It was raining very hard and I saw lightning, intense lightning ahead of me. Then my tape started acting funny, there was a lot of static, then the next thing that I remember, there was a big flash of light, white light over the car. The next day, I found this on my stomach. Jesse gave me a photo he had a fellow worker take. It clearly shows a triangular shaped bruise on his abdomen. Three years later, that flash of light and the unexplained bruise still bothered him. We scheduled a session for November 11, 1993.

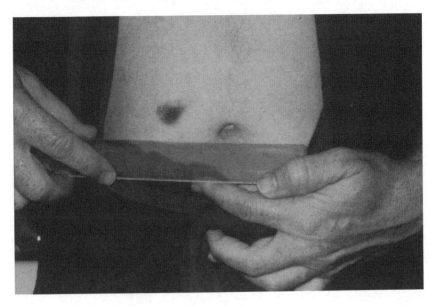

Once Jesse was in a deep state of relaxation, I set the scene as he is driving on Interstate 40, he hears static on his tape and he sees a very bright light.

Jesse: The light's so bright I can't see the road!

He began to breathe rapidly, becoming very agitated.

Yvonne: Ok, Jesse, just take a deep breath. Just report to me what you are experiencing. Remember, you're in a safe place now.

Jesse: I'm under this big light...and I'm lying flat! There are two of them looking at my chest. This one on the right is leaning down far, really close to my chest. I don't like that ...OH, NO, NO! He's got something in his hand!

Yvonne: Can you see what he has in his hand? Just take a good look.

Jesse: OH, it's that, oh how do I describe it, that black circular half of a circle object with the spikes sticking out of it, they just sat it on my stomach.

Yvonne: What part of your abdomen?

Jesse: (*starting to cry*) I don't know what that was for. There's like light being directed right into that thing on my stomach...and it hurts!

Yvonne: What's happening, Jesse, just tell me what's happening.

Jesse: Oh, you know what they did.

Yvonne: Go ahead and verbalize it.

After a long pause...

Jesse: It was an anal probe...my legs hurt and it...instantly, I was hot up to my chest, it's like they just turned on the heat, my groin area, my stomach...oh, I thought I would get away without them doing that this time. Oh, the room's gotten darker and now they've stood me up, but I'm still attached to the table, it's like the table has been raised up and I'm almost in a standing position. Oh my God!

Yvonne: What's happening, Jesse, just verbalize what's happening.

105

Jesse: The room got real white and the tall white being just came into the room. He's standing right here to my left and three silhouettes came in. Oh, and they opened the door and a big flash of light just hit me in the face! Oh and there are more filing in...they are standing against the wall, they are to my right. Um, the tall white being is holding out his left arm, pointing at something. He keeps pointing at the ones standing against the wall.

Yvonne: Jesse, how many do you see in the room with you?

Jesse: (*crying uncontrollably*) Oh, there's one, two, three...I see eight of them, children, standing right there. Oh, he's...

Yvonne: What's happening, Jesse, remember, it's not happening now, just verbalize.

Jesse: He's telling me that they're mine... they're all mine...he never said that before.

Yvonne: What do these children look like?

Jesse: Oh, they're very skinny, they all have white hair...different ages (*barely able to talk through his tears*). The tall being...He's oh, he's holding a baby, it's a baby, little baby...oh, he's telling me to hold it...he just put it in my arms!

Yvonne: Tell me what the baby looks like, you will be able to look at it now and just describe what it looks like without feeling any pain or emotion, just detach yourself...Jesse, describe the baby.

Jesse: Oh...he's very pale, very skinny, very fine hair...large eyes...oh, he's...

Jesse was crying hard now...wailing.

Yvonne: He's what, Jesse, what's happening...I'm right here, I'm going to touch your hand, tell me what's happening.

Jesse: Ohhh, I think he's crying...my baby...oh, he's so pale! Oh, he's taking the baby from me...he's thanking me. Ohhh...

Yvonne: I know this is difficult, you're doing fine, just tell me what's happening.

Jesse: The others are coming toward me...they're all touching my hand as they're going out of the room. Oh...the tall being says, "Thank you for them."

> Yvonne: Jesse, we're going to stop right here...take a
> deep breath.

I cannot begin to describe how heart wrenching this session was for Jesse. The deep raw emotion Jesse experienced when he saw his baby and was being told by the tall being that all the children were his! Jesse was very distraught after this session, knowing that he will not be a part of their lives and wondering what will become of them.

Independent confirmation of their abduction is very important for individuals who have experienced contact. During their hypnotic regression as well as in conscious recollections, CERO members report seeing fellow members onboard an alien craft. In fact, it's been the topic of discussion during more than one monthly meeting! (*I will discuss an example of this experience in the cases of Katie Campbell and Renee Reynolds in the next pair of chapters*).

Jesse's experience with encountering another abductee during a "lost time" episode is revealing. It shows that abductees are not completely powerless victims but are conscious of what is happening and who is around them during the abduction, even if the memory is suppressed.

The following is an account taken from Jesse's conscious memory; he dated the event March 24, 1994:

> Jesse: Well I had gone to bed at 1:38 a.m., Thursday night I lay down in bed, turned to my right where I could see my clock and it was 1:38 a.m. I turned to my left side to try to get more comfortable, I couldn't get comfortable. I turned back to my right side and noticed that it was then 5:00 a.m. At that point, I realized that something obviously had happened and I started going back through my memory of what had gone on.

Unfortunately, there was little that Jesse could recall. What had happened to him in the early hours of that morning? He wanted to find out. When I took Jesse back to that night under hypnotic regression, he found himself in a room...and not alone.

> Jesse: Everything is white and I'm so cold in this room. Um, there's three pairs of knees to my left and we are all sitting on a...um, it's a part of the wall that just comes out and forms a seat...it goes all the way around the room...I'm sitting here staring at the floor and I see knees in my field of vision.

Yvonne: Does this feel like a small or large room? Can you describe your surroundings?

Jesse: It feels small, our knees are touching...I don't know if it's our legs making the floor look pentagon shaped, but the room appears to be round like in a can.

He paused as if he were observing what was going on around him.

Jesse: It seems the door opens to the left there, there's a pulsating light emanating from the side near the door...we all freeze staring at the light...oh, somebody takes my right arm.

Yvonne: Who takes your arm? Can you describe him?

Jesse: Yeah, I know who it is...it's John...he's afraid too.

He became increasingly upset and began to cry.

Jesse: He takes my hand.

Yvonne: Does John say anything to you?

Jesse: No...we're just crying...I tell him it'll be over soon...oh, they just took him out...now the room is strobing and I don't see anybody else.

Yvonne: No one else is in the room with you?

Jesse: No...uh, it's not the same room.

Yvonne: You feel that you're in a different place now? Look around and describe your surroundings.

Jesse: Uh, I'm on a table in a larger room and I see four people...no, there are four beings around a person on a table. I can see them, full frame, full vision...there's light coming from the ceiling lighting them up.

He began to breathe very heavily and became agitated.

Yvonne: Now, what's happening?

Jesse: I don't know why they're making me watch this?

Yvonne: What are you watching, Jesse? Just tell me what's happening?

Jesse: Oh, I think I'm looking at a screen because I couldn't be this close! Oh, they're putting a tube on John!

Yvonne: Can you describe the tube?

Jesse: Um, yes, it's one of the regular sampling tubes that's coming out of...oh...where's it coming from? Um, it's like a machine they have rolled in on a little table.

Yvonne: Is John awake?

Jesse: Well...he's not moving. Oh, now my arms are hurting.

Yvonne: What is happening with your arm?

Jesse: Ohhh, it feels like a metal device with a clamp on it...there's two beings looking at my arms. Oh, they're applying pressure to my groin area, oh...it hurts and the pain is giving me a headache.

Yvonne: From where you are laying on the table, can you still see John?

Jesse: Uh, no...oh, it looks like John is standing over me, he's...he's looking down at me...but he doesn't... I think he is just being carried out, I don't know if he sees me.

Jesse's voice quivered as he described John being carried out of the room.

Jesse: Oh, now it feels...something pressuring my temples really hard, like there's something on either side of my temples...oh, it's almost like electricity through them, right between my eyes that's where the pain is, oh, I have a headache. Oh, they've taken that thing off the top of my head and it's aching. There's that pulsating light, it seems like a distracter and above me I see the number 4.

Yvonne: Where do you see this number?

Jesse: Um...it's sort of above me, in the ceiling above, oh, there's a light that flashed.

After the flash of light, Jesse found himself back in his bedroom. He told me that he was seeing an "s" or a "5" when he realized he was seeing his digital clock reading 5 a.m.

Later after Jesse had come out of hypnosis and we were debriefing, he was quite upset about seeing fellow CERO member John. It was difficult for him to understand why these beings allowed him to watch as they performed a procedure on John. At the following CERO meeting, Jesse shared with the group his conscious memory as well as his retrieved memories from the hypnosis session. Tears welled up in John's eyes as he listened to Jesse recount seeing him on the craft. It was very emotional for both men, though John had little to say at the time.

In preparing this chapter, I spoke with John on the telephone. I explained that I was including the incident where Jesse saw him during one of his encounters. John's voice began to quiver as he too remembered seeing Jesse:

> John: Yes, I remember seeing Jesse and it's like we acknowledged each other but not like we do at the meetings. It was more like we were there doing what we were supposed to do. I have also not only seen other CERO members, but other people as well, some I know, some I don't know.

John became emotional on the phone as the call brought back so many memories. Abduction survivors struggle with their experiences almost daily. To be reminded that other people have had similar experiences is reassuring they are not alone and that it really did happen to them. Or as John said on the phone as he struggled with his emotions, *"It's just when you were telling me about Jesse's session when he saw me, that was just more confirmation for me."*

John called me back the next day. He was still processing the memory and the emotions I had inadvertently stirred up. *"I felt a sort of comfort when I saw Jesse,"* said John as he remembered that episode so many years ago. *"I got goosebumps and had a lump in my throat when you mentioned the session when Jesse saw me."*

During the debriefing, Jesse also told me when he was coming out of hypnosis, he saw a vision. I asked him to write it down as I ask all clients to do with strange or unsettling memories or experiences. John's recollection of the vision:

> As Yvonne was bringing me out, I saw a vision of New York City exploding and a castle, cathedral or church-like building also exploding and/or burning. Don't know what that means.

While in hindsight, this vision of an exploding New York City is ominous in its implications, it did not strike me as highly unusual at the time. In fact, I asked Jesse if he experienced these "visions" before and if he considered himself psychic. He told me even as a little boy, he would know or sense things before they happened, something he could never understand. As for Jesse's vision, it would recur, becoming increasingly prior to September 11, 2001. I will discuss this further at the end of the chapter.

B. John Explores Hypnotherapy

Over time, Jesse became familiar with my professional approach and requirement when working with double or multiple witness abduction cases. Although Jesse sought further confirmation about his 1957 experience, he never discussed what he remembered about that day with his brother John or revealed any of the details that had surfaced during his hypnosis sessions. In calls home, Jesse did acknowledge he was exploring his memories of the event with hypnosis but left it at that.

In late summer of 1993 (36 years after the incident) in their family's backyard, John called Jesse. He told his older brother he had been thinking about that episode as well...and was also interested in undergoing regression involving that day so very long ago.

In October 1993, Jesse and I flew to Knoxville, Tennessee to visit John. Jesse missed his family. He was very excited about seeing John, his parents and his two sisters, all of whom still lived in the Knoxville area.

This was also special for me. I was going to finally meet the very close-knit Long family that Jesse had spoken about so frequently. Little did I know, this trip to Knoxville would leave a dramatic impression on all of us.

Jesse and I arrived at his parents' home late that evening. Over dinner, we enjoyed visiting the gathered family, including John and his wife. After dinner, he and I set a time for his first hypnotic regression the next morning.

John arrived at his parents' home the next day around 11:00 a.m. as scheduled. While driving to the house, John heard on the radio that there was a threat of rain later that day. He suggested that if I would like to visit the house he was building, we needed to go as soon as possible before the road to his property became impassable from water and mud. With Mrs. Long driving Jesse and me, we followed John in his pickup truck for the short trip to Raccoon Valley, Tennessee.

Over the previous two years, Jesse told me that his brother had always wanted to live in a "round" house. However, I was not prepared for what I would see that day when we approached John's house. The house stood out, isolated as it was and surrounded by open fields. The house was not just round...it bore a striking resemblance to frequent descriptions of flying saucers.

To say I was startled would be an understatement. There was John's saucer-like creation, appearing dramatically in the middle of the natural wilderness of Tennessee with its wildlife and open country.

John and his wife bought the land in Raccoon Valley, Tennessee in 1984 an he started construction in October 1990. He drew up the plans himself and built his "dream house" to conform to his own mental image.

He had not given it a thought that the result would appear saucer shaped to others.

As I said, I cannot completely describe the impact the house had on me as a hypnotherapist and researcher. John never read any material or, for that matter, had any interest in UFOs, which made the design of his home all the more unexpected and unsettling.

But a second, equally unsettling, surprise was to follow.

Researchers and individuals who study ufology report that many abductees describe alien creatures as having a "praying mantis" appearance. John excused himself for a few moments, only to return carrying a large wooden sculpture of a praying mantis…said he had felt compelled to carve, only to store in his shed. He had never given any special significance to what had motivated him to make it and he was unaware of its significance to urologists. Jesse, hoping his brother would also agree to regressive hypnotherapy someday, had been careful not to discuss the details of his own session, so he would not contaminate his brother's memory with his own recollections.

At the sight of the sculpture, Jesse turned to me and said, *"Oh yeah, I forgot to tell you about this."* I tried to keep my composure but I grabbed my video camera and interviewed John right then and there about his other unusual "creation." He seemed surprised by my sudden interest but stated he had no particular reason for wanting to create such a statue.

In a 2007 email, John added a very interesting note to the story:

> An amusing aside about the mantis I may not have told you (*turning to Jesse*): While in the mobile home on the land there, I had wrapped the mantis in a garbage bag and stored it in the crawl space underneath. Years later when it was time to get rid of the mobile home, I took my mantis out of the bag and discovered a large number, maybe fifty baby praying mantises were in there with the sculptured mantis. They swarmed around a bit and then took off. Odd thing…odd thing, indeed!

My visit was already feeling overwhelming and I had only been there a day. However, as a professional, I knew I could not show any reaction. I had to be as careful as Jesse not to "tip" off his brother that the round house or his self-created praying mantis might very well have subconscious meanings to him.

After taking numerous photographs of the statue of the mantis, we decided to return to their parents' house and begin John's initial interview and briefing in order to prepare for his first hypnosis session.

The Longs had a spare room, which provided privacy for my session with John. Equipped with my reliable tape recorder, I began the pre-hypnosis interview, asking John to describe his conscious recollection of the 1957 event:

> John: What I remember is: We were in the backyard near the sandbox. I think Butch (his nickname for Jesse) was in the sand box or close to it and I was away from it. He said something and we looked up the hill and there was a guy standing there. It looked like he had a hatchet in his hand or something. He raised his hand up like he was going to throw it and I don't really remember anything that follows that sequence. The next thing I remember is looking at a frog in the side of the hill, a bullfrog, and watching his throat constricting and expanding. That's really all I remember about that. I have no other memories of that at all. I got out of the sandbox for a reason, but what reason does a three-year-old need to get out of the sandbox? Butch said something and we both looked up the hill. I have absolutely no memory after seeing the guy standing there.

In preparing this chapter, I asked John by email, why he decided to finally look into the 1957 event and undergo hypnotic regression?

John responded in his own email:

> It never really entered my mind as an adult that I should try to understand what happened that day. In the back of my mind, it had always been like a secret we weren't supposed to talk about. In fact, I don't think my brother had ever mentioned it to me until we were both much older. When he did mention it…" Hey, you remember that time we were in the backyard…the sandbox…someone standing there…" of course I remembered instantly. It was a permanent memory even though blurry and dreamlike. What I did remember and will always remember is that "that day something happened" was important and out of the ordinary, unlike most ordinary

114

childhood memories that are forgotten. Although sketchy in detail, the ordinary was surreal and fantastic.

For example, just prior to seeing the "figure" standing nearby, I remember the grass below my feet, how the sunlight was piercing and refracting through the dew hanging on the blades of grass…it had a taste, it tasted like something but nothing was on my tongue. I can't tell you in words what it tasted like, but I can recall the taste each time I let the memory return.

There were goose bumps on top of my head, but I was not afraid. There was also something intuitive about it and at that age, I didn't question it, but it seemed like there was more than one sun in the sky because the light and shadows were not normal. As I say, it was visually surreal. I knew I would always remember something about that day. It was part of me that would never go away. I let myself forget…though I don't remember why.

John's initial interview revealed to me that both brothers' conscious memories were almost identical. I was eager to learn what hidden recollections in John's subconscious would be revealed during hypnotherapy.

After a short break, I asked John if he felt comfortable about his first hypnosis session which we had moved to the next day. He did not raise my particular concerns.

The next morning, I reviewed my notes with John about the date, location, his age…anything that would help set the scene for his hypnotic regression.

With my tape recorder rolling, I began giving John progressive relaxation instructions, leading him into a deep hypnotic trance. I directed him to concentrate only on my voice. Once John reached a hypnotic state, we went back in time to his childhood in 1957…

Yvonne: John, during this time in your life, you are 4 years old, feel yourself back in that time, as you look down at your feet and allow yourself to see and feel your shoes, the clothes you are wearing, just feel yourself back there as a 4-year-old little boy. As your mind becomes very sharp and clear, take a careful look around you and using all of your senses, describe your backyard where you and Butch play, finding as you speak verbally, the deeper asleep you will become.

After a brief pause, John cleared his throat and began to slowly describe his surroundings.

> John: There's a small flat area with a sharp hill, there's a swing set and sandbox and the hill curves around to the side of the house a little bit and there's some red clay where it has been dug out. And the sand is scattered around outside the sandbox. There's a tricycle, a ball, a shovel.
>
> Yvonne: Now on this particular day, you are playing with Butch. As you are outside of the sandbox, take a look at Butch playing in the sandbox. Feel yourself playing outside and around the sandbox. Allow yourself now to go to that point where Butch catches your attention.
>
> John: He screams, "Look out!"
>
> Yvonne: And why did he scream the words, "Look out?"
>
> John: There's somebody standing up on the hill looking down at us.
>
> Yvonne: John, take a look up the hill and describe who is standing there, are you looking at that person now?
>
> John: I can't...I can't see his face.

John paused as if looking for the word to describe the person standing on the hill.

> Yvonne: Don't analyze anything, just verbalize what you are sensing or seeing.
>
> John: Just a figure, someone standing there above us. It looks like he has a hatchet in his hand.
>
> Yvonne: Now tell me from that point. You see that person? What is he doing?
>
> John: I don't know. It's...it's just a shiny light.
>
> Yvonne: OK, tell me where you see this shiny light.
>
> John: The hatchet.
>
> Yvonne: And what is Butch doing while you are looking at this person with the hatchet, can you turn and look at Butch?
>
> John: He's afraid, just staring.
>
> Yvonne: Does this person say anything to the both of you?
>
> John: I don't hear anything.

> Yvonne: Is he still standing there with the hatchet raised in the air?
>
> John: Yeah.
>
> Yvonne: OK, tell me what he is doing, the next thing that happens as he is standing there with the hatchet.
>
> John: I don't know; I'm looking at this frog.
>
> Yvonne: Where is the frog?
>
> John: In the grass, on the side of the hill, he's just sitting there making his throat bloat out.

After John described seeing the frog, I asked him to look up the hill again and tell me if the person was still standing there. John told me that he no longer saw the person.

I suggested to John a couple of times that we were going to "back up" in this memory to where both brothers are looking at this person as he raises the hatchet. John again described the frog in the grass. I realized we had come to a block in his memory, possibly caused by a post-hypnotic suggestion by "someone" or John's subconscious to protect him from a traumatic experience or event his 4-year-old mind was not equipped to handle.

In my years working with abduction cases, it is quite common to run into a blocked memory. It is often an indication that the individual is not quite ready to confront the source of their anxiety. However, more often than not, a client will give me the "permission" to penetrate the block at that session or a later one. I explain the process to all of my new clients by using the analogy of "peeling the layers of an onion" …how we will slowly and methodically go about uncovering the root of the anxiety or distress.

One more time, I attempted to suggest to John that we back up in that moment in 1957 when he and his brother are in the sandbox:

> Yvonne: Ok, John, go back to the point where you and Butch were looking at this person as you both saw him raise the hatchet…just describe what happens next.
>
> John: I don't know, I think I'm asleep.
>
> Yvonne: Where are you asleep? In your backyard?
>
> John: I don't know, I'm inside myself.
>
> Yvonne: And where do you feel you are?

After a very long pause, John said…

> John: *There's not time, everything's stopped.*

117

After several minutes of questioning, I realized John had spontaneously regressed to another experience as a child...one which his subconscious was ready to bring forward.

This childhood memory involved seeing a very bright "star" outside of his bedroom. During his initial interview, John shared with me...

> John: One thing that sticks out in my mind, but I don't know where we were living at that time. I was in a crib or small bed, I woke up in the night and looked out the window. There were venetian blinds in the window and I looked out the window at the sky. There was an incredible star out in the sky, like the star of David, huge spires, it just took up the entire sky.

With this in mind and using a series of suggestions, I reinforced to John that he was going into a deeper state of hypnosis. We then continued the session.

> Yvonne: Are you ready to go to the memory that you shared with me about the bright star?
> John: Yes, I'm ready.
> Yvonne: OK, John, allow yourself to drift back to that time in your life when you were either at your parents' house in Rogersville or at your grandparents' house in Chattanooga. In this memory, you felt that it was cold outside, wintertime, you remember being in bed. Now as you take some deep cleansing breaths, feel yourself in your bed, become aware of the softness underneath you and the warmth of your blankets. Allow your mind to become very sharp and clear as you allow the memories to come forward.

After a short pause, John cleared his throat, then proceeded.

> John: A brilliant star, it fills the whole sky.
> Yvonne: What color is the light from the star?
> John: It's brilliant white, silver, it's overwhelming. It's a warm feeling, it loves me.

As I continued to question John, he recalled being so excited about what he was seeing that he described himself getting out of bed so he could tell his family. Then he found they were all asleep, he climbed back into bed. He saw that the light was still there.

> John: I said, "Okay".
> Yvonne: Were you answering a question?
> John: I don't know, but I agreed to remember. It's a place where time stops, deep inside.
> Yvonne: Is this a place that is familiar to you?
> John: Yes, it's very strong, very strong.
> Yvonne: Does the bright light cause you to go to that place, John?
> John: Yes.
> Yvonne: Does anything occur in that place that you feel like talking about?
> John: Things move without moving, everything I feel.

C. The Hill

It appeared the memory John was describing was an experience that had taken place prior to their double abduction in 1957. As for the "place where time stops"…John felt it was familiar to him and in an environment other than his bedroom.

Once we left this time and place, I asked John if he wanted to come out of hypnosis or did he want to explore further. John chose to continue, returning to the experience with his brother Jesse. I take John once again to the year 1957, to his backyard in Rogersville, Tennessee.

> Yvonne: John, your mind is very sharp and clear and you will allow yourself to bring the memories forward, as this time in your life is very important to you.
> John: There's someone on the hill. He raises a hatchet up in the air. It's shiny. There's this frog (*he paused*), a crazy frog, just sitting there. There's no surroundings…there's no landscape outside.
> Yvonne: John, look around you, describe your surroundings.
> John: A place in the side of the hill, where he sits, it's like a…it's like a photograph.

He pauses again, longer this time, then almost in a whisper…

> John: Real…real quiet noises. We're…we're up on top of the hill.

Yvonne: You and Butch?

John: (*pausing*) Yeah…inside.

Yvonne: Did you say you are inside?

John: Inside a house.

Yvonne: Take a good look around you now. Everything is very sharp and clear. Just describe what the house looks like.

John: You can see out, but nobody can see in. It's like a dome…like being inside a ball.

Yvonne: Are you there by yourself?

John: No.

Yvonne: Somebody is with you?

John: Yes.

Yvonne: Who is with you?

John: There…there are four…there are four of them. These are different.

Yvonne: Can you describe the ones that look different?

John: They're short, dark. I asked John what was the color of their hair. He answered that he did not see any. I asked if he could see their faces. He answered that it was too dark, he could not see them.

Yvonne: Describe what the fourth one looks like.

John: Like a bug…a big bug!

Yvonne: What makes him look like a big bug?

John: His big eyes…dark eyes and a real small mouth.

Yvonne: How tall is he?

John: Real tall, taller than the others.

> Yvonne: Take a look at him and tell me what he is wearing.
> John: I don't see anything.
> Yvonne: Can you describe his skin?
> John: It's gray.
> Yvonne: The same as the other three?
> John: No. They're dark.
> Yvonne: Can you describe the dark color of the other three?
> John: I can't see them.

When working with clients, I will sometimes ask cautiously leading questions. This is to test whether the client's responses are from his or her subconscious recollection or simply responding to my suggestions...what expert hypnotherapists call "leadable."

For instance, when I asked John to describe what the tall "bug-looking" being was wearing, I was inferring that the being was wearing clothing of some type. John answered that he did not see any clothing; a clear indication that he was not "leadable." I used another leading question when John described the tall being's skin as "gray" and I responded by asking..." were the other three also gray?" Again, he ignored my suggestion and answered in the negative, "no, they're dark." Clearly, John was describing a true, physical event as he recalled the information hidden in the deep recesses of his subconscious.

Debunkers claim that hypnotherapy is useless because they insist that hypnotherapists lead their clients. It is obvious they do not understand when leading questions are or are not appropriate and have never researched the proper procedure for hypnotic regressions by a qualified hypnotherapist. While inexperienced or poorly trained hypnotists can misuse leading questions, they can be a useful tool when used properly to test clients' susceptibility to suggestion or the depth of their hypnotic trance.

John's session continued as I asked about these beings.

> Yvonne: John, what are the three dark ones doing?
> John: They're with Butch.
> Yvonne: Can you see Butch?
> John: Yeah, he's sitting down, they won't let me go over there. I want to go over there and they won't let me (*pausing*) I go someplace else.
> Yvonne: Is someone with you?
> John: Yeah, the tall...the tall one.
> Yvonne: Just describe where he is taking you.
> John: A place where there is no time. Talking without talking.

Yvonne: Is the tall one talking to you?
John: "I'm the protector." I have to keep everything secret.
Yvonne: Using all of your senses, describe everything that you are experiencing.

John paused and took a series of deep breaths.

John: It's very warm…in my belly. It's real warm. It's inside my belly. I feel like I'm flying. I'm about three feet off the ground…I'm floating. He tells me if I remember, I can do this any time. If I can remember. I can't tell anybody.

I asked John if he knew where Butch was. He kept repeating that he did not know and could not tell anybody. I began to give John suggestions about being in a safe place. I emphasized that nothing would happen to him if he verbalized what was happening to him and where Butch was. But before I could finish my suggestions, John grabbed his left ear.

John: He did something to my ear.
Yvonne: Who did something to your ear?
John: The tall one.
Yvonne: Tell me what you felt, what did he do to your ear?
John: (*holding his ear*) It stings, I don't know what he did.
Yvonne: When did he do that to your ear?
John: While I'm floating.
Yvonne: Did he tell you why he did that?
John: It's the agreement.
Yvonne: Is the sting inside of your ear or outside of your ear?
John: On the back of my ear…it's the agreement.
Yvonne: Does he touch any other part of your body? Become aware of your body and describe if you feel anything else on any part of your body.

John took a long pause then suddenly, his arms jerked up violently.

Yvonne: John verbalize what just happened, just verbalize it.
John: I don't know…I don't know. (*pause*) Power!
Yvonne: What kind of power?
John: Complete…total…control.
Yvonne: Throughout your body?
John: Yeah, the warm spot in my belly. I can't tell anybody.

I asked John if there was anything touching his stomach. He answered "no." I asked him where the "tall one" was.

> John: They're all gone.
> Yvonne: Are you still in the dome?
> John: No.
> Yvonne: Is Butch with you?
> John: Yeah.
> Yvonne: Where are you both now?
> John: We're in the sandbox.

I brought John out of hypnosis and began his debriefing. I asked John about the "tall one" who appeared to be his escort and if he represented any "bug," since John described him looking like a "big bug." John responded that this being in fact, looked like a "praying mantis." John's obsession with his round house and his praying mantis sculpture began to make sense to him as we continued our debriefing.

Although John believed that something had been done to his ear, he did not consider it a negative experience. He explained that the "surgery" was part of an "agreement" and he considered the talk being to his friend. For that reason, his experience was "pleasant and fun."

Several hours after we concluded John's first session, the two of us sat at his parents' dining room table. John's mother, ever the gracious hostess, offered us refreshments as John and I continued to talk about the results of this session. One of John's main post-hypnotic recollections was the assurance his praying mantis-like "friend" gave him that he would be able to fly whenever he chose if he remembered to believe he could fly and concentrate.

Mrs. Long's ears perked up when she overheard our discussion. She told me that as a little boy, John always told her that he could fly. She quite naturally assumed it was no more than a young boy's childhood fantasy. Now, as she heard the details of John's hypnotic recollection, she commented how it all finally made sense to her.

Prior to our trip to Tennessee, Jesse had continued to undergo hypnotic regression with me hoping to find answers to his partial memories and explanations for strange and disturbing body marks that have appeared on his body overnight.

However, each time I accessed his subconscious mind to allow his buried memories to come forward to a conscious level, Jesse was only able to gather pieces of his personal puzzle...ever so slowly...particularly if it dealt with his early memories as a child. Jesse had come to almost accept his partial knowledge as his fate, even as he resented being used as a tool for the alien agenda.

While in Knoxville during our visit in 1991, Jesse was finally prepared to relive his childhood experience. He was finding it comforting to be back home after so many years.

After lunch, Jesse readied himself for a session now that he was surrounded by familiar places and family. He quickly drifted into a deep state of relaxation. I regressed Jesse back to that summer day in Rogersville, Tennessee, 1957.

> Yvonne: Jesse, just describe what you are doing.
> Jesse: John and I are building a...we have a bucket of sand that we turned upside down and build buildings. There's a clothesline post not too far from our sandbox...and I see the hill that goes up behind us.
> Yvonne: OK, it was during this time you remembered looking up toward the hill...just allow yourself to go back to that memory...taking deep breaths.

Jesse paused.

> Jesse: I see a man standing there...building something. It looks like...he has an ax in his hand.
> Yvonne: OK, Jesse, as you are looking at that man, just describe the next thing that happens.
> Jesse: I take John by his hand and we go up the hill. We (lowering his voice) go up the hill. There's this strange looking house...and there's people working all around and they're over to the left, there's this one, one big guy standing there and...
> Yvonne: What does that strange house look like?
> Jesse: Uh, there's, uh. It's round and there's, uh, it looks like boards holding up the round, uh, round roof...and people scurrying all around it...OH, there's a light...a light that came out of the house... the light hit me! I'm vibrating all over...and I can't move.

At this point, Jesse's memory jumped forward to describe three small beings.

> Jesse: There's three standing over me...oh, there's three at my feet looking at me!
> Yvonne: What do they look like, Jesse?
> Jesse: They're...oh...they're little people...they're dark.
> Yvonne: Where's John?
> Jesse: They took him into that house and I'm inside...and it's really light...and the ceiling is all curved and white.
> Yvonne: What do these people look like?
> Jesse: The one to my right is dark and he's got a big head...it's real...oooh, he's got big eyes...and he just...what's he doing...he's doing something to my right arm (becoming upset) and there's this guy over here on my left. He's taller and he...he's looking down at my chest.
> Yvonne: Does he look like the shorter ones?
> Jesse: No...well, he stands taller...he's a lot taller. Oh, that hurts! They put something on my chest.
> Yvonne: What did they put on your chest?
> Jesse: This...I don't know...there's light coming out of the bottom of it...that thing is coming out of the ceiling and it's sitting on my chest...feels like a flat box.
> Yvonne: How many are with you?

125

Jesse: Um, there's one here at my right...uh...two at my feet on my right side and there's one at my foot on my left. And then this tall guy on my left shoulder (hesitating then taking a deep breath) this guy on my right...what's he...? Oh, he's got a rod!

He now became excited and upset.

Jesse: He's right down at my feet. He's down at my legs...and I can't see because of the box on my chest...but he's down there with this...long rod! The tall guy on my left keeps looking down at my legs and now he's looking right at me...in my face. He's staring at me right now...just staring.

Numerous abductees describe procedures similar to what Jesse described. The taller being, who seemed to be in charge, began to start deeply and directly into Jesse's eyes. I suspected that this was the moment when the "crystal-like" object was placed in Jesse's left shin. When I asked Jesse what physical sensations he was feeling, he replied...

Jesse: Nothing! I don't feel anything. He's just staring. He's not moving...like I can't NOT look at him! I have to look at him.

My colleague, Dr. David Jacobs in his book, *"Secret Life"* described this same "staring" procedure. David referred to it as "mindscan" with mental pictures placed in the abductee's mind to elicit a variety of emotions. Many of my subjects have described this staring as having a calming effect. Could it also be a form of distraction or "alien anesthesia"?

Colleagues and authors Stanton Friedman and Kathleen Marden (Betty Hill's niece) in their book *"Captured"* wrote about Betty Hill's experience on the abduction examination table during the insertion of a long needle into her navel. As Betty cried out in pain, the being who Betty referred to as the "leader," leaned over her, waved his hand in front of her eyes and alleviated the pain.

Similarly, even though Jesse became agitated seeing a long rod and one of the beings working on his legs. Once the taller being looked into his eyes, Jesse's pain, discomfort and fear disappeared. As with Betty Hill and countless others, this seemed to be their way to control their captives so they could continue their "operation."

I stayed with Jesse, guiding him with questions about the abduction activities surrounding him.

> Jesse: Oh…what is that? They're just moving around my head.
> Yvonne: What is moving around, Jesse?
> Jesse: The little black ones are moving around on either side of my head back and forth. Oooh (beginning to breathe faster), ow, right in the back of my head!
> Yvonne: What's in the back of your head?
> Jesse: He just stuck me with something right in the back of the head…that hurt!
> Yvonne: What part of your head?
> Jesse: Right where my…right in the indentation there in the back of the head…at the neck.

Jesse described feeling an activity on his right as he saw the beings going in and out through a door on the right side of the room. When he attempted to look to his left, the tall being was standing there, staring at him, blocking his view.

> Jesse: Where is John? He might be over to my left, but the tall guy is standing there, looking down at me and I can't see past him…he's staring…he's staring…
> Yvonne: Describe his face, Jesse.
> Jesse: Like a bug…he's just got…he's just real skinny and he's got big round eyes. He doesn't look…he's not sad or he's not happy…he's just looking, just looking at me.

Jesse described one of them carrying John over and holding him up for Jesse to see. Although I understood Jesse's concern for his brother, I sensed that these beings were using the "staring/mindscan" procedure, inserting the image of his brother, John into Jesse's mind to calm him.

> Jesse: (with a sense of relief) That one carried John over here…he's holding John up and John's looking at me. Oh! They took him away. It's like they wanted to let me know that John was way…and he was okay.

Even though John was not physically present while Jesse described the abduction procedure, he had also described the way he and his brother were kept separate from one another during their abduction experience. In

John's words, "they won't let me go over there, I wanted to go over there and they wouldn't let me…"

To check whether my intuition was correct, I asked Jesse:

> Yvonne: Where's John now?
> Jesse: (becoming upset) I don't know…I don't see him now! That tall guy keeps looking at me…and he puts…he's got his hand on my chest …and he's looking down (emphasizing each word) right into my eyes. Really close…Oh! There's a big white light…big flash of light so bright that I can't see anything!

As Jesse's hypnosis session continued, he found himself back in his yard as he described taking his brother's hand and walking back down the hill toward their sandbox.

D. John's Second Session

John was prepared for his second session on the following day. I regressed John for a return subconscious journey to 1957 and to the point in time when he and Jesse were on the top of the hill…

> Yvonne: John, just describe what you see.
> John: We're inside of a dome. It's round but they're not really walls. It doesn't feel solid.
> Yvonne: Do you see light inside the dome?
> John: Just reflection, light reflecting through the dome, you can see outside, the trees.
> Yvonne: You can see through the windows?
> John: I don't see any windows.
> Yvonne: And what are you and Butch doing?
> John: Butch left, three…three people took him.
> Yvonne: Can you describe what these people look like?
> John: Dark images.
> Yvonne: Do you know where they took him?
> John: No, I can't go there.
> Yvonne: Are you by yourself?
> John: No.
> Yvonne: Who's with you?
> John: A tall…a tall one. We go to the other side.

> Yvonne: Can you describe what your surroundings look like on the other side?
> John: No…all I see is his face.
> Yvonne: Does he frighten you?
> John: No. He's funny. He thinks I'm funny…I'm floating off of the ground.
> Yvonne: And how do you do that?
> John: It's warm inside my stomach. It's a special place.

John's frequent reference during hypnosis to a "special place" which is "warm inside my stomach" would suggest that having been regressed to age four, John was no using the language of a four-year-old to explain what he had been told by those who had abducted him…that he could fly if he concentrated with his entire mind and body.

> Yvonne: Is he talking to you?
> John: Yeah, it's a special place. I can always go there. I can go there and be weightless.
> Yvonne: That agreement that you talked about, John, was that the agreement with him?
> John: We agree that I can go there any time, but I can't tell anybody what happened.
> Yvonne: Does the agreement have anything to do with Butch?
> John: Yeah, I can't talk about it.
> Yvonne: You can't talk about what happened to you or Butch?
> John: Right, if I need to, I have to lie about it, make up stories.
> Yvonne: Did you give him permission for you and Butch?
> John: No. Just me.

In the second session with John, I had hoped to uncover more details about what he experienced inside the "dome" where he was taken during his abduction.

He once again described feeling a sting in his left ear "like a bee sting." When I questioned further about what had been done to his ear and if they had given him any explanation, he told me that it was all part of the "agreement." I continued questioning John if he knew the purpose of the agreement and if he knew where Butch was in the dome. He answered, *"I can't remember…I'm not supposed to remember."*

After reassuring John that it was all right to remember, I asked him if there were others with him beside his tall friend. He described smaller beings moving around very quickly. When I asked if they were dark beings he had seen earlier, he answered that he could not "see" them. He said that they were trying to calm Butch down. John added he was not allowed to go in that area of the "dome," but that Butch was "OK."

> Yvonne: Who takes you in there to see Butch?
> John: I just see him in my mind.

Typically, abductees explain communications between them and their captors as being telepathic. John also said that was how they conducted communications with him that his brother was fine.

John's attention once again turned to learning how to "fly and then float". When I asked John if he just floated there with the tall one until they are done with Butch, he replied *"yeah."* John then described asking Butch if he saw the frog, indicating that John's memory had jumped to being back in his yard. When I asked him how they got out of the dome…had someone taken them out? He replied, *"I don't know."*

I asked John to take some deep breaths because we were going to back up in this memory.

> Yvonne: As we back up a little bit to where you and Butch walked up the hill and when you saw it, at that point, can you describe what it looked like to you?
> John: I didn't see it. It's a construction…wood…stuff laying around.

After further questioning, John could not remember how he got inside of the dome, only once he was inside, he saw the four "people," three and the tall one. I questioned John further, asking him if he could describe how he and Butch came out of the dome. Again, he replied that he did not know, only that he was laughing when he saw the frog.

Once I brought John out of hypnosis, he reflected on what he now consciously knew based on his two sessions:

> John: That agreement not to tell is like breaking a promise. That dome is like it's not even there, like a membrane that's not even there. The light and dark beings moved around in there. They weren't always in the same place.

On our last night in Knoxville, we all enjoyed dinner at a local restaurant and avoided talking about the dramatic recollections that John and Jesse had uncovered in their hypnosis sessions. During my return flight to California with Jesse the next day, my thoughts continued to dwell on the past three days and their many revelations. I could not concentrate on the meals being served or the in-flight movie. My mind was too busy replaying the brothers' hypnotherapy sessions. I stared out of the window and down on the billowy clouds below. I chuckled to myself as I imagined a UFO making a sudden appearance and realized that my involvement with post-traumatic stress victims following their close encounters would be my life's work.

E. Post Note

The producers of the television program, "Encounters: The Hidden Truth" contacted me expressing an interest in doing a program about abductions. The hour-long series featured real-life stories about paranormal phenomena and the producers were quite interested in the two brothers' experiences. Jesse and John gave their permission and the necessary arrangements were made. The producers flew Jesse and me back to Tennessee, the brothers were interviewed on camera and they shot footage of John's round house and six-foot praying mantis. At the executive producer's request, I conducted an on-camera regression session with John. The show aired nationally.

Most Individuals who experience abductions prefer anonymity to avoid possible ridicule. Still Jesse's and John's willingness to publicly discuss their many encounters has not only helped build public interest and awareness about UFO abduction, but has also contributed to a greater understanding that multiple abduction cases are a reality worldwide.

F. Returning Home

In the summer of 2005, I flew to Knoxville on my way home from a meeting in New York. Jesse had recently moved back to Tennessee to be closer to his family. Since I had not seen both brothers for a few years, I was looking forward to my visit. Jesse was not a proud homeowner. As we waited for John to arrive, he gave me the grand tour of his lovely home.

Shortly after Jesse moved back to Knoxville, he called to tell me that John was busy with some very interesting inventions and suggested that I talk to him. Always curious, I called John and listened as he brought me up to date about his latest ventures.

When John arrived, the three of us sat down to catch up on each other's lives. John gave me copies of abstracts for his inventions as well as copies of the four patents that were pending. One of his more interesting patent applications was for (*what he called*) the "Magnetic Eccentric Drive."

John's "Magnetic Eccentric Drive" appeared to stir up more than its share of interest as excerpts from our conversation during my visit to Knoxville demonstrate...

> John: Unusual thing about the last pending application...I have been denied permission by the USPTO to file worldwide applications on this one for a period of at least 6 months as government officials review and decide whether or not to issue an Order of Secrecy. If I receive such an order, I will be required to tell them who I have shown the device to. The device applies to satellites, space probes and surveillance craft. Odd for a guy like myself who only graduated high school.
>
> Yvonne: It has been a while since your regression, did you come up with these inventions after your regressions and after you came forward publicly when we were featured on the "Encounters Show?" And how did these ideas come to you?
>
> John: Yes, this all happened after the regressions. I never have been able to follow my own thought process, no answer for that. I have always been obsessed...driven.
>
> Yvonne: The same way you were driven to build your round house?
>
> John: Yeah, a childhood memory that kind of relates to what I'm doing. My brother and sisters and I used to walk to the store which was a quarter mile away. I was always looking down at the gutters, counting the bars and looking at things. I would pick them up saying, "it's not right...that's not right, something about it is not right." This was in Florence, Alabama, when I was 10-11 years old, this memory sticks with me. I would look at things, the mechanical processes and I'd be disappointed saying, "it's not right." It would be a piece of something, I didn't even know what it was.
>
> Yvonne: When did this childhood memory come back to you?
>
> John: Something that has been in the back of my mind for many years, I guess.
>
> Yvonne: So, after we did your regressions, did these memories and information come to you in a dream?

John: I think…I do a lot of reading. I think it was an article about problems converting different types of motions, random motion into electrical power very easily, mechanically. So, this is really most of what all this stuff is, is a way to convert motion and produce energy without having to have a gearbox. In fact, one type of motion can be converted into another type of motion without physically touching each other. And I just got hooked on that and I just kind of obsessed with it. You can theoretically have an engine out there that would last indefinitely because you'd have no wear and tear on parts because they don't actually touch each other. So, I just got absorbed in that. And that's where the last one came from.

Yvonne: When you filed and were denied…

John: No, I couldn't file, they let me file a provisional application. That application would just be 12 months before I have to file the real patent and what they are normally, they give you a license number because you only have so much time before you can file for worldwide patents. Normally, they give you a license number that allows you to do that, but in this case, they wouldn't give me one and if you look up the code, it's really funny, the way they word it. It says that within 6 months, you may receive an Order of Secrecy and you will be required to divulge every person that you have shown this to. I doubt that they're going to do that, they may not do it. Altogether, they can basically steal it.

Yvonne: Oh, no! Can they actually do that?

John: Oh, yeah. There's a chance they might compensate for it, but they can do whatever they want to do. Especially the Defense Department or the Department of Energy.

Yvonne: How did you react when you found out?

John: Well, that was the first time that ever happened, all the other ones went OK. At first, I thought it's just a mistake…maybe it's a glitch in the system or something. But then, maybe they see something about it that there's something in the satellite they want to keep secret.

Yvonne: Yes, like threatening national security.

John: Yeah, they don't want other countries to have that technology so they basically take it and use it. I just thought that was odd 'cause it never happened before…It just seemed kind of strange.

Yvonne: Another question, John, do you still have that object behind your ear?
John: Yeah.
Yvonne: It's not bothering you?
John: I never even think about it.
Yvonne: Since your regressions, have you kept track of your dreams?
John: They're kind of hard to keep track of, I have really bizarre dreams, they're too many.
Yvonne: Really? Like what?
John: The sensation of being weightless, float around, hovering above the ground. Those are my favorites.
Yvonne: Like an "out of body experience?"
John: Well, they're pretty physical.
Yvonne: I remember after your first session, your Mom told me that when you were a child, you always told her that you could fly...she just volunteered that bit of information to me. And in light of what you recalled during your session, your Mom's comment was very compelling, particularly since she was not present during your session.

John now feels that he is expressing his life purpose. He describes it as "light bulbs" turning on, receiving knowledge. John feels that the object, which remains behind his ear, is providing information to him. He has not had the object removed because of the "agreement" he made with his "tall friend" during his abduction experience as a young boy.

In 2007, John updated me on the "Magnetic Eccentric Drive" with an email...

>   I did a "back-door" on the patent office as follows: I dissected the entire thing, split it into more than one patent and filed again under a different title as separate applications which it now is. "Magnetic Eccentric Drive" is now "Radical Magnetic Cam". Apple. No.11/602,001. It was received as a provisional application and is currently in the "publication" stage where it will remain until official examination. Two more applications will follow to reconnect the original in its previous form. There is more than one way to skin a cat.
>   I keep coming up with new devices faster than I can apply for patents. I routinely do patent searches to see

*what has been done before with magnets and can't believe
a lot of these things have never been one before or are in
forms that show a total misunderstanding of magnetic
fields. Looks like I have lots of work to do still.*

*Maybe I'll come up with the "holy grail" of physics.
Over-unity, free energy. The first and second laws of
thermodynamics need a good kick in the butt from what I
can tell.*

Keep in touch,
John

As for Jesse, last year I asked him to draft an update on his life with
any reflections he gained from his experiences. I find these to be beneficial
for understanding the long-term effects of abductions.

On August 16, 2007, I received Jesse's letter in response...

Since my sessions with Yvonne, I feel I have grown and
gotten better in dealing with what has been happening to me.
I'm at the point now that my encounters don't affect me like
they used to...I'm not afraid anymore. Now they are just a
part of my life...an occasional experience that comes and
goes. Granted, I don't have the answer to "why me?" I
guess I'll never have that. But, I'm rest assured that
whatever THEIR reasons, I had to be a part of it and perhaps
future generations will know and understand what small part
I've played.

In a follow-up phone call, I asked Jesse if he feels that his psychic
abilities were a result of his abduction experiences or not...

Jesse: I know that I had mentioned to you that my psychic
abilities seemed to be enhanced after starting my sessions
with you. I think facing up to what is happening to me
"opened up" my mind and allowed other abilities to grow.
Of course, I've known since I was a child that I could
"know" ahead of time when things were going to
happen...when people would die or other tragedies would
occur. That ability increased significantly after facing my
"abduction" fears. I can't say that my encounters with
"them" is what "caused" my psychic abilities is partially
why "they" chose me to begin with.

The reason I asked Jesse about his psychic abilities goes back to his vision of an exploding New York City. That vision would recur with increasing regularity in the following years.

For example, I was visiting Jesse when he described seeing a plane hit the World Trade Center. He excused himself and left the room for a few minutes. When he returned, he handed me a drawing from a dream that he had in 1991. It was an image of a crack in the towers before they pancaked to the ground. The drawing was dated July 17, 1991.

As it grew closer to 9/11, Jesse kept telling me that he was having other "dreams" and "flashes" about an impending event in New York…and that his sister was present in the images. He couldn't figure out why she was there or what it all meant. It wasn't until after 9/11 that these dreams, flashes and visions suddenly made sense.

The morning of September 11, 2001, the alarm rang at 5:30 a.m. I jumped out of bed and turned on the television in the family room to catch up on the news, weather and traffic. As I was making my morning coffee, *Good Morning America* announced that a plane had hit one of the twin towers in New York. My first thought was, "How horrible, the pilot of a small plane must have veered off course and hit the building!" While the coffee was brewing, I woke up my younger son, Brent and made him breakfast, then I jumped in the shower so I could be ready to drive him to school.

When I walked back into the kitchen to pour myself a cup of coffee, the second plane had hit the other tower. Brent and I looked at each other in stunned silence. As our attention turned back to the television, the first tower went crashing to the ground.

At that very moment, the phone rang. It was Jesse calling long distance from Tennessee. He was crying hysterically, asking if I'm watching the news. I tried to understand what he was saying through his tears. He was shouting over the phone, *"That's what I saw! The plane going into the building, oh my God, my vision, the plane going into the building!"* As we would find out later, his sister's son's birthday is on September 11th.

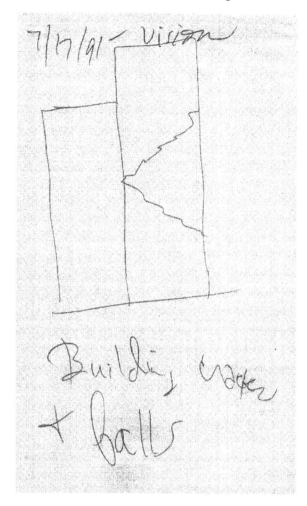

CHAPTER 6: Renee Reynolds

"He looks different than they do….
I don't want to see him."

In February 1991, I received a phone call from a young woman named Renee Reynolds. She was referred to me by my colleague, researcher and author of *The Tujunga Canyon Contacts,* among other books, Ann Druffel. For several years, Renee had been bothered by some disturbing unexplained scars and marks that appeared on her body, episodes of time lost as well as suffering from debilitating panic attacks while driving to Palm Springs, California to visit her grandmother; her breathing becoming erratic, difficulty breathing and swallowing, her hands feeling tingly and cold.

At the time, Renee was a young mother of two sons; Robert age 2, Carl, Jr. age 9 and a daughter Samantha age 11 and along with her husband Carl, Sr. enjoy a busy life raising their three children. Even though Renee cherished her role as wife and mother, she could no longer ignore her suspicions that "something" inexplicable may have happened to her.

On April 24, 1991, I met Renee for the first time at my office for her first hypnosis session. I was struck by her simple outer beauty. She was about 5'8" tall with shoulder length blond hair, very little make-up, yet there was something about this young mother's inner beauty that made her fair skin glow. I was struck, but not surprised about how nervous she was, twisting her hands and wiping the perspiration from her hands and face as I went over some necessary paperwork prior to the hypnosis. I explained to Renee that to relieve her from her panic attacks when she drives to visit her grandmother, it was necessary to find the cause of her anxiety. I suggested that I regress her back to one of her trips to Palm Springs, after a few minutes of questions and discussion, Renee agreed.

Renee was curious about why her truck's engine, as she describes, "went strange" during a trip in the summer of 1980 when she was a 19-year-old. Shelly, her close friend, decided to join Renee and her 6-month-old daughter Samantha on this trip to keep Renee company and help with the baby. Renee packed up her truck. They were on their way at 4:00 p.m. The following transcript is taken from Renee's hypnosis session on April 24, 1991:

> YS: Renee, just feel yourself in your truck, feeling the seat underneath you, your hands are on the steering wheel, feeling the bumps in the road, using all of your senses,

everything is very familiar to you. You are comfortable, confident and excited about seeing your grandmother. Now just take some deep breaths and describe everything that is happening.

RR: Traffic is very heavy, I hate leaving this time of day...we're getting on the freeway, and we're going to sit in traffic for hours.

(Renee's most severe panic attacks would occur when driving through the 134 freeway through Pasadena, California until she reached the 10 freeway)

YS: OK, just continue describing where you are.

RR: I'm going to take the 5 to the 134 and we're hitting traffic...I knew it was going to be like this. *(Renee continues to voice her frustration with the heavy traffic...after a few minutes, she begins breathing very rapidly)*

YS: What is happening, Renee?

RR: *(whispering)* I don't know...my truck doesn't feel right...something is wrong with my truck...I'm scared!

YS: Are you still driving on the 134?

RR: No...I don't know where I am. *(beginning to cry)*

YS: Are you still in your truck?

RR: *(sounding confused)* Yeah...we're sitting in the truck...we're parked somewhere? I don't know where I am!

YS: Take some deep breaths and look around you...is it still daylight?

RR: *(breathing heavily as she looks around her)* It's getting dark...it's so quiet...it's so desolate...I don't know how it could be so desolate!

YS: Is Shelly still in the front seat with you?

RR: *(pausing)* Yeah...she's sitting there just staring...just staring into space...*(confused)* she's like...she's asleep or something.

YS: Look all around you...you are able to sense everything...see, hear everything clearly.

RR: *(very agitated)* I'm scared, I'm going to hold the baby...it's really quiet and it's starting to get light...it's light all around me...there's light everywhere around my truck! The baby is still sleeping, she's not waking up with this light in our face! *(gasps)* The truck's door is opening!

YS: Shelly's door is opening?

RR: NO, NO...my door's opening!

YS: Are you opening the door?

139

RR: NO! It's opening by itself and I'm holding the baby, I can't drop the baby! (*very upset, crying hysterically*) We're getting out of the truck. It's summer and I'm cold! (*shivers*)

YS: Renee, you are safe, you are just reporting what is happening. Why are you getting out of the truck?

RR: Cause I'm supposed to. (*her tone almost calm*)

YS: Is there anyone with you?

RR: (*whispering and looking around her*) Yes...yes, some people, I can see them.

YS: Are they people that stopped off the freeway?

RR: No...no, they're not people like that. (*gasping*) They look different. Some are small and some are taller.

YS: Are you out of the truck?

RR: Uh-huh, we've been out of the truck...we're walking...and they have the baby. They're holding her so I don't drop her. It's alright...they're very kind to me. They're very soft spoken. They don't talk like we talk through our mouths. They just think and we feel and can sense and know what they're saying. (*shivers*) I must be nervous...I'm so cold.

YS: OK, Renee, just go on describing what is happening.

RR: (*whispering*) I just feel scared...I don't really like going with them. I don't like being here with them.

YS: Is Shelly with you?

RR: No, she's back in the truck. They didn't want her. It's always just me. (*shivering*) Ohhh, we're going in...in this big thing. It's huge!

YS: You are doing just fine, just keep describing what is happening.

RR: It's like a ramp of some kind, you stand on it and it goes up. It's like a grill underneath my feet. I'm going up. (*long pause*) I'm...I'm walking down a hall. It's pretty bright, like white. I'm with them. I'm following them. (*shivering uncontrollably and agitated*) I can't move my feet now and I can't see Samantha...where's my baby!

YS: Take a deep breath, now, remember you are just exploring this, knowing that the baby is alright, she's eleven years old now...allow yourself to describe everything that is happening.

RR: Ahh, yeah, she's alright. (*breathing more normally*)

YS: Are you still walking down the hall?

RR: (*gasps*) Oh…No, I'm laying down now. I can't move my arms and my legs are going numb. Oh, I feel this real tingly feeling from my knees up to my thighs and my buttocks…very, very weird feeling!

YS: You're doing fine now, Renee, just keep describing what you are experiencing.

RR: Oh my God…they're spreading my legs (*crying*) My knees are bent up. Ohhh, there's a sharp pain in my leg. Oh, there's a needle in my leg!

YS: Who is doing this to you? Renee, look all around you.

RR: They are, there's four of them…there's one to the right of me talking to me. I know this one…I know him.

YS: What is he saying to you, Renee?

RR: He's asking me how I have been. He's telling me that the baby is beautiful…that we will be alright. He's talking to me and…and they're doing something to my pelvic area!

Renee almost became inconsolable as she felt the beings doing something to her vaginal area. She began screaming that it wasn't right what they were doing to her. It was at this point that I received confirmation once again that the abduction agenda is more complex than any of us ever imagined.

YS: Knowing that you came out of this safe, you will be able to experience this without feeling any pain or fear. Now, are they still in your vaginal area?

RR: (*crying*) Yes! He's inside of me!

YS: They're putting something inside of you?

RR: NO, he's inside of me…and she's holding my head and he's inside of me…get off of me! She's holding my head so tight!

YS: Who is inside of you?

RR: (*crying*) He looks different than they do…I don't want to see him! They are all around me and I feel so dirty…I don't want to see them anymore…Oh God, help me!

Because Renee was so distressed, I decided to end the session and slowly bring her out of the hypnotic state. During the debriefing, she told me that she remembered arriving at her grandmother's house around 11:30 p.m., "I remember my grandmother yelling at me because she had dinner waiting and she was very worried." There were no cell phones in 1980 and because her truck did not have a clock, Renee was unaware that so much time had passed, the thought never occurred to her to call her grandmother. I questioned her about the being holding her head. Renee told me that she "felt" female, although there was no physical difference.

During these examinations, a female alien being is often described as standing close, often staring into the eyes of the abductee creating a sense of calm. The disturbing "sexual" act that Renee was describing has been reported in many of my cases as well as those of my colleagues. Renee reported the being who was having relations with her as being "different" from the others. Typically, alien beings, whether male or female, are all described very much the same. Usually, 3-4 feet tall, although some are taller, hairless, large "wrap around" eyes, slight build with no discerning sexual organs.

There are also beings which are described as very human looking, even some are described as exceptionally attractive. Throughout all of these years of research, we have come to learn that these "human" looking beings are actually perfected "hybrids." As one of my clients commented after her session, "if you passed him on the street, he wouldn't stand out, except that he was gorgeous!"

On May 20, 1991, Renee returned to my office for another hypnotic regression session. The information that came forward in her first session was disturbing to her and at the same time, Renee was determined to find more answers and to confirm that her partial memories are true experiences. Her first session was very painful for her, she was still trying to process all of the information that came forward, her emotions telling her that it was just a nightmare, but her intellect told her that it was not.

Renee called me after an experience she had on May 13, 1991, this is what she told me:

> "I went to bed around 11 p.m., I was tired. My husband, Carl, was asleep next to me. Around 2:30 a.m., something bumped the waterbed. It woke my husband, he got up and went to the bathroom. I remember seeing a figure, dark silhouette, no hair, very large head, long neck, thin arms and waist. His height was about my daughter's height, under 5 ft. tall. The figure just walked by, then I went to sleep. When I woke up in the morning, I was bleeding from my vagina (*a brownish-red fluid*). I felt no pain, but I bled for 3 days."

Renee was anxious to schedule another session as soon as I had an opening. She was convinced that after her May 13th experience, they were aware of her sessions with me.

> "They know what I'm doing, they told me not to tell anyone, I wasn't supposed to tell you…how dare they, I have the right to know what happened to me!"

Renee's second session was scheduled on May 20, 1991. She was anxious to explore a very clear memory that she shared with her son, Carl, Jr.

The date was May 13, 1988.[9] Renee was 27 years old living in her father's trailer on Lake Hemet with her two children, her daughter Samantha and her young son, 5-year-old Carl. She prepared the kids for bed and, shortly after, they all went to sleep. The next thing that Renee remembered is waking up and seeing a "fireball" or bright orb hovering above her head, little Carl woke up and saw the "fireball." As they watched it float out of the window, Renee looked out and remembered seeing an owl. She thinks they went back to sleep. This memory particularly bothered her because her son was also involved, but to what extent, she did not know.

After my usual induction, I began to regress Renee back to May 13, 1988:

> YS: Renee, you will be able to see and sense, hear and feel everything, very sharply, very clearly. When you are there on Lake Hemet, just describe what you are doing in the trailer.
>
> RR: It's really cold up here, the kids are getting ready for bed in the back of the trailer, I'm so tired. I turn on the heater and we all fall asleep.
>
> YS: OK, Renee, using all of your senses, just report if anything happens next. Take some deep breaths and sense all around you.
>
> RR: We're just sleeping…and it's getting very bright in the trailer, very bright. Oh my God, the door is opening up! (*long pause*) I'm outside…it's very bright outside, brighter than day. It's so strange. (*seems very calm, almost in awe*)
>
> YS: Do you know why you went outside?

---

[9] Renee had two experiences on May 13th. First was 1988 and the second 1991. What makes this date so significant?

RR: I'm supposed to. Everything is so bright. (*startled*) I'm going up...I'm kinda floating up!

YS: How are you floating up?

R: In the light...just floating up. Ohhh! I can look down and see the ground and the top of the trailer. I can look through the trees. I'm as high as the trees almost! It's so cold. Oh, my God, where am I?

YS: What are you seeing? Renee, just look around you and just report what is happening.

RR: (*becoming agitated*) I'm in a room! The room is so white, bright...and I'm lying down, how did I get in here (*breathing heavily*) It's so weird!

YS: Is there anyone there with you?

RR: I feel one behind me...and I feel another one, but I feel a lot of other people watching.

YS: Can you describe what they look like, these people?

RR: They're small and they have beautiful eyes; very deep and dark and soulful, just beautiful eyes. They have nice sharp chins and silky skin. It's so soft looking, but it's different. It's so hard to explain. It's not like our skin. It's so soft, but it's kind of a pasty color, gray color, but not gray.

YS: Do you see Carl in the room with you?

RR: Yes, yes I do...he's upset, he's on a table like me and he has somebody with him and they're calming him down. They're examining him. They're looking at his chest. They're doing something to his ears. I can't get up and do anything for Carl. I don't want to frighten him 'cause I'm frightened!

YS: OK, you know that you and Carl came out of this and you both are fine and healthy. Just continue to describe what is happening.

RR: Oh! They're touching me down there. They're examining me. That's why my legs feel funny...they're examining me and my legs feel funny! I can't lift my head...but he's examining me and he's taking something. He's taking something. (*becoming hysterical*)

YS: Renee, you will be able to report what is happening without experiencing the pain. Tell me what is happening.

RR: (*crying*) They're going to let me have a baby. They're telling me when my husband comes up this weekend, that I would have a baby. It's ok. They're going to let me have a baby!

YS: Do you understand what that means? They're going to let you have a baby?

RR: Yes, no, I don't know...I don't know! (*feeling very confused*) There's people around me...and they're putting something in my arms.

YS: What is it, Renee?

RR: I feel it in my arms...I can feel its little legs. (*breathing very heavy*) Oh my God, Oh my God, Oh my God!

YS: Renee, listen to me, you will be able to experience everything very clearly without the fear. Remember, whatever happened to you. You came out of it and you are alive and healthy. Now, tell me what is happening.

RR: (*trying to breathe normally*) There's a baby in my arms! Whose baby is this...oh my God...there's a baby...oh my arms are numb, I'm afraid I'll drop this baby...oh...this baby in my arms!

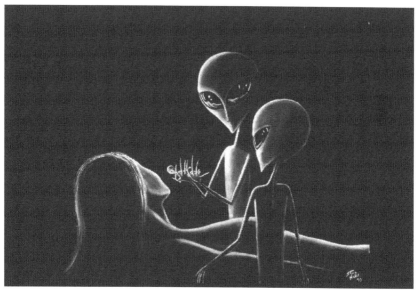

Artist Steve Neill

Renee was so upset and crying in disbelief that the beings have given her a baby to hold. Renee's love for children is very apparent as she describes the baby.

YS: Renee, take a look at the baby, describe what the baby looks like.

RR: (*Long pause as she looks at the baby*) This baby is so small...small and very skinny. Oh, I don't want to drop this baby. It doesn't have as much hair as my children. It's so thin and its color is different. (*crying*) I can't believe...this child is pasty, white, really white and it's cold. I can feel it laying on my chest...ah it's so nice...I love babies. (*crying*)

YS: Renee, are the others still in the room?

RR: Yes...they're all looking at me...looking at how I'm reacting to this baby. (*crying*) I love children. I would like to have lots of children. Oh, I'm shaking...and this baby is so quiet. I don't want to scare this baby.

YS: Can you tell if it's a girl or boy baby?

RR: Oh, it's a boy. It's so small, so little. Oh, I'm freezing. I'm so cold. (*Begins to breathe heavily, getting very upset*) They're taking it from me! Please don't take it!

YS: Where are they taking the baby?

RR: (*very upset, crying*) Out through the door...PLEASE, don't take him, don't take this baby. Let me have this baby. You don't know how to take care of a baby! (*screaming and crying*)

YS: Are they answering you about the baby?

RR: (crying) They won't let me get up. They're telling me that the little baby will be ok. Oh, my God, why can't I have this baby!

YS: Renee, take some deep breaths, you're doing fine. What is happening now?

RR: (*a little calmer*) I'm standing up and I'm walking. I'm down a hall. I'm walking down this hall then I stand on, it looks like nothing is there, but there is something holding me up. I'm inside this room that's different, feels like I'm standing on the sky. It's getting bright and I feel myself going down. They're helping me and Carl...putting us back in bed. (*pausing*) Oh, there's a fireball. Carl sees it too. It's hovering over our heads! I watch it floating out the window. I look out the window and I can't believe it. I see this beautiful owl in the tree. This owl is gorgeous. I have never seen a more beautiful owl in my life. (*yawns*) I'm so tired. I just want to sleep.

When I brought Renee out of hypnosis, she was very emotional. It took her a while to compose herself enough to drive home. It was apparent to me that her conscious memory of the "fireball" or Orb was the end of her experience. Abductees usually consciously recall the beginning of an abduction or the end when they are brought back. The Owl is used over and again as a "screen memory," a memory that is artificially induced by the aliens.

As I brought Renee out of hypnosis, she was very emotional. It took her quite a while to compose herself enough to drive home. As her hypnotherapist, it was heart wrenching to watch her relive the interaction with the "baby." Her pain and confusion of why they would not let her keep the baby came through in her session in verbal and non-verbal communication. During the debriefing Renee stated that she felt violated. She also had many questions about the baby which I tried to answer and at the same time, give her confirmation that I have worked with many cases involving men and women being shown babies and that this is an integral part of the alien program. After hearing this, Renee felt some relief, but was little consolation for her; she was truly concerned about the well-being of these babies. "They told me that I could keep my other baby...how dare they, what gives them the right?" Shortly after this incident, Renee became pregnant with her youngest son, Robert who was born in March 1989.

Renee's sessions sparked another memory of the night she feels she conceived her daughter.

> "I was lying in bed with my husband, and suddenly there was a blinding light. We thought it was a lightning storm, but the light was so blinding that we couldn't see for a while. I can't remember anything else."

I worked with Renee for about two years. The information that came forward was helpful to her, particularly putting together the pieces of a missing time episode she had with her boyfriend at the age of 15, at which time, she experienced her first very painful pelvic exam. The beings told her that she "was ready" and that she had "come of age." As I questioned her, the more resistant she became: "I can't talk to you, I'm not supposed to tell anyone."

Renee knows that she has "helped" them with their project all of her life. The realization that she may have numerous hybrid children that she is not aware of tortures her every day. A part of her is up there somewhere away from her and as a mother she worries about what will become of them.

Renee moved on with her busy life and like so many others living with this secret, one day she will know. According to the aliens, when the time is right, we will "know" the purpose of the massive "hybrid breeding program." Now, Renee drives to see her grandmother free of panic attacks.

CHAPTER 7: Katie Campbell

**"I can't stand my husband to touch me sexually.
I feel I am destroying everything good around me.
I have anxiety attacks; I want to have a normal life."**

Katie Campbell was referred to me by CERO member, Jesse Long. When she telephoned me, she told me that she was bothered by some memories and dreams that have bothered her for many years and was finally ready for some answers.

I interviewed Katie in my office on April 20, 1992. Katie was married, 29 years old; about 5' 7", with shoulder length light brown hair, fair complexion. Although she did not have on a stitch of make-up, her skin looked flawless. Her warm and polite personality made it easy to establish an easy rapport. She told me that she was finally ready to confront her fears whether something actually happened or not. She felt that it was better knowing the truth, half kidding she said to me, "I am ready to find out if I'm crazy."

Katie could not believe her good fortune when she met Jesse Long while working as a Production Assistant on a major film where Jesse was the Script Supervisor. One day while having lunch together, their conversation somehow led to the subject of UFOs and abduction. Katie couldn't believe that she was finally talking to someone about her many very strange and disturbing memories without the fear of ridicule. Jesse shared with Katie about the many years he worked with me in private sessions and told her all about the very special people in CERO. Katie knew that it was no coincidence that she and Jesse happened to be hired for the same film.

During her interview, Katie explained that for many years, she suffered from stomach trouble and insomnia. She often experienced shooting pain in her left ovaries through her hips and down her legs. Her doctor felt a lump on her left ovary, but was not detected on the ultrasound.

Katie's earliest memory was when she was 5 years old. Here is what she told me in her own words:

> "I had a recurring nightmare of playing on my street, a *cul de sac* and someone, a man, would take me away to the end of the street where there was a rectangular booth or box about 6 feet long and about 4 feet high. All the neighbors were outside doing yard work and I would scream, but no one would hear me or see me. This man would take me behind this box, then I would wake up."

At the age of 7 years old, she would see a funny looking character she named "Monster McMillen:"

> "He was a funny looking thing with a very large head made of grayish brainy material with very large eyes, no ears and a small mouth. His body was very thin and long and long skinny arms. He stood about 4 feet high and seemed to dance or waddle around the room. I was never afraid of him and always seemed happy and had soft eyes. I would always see him at my cousin Greg's house in the basement and I saw him in my bedroom too. Greg saw him too, but none of my other cousins whom I played with ever saw him. He would communicate with me, but I don't remember what was said. I would bring food to my room at night thinking if I fed him, he would go away. I don't know how long this went on, maybe a couple of years."

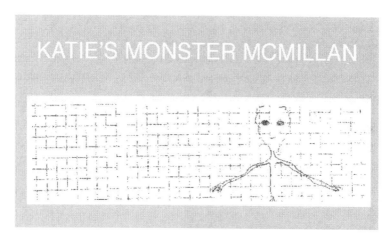

Katie was also bothered about recurring dreams that she had about a "bubble family." In this dream, they would always talk to her, but "not with words, I don't remember what they said. But it was at that point in my life where I started to feel that I didn't belong. I felt that my parents were just my guardians and I started to feel uncomfortable and like I could not fit in with anybody.

It was now she felt she was having "out of body experiences" and episodes of paralysis, after these episodes, she was always so exhausted, "I would wake in the morning and I felt like I was run over by a truck."

The memory that disturbed her the most was when she was 19 years old. During this time in her life, she said that she was obsessed with the "devil". She was afraid to be alone and could not fall asleep at night unless every light in the house was on.

> "I had a dream one night that I was in a room with just a table or dentist's chair reclined. I was strapped into this chair or table and the "devil" was tormenting or torturing me. My parents were there helping the "devil." I woke up the next morning and I was very sore and swollen. My vagina was sore and swollen. My whole body felt like I had been beaten up. It seemed so real. I didn't get my period for about six months after that. I did a pregnancy test at home, even though I did not have a boyfriend at the time, the test was negative."

Her mother would talk to her about experiences she remembered about a bright light coming through the window. Because her father was a devout Catholic, Katie decided to see a priest. He told her that she was obsessed with the devil and talked to her about an exorcism. Katie became frightened by his suggestion and never went back. She felt very alone.

During her interview, Katie told me that for many years, she suffered from stomach trouble and insomnia. She often experienced shooting pain in her left ovaries through her hips and down her legs. Her doctor felt a lump in her left ovary, but was not detected on the ultrasound. What bothered Katie the most was the fact that she does not want to have sexual relations with her husband, "I don't want him to touch me, it hurts to have sex."

She truly loved him, they were very compatible in every way, except for sex. She feared that this could destroy her marriage, but at the same time, she could not explain why she felt this way. Her family therapist asked her if she had ever been raped. With tears in her eyes, she asked me to help get to the bottom of all these disturbing and confusing dreams and memories but most of all, she needed some understanding about why she did not enjoy being touched by her own husband.

I reassured Katie that hypnotherapy is a very useful and safe tool and that she was indeed in safe hands. I explained to her that the important thing is to find the cause of these recurring dreams, once that is accomplished, she will be able to get on with her life and enjoy a fulfilling married relationship.

Katie scheduled her first session on April 29, 1992. Although she was very nervous about her first hypnotic regression, she was anxious to explore the "Devil Dream" because of the physical effects she suffered the next morning. Katie allowed herself to drift down into a deep sleep as I slowly took her back to the age of 19. She described her home with the beautiful tree-lined backyard and the delicious smell of her mother's cooking. I moved Katie forward to the night she had a very vivid dream of being strapped to a chair or a table. The following account is taken from the transcript from her first session:

> KC: I feel pain in my right arm. (*long pause*) I don't know, it feels like something's electrocuting me or something.
> YS: Are you in your bed?
> KC: (*taking a deep breath*) I'm on the table. It's not flat. It feels like I'm kind of reclining. There's people going out the door. People are scurrying.
> YS: Do you know these people?
> KC: I can only see the backs of them. They look like eggs. Except the one standing on my left.
> YS: What does that person look like?
> KC: I don't know...I just see black. Oh, I see eyes, black eyes. Oh, I feel like I'm being strapped down!
> YS: You can feel the straps?
> KC: I feel like I'm restrained. I feel uncomfortable in the straps.
> YS: OK, just tell me what's happening.
> KC: I'm sitting in a dentist's chair...or, it's not a dentist's chair, it's like a contoured chair, but it's lying down, but not completely flat.
> YS: Using all of your senses, just describe everything that is happening around you.
> KC: There's something attached to a piece of tube. (*complaining of pain*) It's being poked up my shoulder, my right shoulder. It's long and really skinny and the black thing is still beside me, on my left. (*The being on her left, only seeing his eyes*)
> YS: Become aware of the rest of your body, do you feel pain or discomfort in any other part of your body?
> KC: (*tension in her face*) It feels tight, all tense. I have pain in my legs. (*becoming upset; begins to thrash around on my couch*)

Because Katie was becoming extremely distressed, I decided to end the session. Like so many of my clients who have undergone regression, Katie commented that she thought she was making up the events, there was only one problem, she felt the physical and emotional discomfort. "I feel there is more there."

Katie's next session was booked for May 13, 1992. Having been through a regression before, Katie easily drifted into a deep sleep. I once again regressed her to the age of 19 years old, back to her memory of herself on the "dentist chair."

> YS: OK, Katie, as your mind begins to focus, knowing that it's safe now to explore, your mind is very sharp and clear...describe your surroundings.
>
> KC: It's like a hospital room, like clinking and stuff...there's light, it's bright. There's machines and stuff over there on the left and the same door is on the right. I keep seeing those "egg people" and I don't know what they're doing. (*She begins to breathe rapidly, starts to cry*)
>
> YS: Take deep breaths, Katie, you are safe, just continue describing, just verbalize.
>
> KC: (*very upset*) I feel like I'm having an operation. Someone is standing between my legs. He's looking at me. I don't know what's he's doing.
>
> YS: That person who is looking at you, can you describe what he looks like, is it male or female?
>
> KC: It looks male. They all look the same, it's just a feeling. His head is big. His eyes are halfway down his head. They're in the wrong place (*voice rises, begins to cry*) I don't want to look at him anymore! (*crying*)
>
> YS: Katie, you will be able to describe everything without any fear, remember, you came out of this and you are alive, safe and healthy.
>
> KC: (*Becoming a little calmer*) He's looking at my stomach or something. My legs are spread apart and he's holding something in his hand.
>
> YS: Just focus in on what he has in his hand, just report it.
>
> KC: (*Pauses as she studies the instrument*) It's silver. It has little lines on it, like a little opening sort of...I think...like as if it's going to open up inside of me or something. (*sobbing*).

YS: You're doing fine, Katie. Just report what is happening. You are going to get through this. Now take a look at that silver thing.

KC: (*Takes a deep breath*) Ok, now it looks like something that's got all kinds of little fingers. It's going up like that (*uses hand gestures*) and I can see the dark spaces between it. He's just looking at me. He has no expression. I don't know if he's mad, happy or sad. I don't want to lay here anymore. (*Tries to move*)

YS: Are you trying to get up?

KC: No, there's something over my arms...a strap or something.

YS: As you feel yourself lying there, describe what is happening all around you.

KC: There's a machine over here. Uh, it's got all kinds of buttons and stuff and lights and it looks like a computer, kind of. And there's all kinds of stuff against the wall, over there...and then there's counter here and here and the door (*motions with her hands*) and all this stuff is out there, but I don't know what's going on out there...and there's kind of grids on the walls. It looks like metal and silver. There's no decorations or anything. It just looks so cold and steely.

YS: OK, take a look and tell me if the one is still standing between your legs.

KC: Oh, he's just looking at me...and he's reaching for something. (*becoming upset again, breathing heavily*). I don't know what he's doing. There's people going in and out and moving all over the place...and nobody's paying attention to me...like I wasn't there!

YS: Just keep reporting what is happening...you're doing fine.

KC: They all look the same. I can't tell one from the other. They're carrying something...like little trays.

YS: And do you know what is on those trays?

KC: Um, I don't know what it is. It's like little round pokey things and stuff. It all looks different.

YS: Those little round things. Are they large? Are they small?

KC: Uh, like tong sort of things and little pokey straight things and little like magnifying glass-looking things. They look this big. (*shows size using hand gestures*)

153

About this big; they look like little instruments…the machine is still beside me…on my left."

YS: Is there anyone operating that machine, just take a look over to your left.

KC: There's lights on it. I keep seeing a number 4.

YS: Where do you see the number 4?

KC: I see it on the machine…and zeroes.

YS: And down in your pelvic area and your stomach…how does it feel?

KC: Oh, it feels empty and sore…like a vacuum.

YS: Like a vacuum? How does the rest of your body feel?

KC: It hurts mostly on this (*left*) side. It feels cold on my back, kind of prickly. The machine keeps saying number 4. Everything seems really confusing.

Katie indicated that she did not want to continue. When I brought Katie out of hypnosis, she was visibly shaken with the fact that she was feeling the discomfort in her vaginal area. I explained to her that the body retains memories and what she experienced during the course of her regression was a "memory" and not a "dream."

The next session with Katie was one of the most intense experiences I had ever experienced with a female client. She returned to my office on July 30, 1992. When Katie was 23 years old, she experienced a very disturbing lapse of time which she could never forget.

"When I was 23 years old, I went to my bedroom one afternoon to call my friend, Helen. I picked up the phone and looked at the clock. It was 1:05 p.m. The next thing I knew, the phone was on the bed and the clock said 2:30 p.m. I have no idea what happened to the time. I called Helen and asked her if we had spoken earlier, she said 'no.'"

As Katie made herself comfortable on my couch, I began giving her suggestions for deep relaxation as she gently drifted into a very deep sleep.

YS: Feel yourself back in your apartment. Look all around you. Everything is becoming very familiar. Feel yourself in your bedroom. You are 23 years old. Your mind is very sharp and clear. When you are ready to speak verbally, you will find that as you speak; the deeper asleep you will become.

154

KC: I feel like I'm shaking. I feel like all time has stopped. (*Begins to breathe heavier; long pause*) There's something at the end of the hallway.

YS: You see a hallway. Tell me what is at the end of the hallway.

KC: It turns to the right. I see, I see kind of benches and sort of doors on the right, kind of, elevator doors. Oh, ok, I see a lady. She has long brown hair. It's kind of parted in the middle. And now I see a little boy in a red and white striped t-shirt; but I can't tell if they're part of the same family. Oh, it feels really cold.

YS: Ok, you are doing just fine. Just tell me the next thing that happens. Are you still in the hallway?

KC: Yes...I think there's something at the end of the hallway that's a big open space, almost like an auditorium...and it's round.

YS: Can you describe what it looks like?

KC: It's round and it kind of looks like a funnel and it's got seats that go around, and they kind of go down. There's nobody in there right now, it's empty.

YS: Do you see anything else in the hallway?

KC: There's people shuffling in the hallways and in all the rooms on both sides. The hallways are close to this big auditorium.

YS: Can you see or sense anything inside of those rooms?

KC: I'm walking over here and I want to look over here, but I can't see anything inside of that room. It's real fuzzy. But over here is really bright, that's where the hatching things are, on this side.

YS: And why do you say hatching?

KS: I'm not allowed to go in there, but I can sort of see the bubble things.

YS: Can you describe those bubble things?

KC: I think so, but I'm not allowed to look. There must be something inside of them. I think there's about...hmmm, there's about four of them. Um, everything is going fuzzy. There's about four and then this big thing. Then there's more on the other side and there's kind of like these windows, but there's light coming in...it's not sunlight. It's like a heat light, sort of?

YS: Do you see the source of that light?

KC: No, it's likely it's coming through a mirror, kind of? It looks like it would look like in a hospital room. It's really bright. The room is really bright.

YS: Is there anybody inside of that room?

KC: Yeah, there's people along here, and they keep looking at the little egg things. I know there's eggs in there. I can tell.

YS: Do they look like eggs?

KC: I can't see them, but I can feel it. And this big thing in the middle, is kind of white and silver and it kind of comes like a gigantic vacuum cleaner, sort of, and it's got all these tubes coming from it and it goes into these little things. I think there's about nine along here.

YS: Is someone with you?

KC: I think so. I don't see anybody, but I feel like somebody's there, but I just know that I'm not allowed to go into the room. And there's kind of like another room and they all have glass and there's a door over here. Now, I'm going down the hall more. There's people here who are really uncomfortable. They don't know why they're here.

YS: How many people do you see?

KC: I can't see them, but I can tell that there's people there. They're scared because they're screaming. The whole place just has this sort of real tense feeling. But the egg people just go on about their business and they don't pay any attention to if somebody's hurting or somebody's crying. It doesn't matter. They're like robots.

YS: Katie, are you still moving along the hallway?

KC: Now I'm in the other room.

YS: And what does that room look like?

KC: It's kind of weird. (*sighs*) I'm getting real anxious. (*begins to breathe heavily*)

YS: Ok, Katie, you are doing just fine, why do you feel anxious?

KC: (*Becoming upset*) Cause nobody will tell me what I'm doing here.

YS: How many people are in that room with you?

KC: There's a few people, or whatever they are…the egg people. I see the lady one, she's the only one who's real nice. Her eyes are bigger. She's real nice to me.

YS: Is she talking to you?

KC: No, she's looking at me and she's touching me and she's staring at me.

YS: Is there anyone else touching you?

KC: No, she's looking in my eyes.

YS: Is she talking to you?

KC: Mmm, no she's not saying any words, but I feel really comfortable. I've seen her before. I've seen all these people before. Some of them do mean things and some of them are just there and don't do anything.

YS: What kind of mean things do they do?

KC: They torture people.

YS: Do you see them doing that? How do they torture people?

KC: They stick things in them and they make them scream and they don't care when they do operations, if the person can feel it or not. They just do things and don't care, but the lady cares. I think 'cause she never does anything to hurt me."

YS: Take a look around and describe what you see in that room.

KC: Some kind of instruments, maybe, like silver things and I keep feeling like I'm going to have a needle in my arm, but that's ok.

YS: Do you feel pain?

KC: No...I feel like there was something there, but it's gone now. (*sharply draws in breath*) Oooh!

YS: What's happening now?

KC: Somebody else just came to take me away.

YS: And who is that?

KC: Some mean guy...they all look the same, and I just feel something and I'm scared of him. I don't like him. I wish I could go back there with the lady. I know there's other people being tortured.

YS: Can you hear these other people?

KC: (*Begins to cry*) They have things taken from them. They have things put in them and taken out!

YS: Do you know what those things are?

KC: (*Crying hysterically hardly able to talk*) LIKE BABIES! I can't see them right now, but I've seen it before and I can hear them screaming and I know that's why they're screaming cause I've seen them do it before! (*Sobbing*)

YS: Katie, you are safe now. I'm going to touch your hand. I am right here, take some deep breaths. Now you have seen these operations. They let you watch?

KC: (*Quietly sobbing*) I was in a room with other people having operations and I was having something put inside of me…inside of me, but I could see what they were doing to other people…they were putting things inside of them and taking things out.

YS: Did you see men and women in this room?

KC: Yes, but with the men they do something different…they hook men up to machines.

YS: What do the machines look like?

KC: They're big black machines and they have probes coming from them and little attachment things. I think they're testing. It seems like a pain tolerance or something. They won't ever tell me what they're doing but right now; these people aren't very nice because they don't tell you anything, they don't tell you what they're going to do and why…makes me angry!

YS: Do you know what they did to you when you were there before?

KC: Yeah, uh-huh. Sometimes they would just observe me and stare into my eyes. The lady would always make me feel comfortable, then I didn't care what they did to me, but when she wasn't there, sometimes they would hurt me.

YS: Katie, how would they hurt you?

KC: They would put things inside of me, instruments and vacuum sort of things and pokey things in my arms, and …

YS: Do you know why they were putting things inside of you?

KC: (*Pauses*) Cause they wanted to see, I think, if I could have babies.

YS: Did they tell you that?

KC: They don't talk to me. They just plant feelings inside of me, but they don't speak. (*Becoming distressed*) Why can't, I don't like it when they put things in me!

YS: Do you know how old you were the first time they did this?

KC: (*Beginning to cry*) I think I was a little girl. I don't want to see them!

YS: Katie, take a deep breath now. Whatever happened to you when you were a little girl, you came out of it and you are fine, healthy and loved. Now describe what is happening around you.

KC: (*Very upset*) I don't want to see these people anymore. It's not fair! I feel bad for those poor other people, 'cause some of them have never been here before, and they're being tortured for the first time. Oh, uh, I keep seeing a blonde lady on a table beside me!

YS: A blonde lady? Do you know her?

KC: Oh…she's screaming!

YS: Can you describe what they are doing to her?

KC: They have these weird machines that take things out of people. They have tubes and stuff that go into needles in people's arms and shoulders.

YS: You're doing fine, Katie. Keep describing what is happening.

KC: (*Very upset*) There's three egg people with her. There's one touching her head and the other one is down here." (*points to her private parts, begins sobbing*) She's screaming about her baby!

YS: What is she saying about her baby?

KC: (*Sobbing*) She's screaming 'not my baby, please let me have my baby'. Maybe they're stealing her baby. I don't know. I don't want to watch the lady anymore. I feel sick to my stomach.

Katie was so upset by this time that I gently brought her out of hypnosis. During the debriefing, she was so upset with the realization that she had been a part of their program since she was a very young girl. She felt violated. It was finally clear to her why she did not enjoy being touched. During each of her sessions, I gave Katie suggestions for a healthy sex life with her husband who she truly loves.

Katie immediately felt comfortable at her first CERO meeting. She was struck with the familiarity when the members were sharing their experiences with each other. But the biggest surprise for Katie happened when she was introduced to fellow CERO member, Renee Reynolds. Katie was visibly shaken as she asked to speak to me in private.

"Oh, my God, Yvonne, Renee is the woman that I saw on the table next to me."

At that very moment, a chill ran down my spine as I thought back to Renee's intense regression sessions and how she cried and begged "them" to let her keep her baby.

Over the years, CERO members have had vivid "dreams" and memories of seeing each other on the craft during abduction experiences. Katie recognizing Renee lying on the table next to her on the "craft," once again, gave me the confirmation that these experiences are not the product of an overactive imagination. The question is, what is the purpose of this breeding program, where are all these hybrids, have they been encountered here on earth?

CHAPTER 8: The Hybrid Program

Part One chronicles the "Hybrid Program." The stories told are typical of those who have been *Chosen*. Most of the regressions were done in the early 1990s when knowledge of the Hybrid Program was still in the discovery phase. Today, the common aspects of the Hybrid Program are well known but, at the time each of these brave people came forward looking for answers, it was still a mystery. Only a few of us around the world were trying to find answers. At that time, most of those *Chosen* had no place to turn.

Today, the common aspects of the ET-Human interactions are part of popular culture. Greys are now in commercials, abducting people because they have the "right" car or because they want to drink a soda they don't have on their spaceship. Children watch cartoons with Greys or play with Grey dolls. People know that they landed in Roswell and probably live in Area 51. Popular culture has adopted them while they are still denied by the government and science. Even the Vatican believes they may be real.

The Hybrid Program is also known to many. The common elements can be found in hundreds of books, television and web-based programs. With a little bit of research, people know that Greys and other species can walk through walls; take people from their bedrooms; perform medical procedures; and create a hybrid race. Many details such as hybrid baby presentations, implants, virtual reality view screens and other common aspects can be discovered with little effort.

Just as we begin thinking that we may be getting a handle on what they want, things begin to change. This seems to be the trend where every time we think we know what it all means, something new arises to add to the mystery. In the 1890s, the great airship mystery was about strange people in slow moving "airships" complete with anchors and other recognizable features that fascinated the nation. In the 1950s, many came forward with stories of meeting Venusians who came to warn us about nuclear weapons. Later, large waves of craft with occupant sightings made national and international news. Washington D.C., Michigan, Hudson Valley, Belgium, Phoenix, Mexico City and many other locations each took their turn as being the place where UFOs showed themselves to thousands of people. The eighties and nineties had the abduction phenomena, Roswell and Area 51 dominate the headlines. Every time the people start studying one aspect of the phenomena, another emerges. To paraphrase scientist and UFO pioneer Jacques Vallee, it would be unfortunate if they were only people coming from another planet in cans.

Once again, a new trend appears to be emerging. Unfortunately, this trend has many negative aspects. These negative portions of this new trend are not about "evil aliens" coming to invade planet Earth as they have done so many times in Hollywood. The negative aspects are about us. Warnings to Experiencers about what we are doing to ourselves and what we are doing to each other. These warnings are not new. However, they are taking on a more urgent tone and Experiencers are reaching out to me in increasing numbers to say that "time is running out."

About 2011, I noticed a shift in message that Experiencers were conveying to me in their regression sessions and from their conscious memories. Most stated that they were uneasy and felt they had to "do something" but they did not know what it was. A new "urgency" came out of them to act and warn others. I did not publicly mention this trend until an interview I gave to LA Weekly Magazine near the end of 2013.

> Other revelations are less amazing than chilling. In the last two years, Smith says, abductees have been describing a cataclysmic event that is going to happen. Scenes are projected onto a wall or images placed in the mind of explosions, atomic bombs, tsunamis, floods, diseases, large cities underwater, infrastructure destroyed—the whole post-apocalyptic nightmare scenario. "Just utter devastation around the world," she says. "They don't know what it means. Only that it's coming soon."
>
> They are told they are being prepared for something. That they have a job to do. They have recurring dreams of a vast armada of UFOs covering the sky, of leading large groups of people somewhere. They don't know where, or why. But when the time comes, they are told, they will know." (Alimurung, Gendy: *"A Hypnotherapist Built a Career on Alien Abductions, and Her Experiences May Unnerve You" LA Weekly Magazine* (December 5, 2013)
>
> (http://www.laweekly.com/news/a-hypnotherapist-built-a-career-on-alien-abductions-and-her-experiences-may-unnerve-you-4137401.)

Since the interview, the trend has continued. Some have specific predictions. Others only have a sense of dread and "know" they have to do something. It is generalized for some, like "John" (Ch. 4 (Pt. 1) & Ch. 10 (Pt. 2)), who have only "feelings" that they need to get ready. My co-author,

James (Ch. 12 (Pt. 2)), has a need to "do something" and is acting on that "urgency" despite possible damage to his career in law.

Part Two starts the analysis of this new trend. Every researcher who works with Experiencers that I have discussed this new trend also believes "something" is going on. With Part Two, we begin to look for answers.

PART TWO
A Shift In
The Alien Program
Experiencers And Their
Urgency To "Do Something"

CHAPTER 9: The Urgency Shift Begins (Yvonne And James)

About 2011, I began noticing a pattern among Experiencers.[10] This pattern emerged both during regressions and from persons who consciously remember their experiences. Also, new people were seeking me out with these "hard to explain" feelings. They all were echoing a common theme. They were supposed "to do something." What they were supposed "to do," most did not know.

This pattern has become stronger over time and was not restricted to CERO members. The pattern also manifested itself in Experiencer Sessions[11] at conferences such as the International UFO Congress. My first public discussion of this new trend was in an interview for LA Weekly Magazine in December 2013. I was asked if there was anything new on the horizon that I was getting from my sessions with Experiencers. I answered the reporter's question by discussing this new trend of people urgently trying to figure out something they are supposed "to do."

Age, length of experiences, gender, political identity and other factors do not make a difference. Most of them feel they have an important task to perform. As opposed to previous "messages" that Experiencers have received from their interactions with ET, this wave of urgent messages made them feel that they need to act very soon. However, most do not know what task they are supposed to perform. Even if they cannot explain their feelings, most know they must act and that "time is running out." Time for what?

While these ET messages of future earth changes are not new, these warnings have taken on a more "urgent" tone. In 1992, I first heard of this "urgency" from Experiencers. It was at the first conference on the study of Abductees/Experiencers. I had the honor of being invited to speak at the "Abduction Study Conference" at the Massachusetts Institute of Technology ("MIT") in June 1992. It was co-chaired by Harvard Medical

---

[10] This pattern, for some, may have started earlier. In Chapter 4, Alfonso Martinez expressed these "feelings of urgency" in 2007.

[11] Experiencer Sessions are gatherings only open to Experiencers or persons who think they may have had interactions with ET. They are closed to the press and public. At these sessions, people share their experiences with each other in a nonjudgmental environment. For example, at the International UFO Congress, the one hour sessions are held once or twice a day. The attendance varies from 60 to 150 Experiencers per Session with an average attendance of about 100 persons.

School Professor of Psychiatry, Dr. John Mack, and MIT Physicist David E. Pritchard. It was the first academic conference about alien abduction. Its program brought together researchers, hypnotherapists, academicians, and experiencers. Most of the pioneers in the field were present.

One of the highlights for me was the "Experiencer Panel." These brave souls were the early voices of the Abductees/Experiencers. Looking back, one stood out. "Susan,"[12] a speaker on the abductee/experiencer panel described how she acted based on the messages she was given that sound very like those of today. Aboard a ship, she was shown a large "viewing screen." It showed one scene of land being planted in the Middle East. Another scene was of barren land that once had a rainforest in South America. She was told that a massacre had occurred, which she understood to be an ecological massacre. She stated:

> "I don't remember being given any specific information about what I had seen. I remember feeling that time was running out and something needed to be done."[13]

Following her two visits to an alien ship where she received these environmental messages, her "need to do something" prompted her to design an environmental awareness program for three elementary schools which included planting 300 trees. Her actions were extraordinary for the time as she had no background in environmental issues. Later, those schools instituted recycling programs.

Susan saw the messages she received as being very "positive" and intended to help us help ourselves. She disliked the term "abductee" and liked "Experiencer." When asked if she had talked to her hypnotherapist, Budd Hopkins,[14] about these issues, she said that she did not. Her reason was that either she was not ready to tell him or he was not ready to hear it.

---

[12] "Susan" was not her real name.

[13] Pritchard, Pritchard, Mack, Kasey, Yapp Editors., *"Alien Discussions: Proceedings of the Abduction Study Conference Held at MIT, Cambridge, Mass"*, North Cambridge Press, 1994, p. 153.

[14] Budd Hopkins was one of the early pioneers in the field. Prior to his passing in 2011, Budd wrote several books on the alien abduction phenomenon. (*i.e. "Missing Time: A Documented Study of UFO Abductions"*, Ballantine Books (1988).) He used hypnotic regression to recover memories from abductees. His view was that the purpose and nature of the alien intervention was negative. "Carol" disagreed with Hopkins' conclusions, making it highly unlikely that she was subject to any suggestions from him with regards to her "urgency"

This early use of the term started to gain wider usage after the MIT Conference. During the MIT conference, the term "Experiencer" was the preferred term used. I first heard this term from Dr. John Mack. It reflects a more positive view of the phenomenon and its impact on those who interact with ET. However, at the time, most of the researchers saw the experiences of those who interact with ET as negative. The focus was on the types of examinations performed and the seemingly cold and uncaring attitudes of ET.

The use of the term "Experiencer" is indicative of a positive view of Human-ET interactions. It would be consistent with the passage of messages that ask Experiencers to act to assist others in a time of crisis. "Susan," in particular, took her messages and turned them into positive actions that help our planet.

A. Susan's Parallels With Today

Susan was called to action through her experiences. Even though Susan's experiences were often frightening, she talks about the many changes that have occurred in her life, one of which caused her to take steps to preserve the environment. She used the phrase "need to do something" to characterize her feelings. She stated she does not remember being given any specific information but it was more of a "feeling" that she should act, apparently arising from her subconscious. The ideas were not conveyed in the way we pass information. The use of "viewing screens" seems to convey more information than a typical earth-based TV screen. Rather, it appears to be a telepathic conveyance of information directly to the subconscious. This seems to be the predominant way that the current group of Experiencers receive the same urgency "messages" or "feelings."

There are two primary methods of conveyance. One is the use of a viewing screen like the large screen televisions of today. However, according to those who have participated in these presentations, it is a rough comparison in that the Experiencer "feels" that they are present in the scene being presented. More information appears to be transferred to the Experiencer than viewing a normal TV. The second type of information conveyance is what Dr. David Jacobs has labeled "neural engagement."[15] It is when the alien, typically a "Grey," will gaze into the eyes of the

---

to help our planet and her environmental ideas conveyed in two visits to alien ships.

[15] Jacobs, David M., *"Walking Among Us: The Alien Plan to Control Humanity"*. San Francisco, CA: Disinformation Books (2015).

Experiencer from a couple of inches away. Information appears to be passed directly into the mind, primarily the subconscious, of the Experiencer.

With so many common elements found in ET/Human interaction that crosses cultural, religious, ethnic and socioeconomic boundaries, the phenomenon is not limited to any group or region. This makes it more likely that people are willing to listen to the messages of Experiencers than in the past. The worldwide testimony of Experiencers should be recognized as more than coincidence. The same information is gained from those who recover memories during hypnosis and those who consciously remember their interactions.

Susan's "need to do something" finds a parallel with many of today's Experiencers. While the "need" to act was a common feeling among Experiencers, my research shows that the frequency of these messages and urgency felt by Experiencers recently is striking. The feeling of "urgency" was not present with most Experiencers in 1992 like it is today. They tell me about their concern for our environment, but I see, time after time, that the "urgency" has extended beyond environmental concerns.

B. Early Experiencer James Sparks

Another Experiencer who came forward in the 1900s had some of these same urgent concerns. James Sparks wrote about these intense feelings to act in one of the first books written by an Experiencer. In *The Keepers: An Alien Message For The Human Race*, he was told, "Your planet is dying," and to, "Correct the environmental condition of your planet." His conscious memory recalls this message:

> "Our dear blue and white jewel of a planet is dying because of our own mismanagement. While our problems are clear enough, the solutions are not." (Sparks, *"The Keepers: An Alien Message For The Human Race"*. Columbus, North Carolina, Wild Flower Press (2008)."

James Sparks is one of the few Experiencers who consciously remembers almost every experience without hypnosis. He was a patient of Dr. John Mack and helped influence Mack's belief in the positive aspects of the phenomenon. Mack found common threads in many of his patients who brought back messages and an understanding that future actions will need to be taken by Experiencers to help save humanity from catastrophe.

An example of this is found in Dr. Mack's book, *Passport to the Cosmos*,[16] Chapter Five (*Protecting the Earth*), lays out general concerns received by Experiencers from various ETs during interactions on board a ship or conveyed directly to the Experiencer without the typical abduction scenario. These were calls to humanity to change its path towards destruction of Earth.

Most of these early communications were generic, rather than passing along any specific information about upcoming events. The specificity of "Susan" and James Sparks were exceptions. The messages being passed to Experiencers pre-2010-2011 were typically generalized concern for the planet and the path towards destruction we have been taking.

Since around 2011, most of my clients have come forward with a similar urgency that was felt by James Sparks. They are looking to act in some fashion like "Susan." The messages are now more pointed towards a specific occurrence about ready to happen requiring specific action by the Experiencers. One can consider Mr. Sparks to be unique in that he possesses the ability to consciously remember almost everything that occurred during his ET encounters. This may explain the specificity of his memories, as compared to the typical Experiencer who has fragmentary or no conscious memories of their encounters. Suffice it to say that the current group of Experiencers with feelings of "urgency" are more numerous and have more specific information about potential future events.

C. Shift In The Specifics And Quantity Of "Urgent" Messages

As compared to the first twenty years as a researcher, there was a definite shift in the experiences of my clients. This urgency to act is now found in every Experiencer group I meet. It was not an isolated trend for CERO members only. While in the past, many people I worked with would say they had a feeling that they must follow through with some task, but it was not something that was so "urgent" as those coming forward today. Some would talk about telepathic communications where they were told "when it is time, you will remember." For many, the time seems to be now or very soon.

I have been asking this question about the need to take urgent action at every Experiencer group I oversee for the last five years. According to experiencer groups at the International UFO Congress, I estimate 70 to 80% of Experiencers now feel a need to do something. If there are 100 people in the room a strong majority will raise their hands when I ask about an

---

[16] Mack, *"Passport to the Cosmos (Commemorative Edition): Human Transformation and Alien Encounters"*, Kunati, Inc. (2008).

underlying urgency to act. No other question gets a similar response. Most feel that "Time is running out." They must act. However, they are not sure how or what to do.

Over the 25 years of working with Experiencers through regression sessions, have stated repeatedly, that the alien beings are telling them they are being trained and "when the time comes, they will know what to do." Experiencers have told me they often have vivid dreams of leading large groups of people…where? They do not know. Purpose? They do not know.

The 2016 Presidential election results prompted much concern among Experiencers, yet, I have consistently heard that the "urgency" was accelerating prior to the tumultuous election. These "urgency" feelings did not start with Donald Trump's election.

The following are some examples I have received from my CERO members. When I reached out to the membership on this issue, many were expecting to receive my request before it was sent. These examples vary in the type of information that the Experiencer receives. Some of these CERO Experiencers are willing to go "on the record" about their experiences. Others, because of sensitive jobs or just the need to maintain their privacy, choose to remain anonymous. Each of these CERO members has felt the need to speak out about their recent urgent feelings that they must "do something" soon. Some have an inkling about what is about to happen while most do not know or "feel" they know.

D. Recent Examples

Linda "Cortile" Napolitano *(*Subject of Budd Hopkins book, *Witnessed: The True Story of the Brooklyn Bridge UFO Abductions)* wrote to me, explaining her feelings:

> "It almost feels like, 'When sitting in the reception room at the doctor's office and waiting for your name to be called.' As it seems, with each passing year, the feeling of urgency gets stronger. At this point, I'm at my wits end. Whatever it is that has made me feel this way, seems a lot closer than it has ever been. I believe that the New Year (2017), will be the year that we'll find out. Quite honestly, I don't know why it worries me because whatever is going to happen, is something I'm not sure of. I can't get a feeling if it's good or bad.
>
> The feeling of urgency that I've felt, and still feel, even stronger now, is a feeling of "future anticipation."

It's funny that you've asked because I've been thinking about it a lot. I haven't been sure if it's good or bad but I'm now leaning toward, "Dread." I've been buying water and freeze-dried food.

I don't know if this feeling has anything to do with the environment or our planet. However, there are three things I've "unwillingly" been concentrating on. It's almost as though I'm being forced to concentrate on them. I'm not certain of which one it is:

1. An attack - chemical, biological or nuclear.
2. A weather catastrophe - Earthquake or a Hurricane.
3. UFO Disclosure in an unusual way, which may cause panic, and rioting, but I'm not sure if the disclosure will be authentic.

Yvonne, I'm swinging toward #3."

Linda is an Experiencer that has been the subject of one of the highest profile abductions ever. As chronicled in the Hopkins book "Witnessed," she was floated onto a ship out of a multi-story apartment building that was witnessed by at least a half-dozen people. One of the witnesses is alleged to be the former Secretary General of the United Nations, Javier Perez de Cuellar.

The abduction appeared to have been staged for the benefit of the Secretary General and his security detail. There were other independent witnesses who also saw Linda floated out of a window into the waiting craft. The ETs lit the entire incident, which made the incident visible to people on a nearby highway.

Ms. Cortile's role in this important incident makes it hard to ignore her current "urgency" to talk about potential coming events. She played a leading role in ET-Human interactions. Now, she is now having these feelings of "urgency" and has brought forward some possible alternatives of future events that she believes may be what her "urgency" is about. Her description included an expectation that I would ask her about her "urgency" feelings. While most do not understand why they believe they have a role to play in a near term drama, Linda has definite ideas about the source of her concern. She feels a need to communicate her concerns and feelings of "urgency."

Anonymous Married Couple (CERO Members)

"My husband and I both have nightmares/visions. We both wake up and talk about seeing and certainly feel upcoming…

A nuclear attack.

A weather catastrophe-Earthquake

We have already bought several items from Costco storing up on food, water and a generator. This is very interesting that others are feeling, sensing or seeing the same thing."

This California couple are both Experiencers. They have had the typical abduction experiences of being taken and subjected to examinations on board a craft. They have had the up close, neural engagement by a Grey "doctor" where information appears to be conveyed to them.

The content of their visions mirrors the Linda Cortile message. They are not in a "waiting room" like Linda, but are acting on their visions. They fit into a common pattern of those who seem to have more knowledge of why they are feeling the "urgency" to act. These feelings also predated the most recent election.

Artist Steve Neill

Another CERO Married Couple

"We can't seem to stop talking about it lately ("urgency"). It's almost an all-consuming topic that eventually makes its way into every conversation we have with each other.

Before reuniting three years ago, we both separately felt something was going to happen in the future. But since reuniting and, especially the last year, it's so strong that we find it to be perpetual and invasive. We have also had a sudden increase in encounter activity the last few weeks."

This couple has increased ET activity at the same time as their increased anxiety and feelings of the "need to do something". As their feelings intensify, they do not know what they are specifically supposed "to do" or why they are "supposed to do something." This seems to be typical of what I have been hearing from other Experiencers. They know that they are to act, but still do not know how or when. Only that the feeling is that their actions will be needed very soon.

Mary Palomar (Part 1; Chapter 2)

"I have always felt "on edge" about something I can't put my finger on and have no idea what I'm supposed to do about it—and feeling like, if whatever it is comes to pass, I will know what to do. Like so many of us, I am quite apprehensive about changes our species is making to the global environment that supports our existence and that of all the other species here on Earth with us (including the "critters" who told me they were "naturalized citizens of Earth" and, presumably, dependent on our planet to one extent or another, too).

One odd thing has been going on for maybe two or three years now and accelerating over the course of the last year. I'll be doing something ordinary, driving to work or doing something on a work-related project and I "hear" things interjected in my internal chatter, such as "the United States has just ended," "The American project is over," "Where can we move the project now?"

It is coming with more and more frequency and urgency: maybe a couple times in an hour.

173

No doubt the appalling election cycle would be a context for it, but it started earlier than the buildup to the election. I do think this election is a major waypoint in whatever is bearing down on us, but the urgent little internal chatter started two-three years ago."

Mary addresses how her "urgency" predated the 2016 election cycle. Also, her pre-2007 experiences, chronicled in the original *Chosen*, detailed none of the issues that are the result of recent encounters.

As discussed in Chapter 2, Mary has had encounters for decades. Her contacts in the 1990s generally referred to ET concerns about our planet. The concerns, however, did not involve any specific urgency or messages but stated:

> "I sensed fear, anger and sadness from them and frustration and admiration (of our Earth). But these sensations were not very intense. The images and the feelings I can sort of represent as words in what follows, but they were not verbal at all and I'm sure there have to be distortions in my interpretation of what I felt and saw." (Smith, "*Chosen*" (2007)

In 1991, her understanding of the feelings conveyed were "not very intense" in 1991. As discussed in a later chapter, the intensity of the messages received from the ET who still interact with Mary are much stronger and more task oriented.

Another anonymous CERO member

> "Since what I call my awakening, I have felt this drive to find out what I am supposed to be doing with my life. I have never felt that I belong on the planet (I know this sounds strange), but I just don't feel like I am supposed to be here. I am not close to my family and feel drawn towards the stars.
>
> I have also been doing more and more research on the UFO/Alien connections. I was searching through the internet one day and found the UFO Congress in 2016. It was a last-minute thing. I brought my brother-in-law (who has also had contact) and we spent the next 4 days glued to our seats. I then

attended one of your Experiencer Sessions and I felt "this is like home to me.

The people there were searching for the same answers...What is going on with us and why are we drawn to many of the same things. As soon as I got home I emailed you and set up an appointment with you. Jumped down the rabbit hole as they would say. I have never felt fear about what is happening to me (believe it still is happening due to memories I have) and feel they are here to teach us something, like how to save our world. I feel it is too late for our planet and I think they are giving us the tools we are going to need when the "shit hits the fan." I feel that they will make their presence known soon enough. Humans are going to destroy this world and feel they know it.

I had a very bad feeling about Trump five days prior to the elections and had it for about a week. I have not had any visions or visitations specific to this, but just have a deep dark bad feeling. I think Mother Earth is going to have enough of us humans very soon."

This Experiencer is younger and has already had the feelings of an uncertain near-term future. Much of what she (or he) says is like pre-urgency period Experiencer statements. For example, Dr. John Mack talked about how many Experiencers felt that they had a mission, but that it was sometime in the future. They would discuss interactions with ETs, primarily Greys, who answer their questions about jobs they were supposed to accomplish in the future. The ETs would often state: "You will remember when you need to know."[17]

The primary difference is that the Experiencers I now talk to say that the time is approaching with some saying that their roles will begin now or very soon. "Very soon" is another phrase I hear from Experiencers. Until recently, the call to act was within their lifetimes. Now it is "very soon." Some have very specific tasks, others are anxious but do not yet know what they are to do.

CERO Member Jason Friend: One of his earliest memories

"Before long a third being came forward. This being was more like six feet tall compared to the other two who stood

---

[17] Mack, "Abduction: Human encounter with Aliens" Maxwell Macmillan International, New York (1994), p. 53.

more like four feet tall. The appearance of the taller being was distinctly different, a more elegant and a more consciously engaging experience. I could feel her emotion. She walked forward slowly engaging my mind and my soul in a way I could never forget.

I was shown a screen. Oddly enough the screen itself was quite similar to the flat-screens we have today. On it there were all manner of scenes of environmental destruction and human misery; terrible pollution, dead and dying ecosystems, oil disasters, nuclear disasters, war, mass-death, bombs, airplanes, famine, drought, unbelievable conditions. I recall seeing deforestation on the continents. I recall seeing something very closely resembling the oil fires seen during the first US invasion of Iraq nearly a decade in the future. Essentially, they were there to plant a seed of awareness and urgency about a slough of dire conditions that needed correcting, and still do. It seemed I was given a download to last a lifetime."

Jason's messages of environmental doom are common among Experiencers. As a millennial, he seems to be receiving more dire and direct warnings about the future than Experiencers of previous generations. His memories fit the general pattern of an increase of the persistence and urgency that Experiencers are now receiving.

Artist Steve Neill

E. Preliminary Conclusions

The "need to do something" has been around since the abduction phenomenon was first discovered. However, it has not consumed so many people's thoughts and motivations. In the last five years, my clients and many other Experiencers are all coming forward with the same "urgent" feelings. They are to "do something" but they do not know what it is.

It has rapidly accelerated both in numbers coming forward in the intensity of their feelings. The Dr. Edgar Mitchell Foundation For Research Into Extraterrestrial Encounters (FREE) conducted a survey in 2016. The survey was based on conscious recollections. The Survey validates these preliminary conclusions. In a survey of nearly two thousand Experiencers, most have these general feelings of a need to act.

39% were given an environmental message.
34% were told about future natural catastrophes.
53% were shown a vision, a video or picture.
25% were told their "mission" on earth.

In his book *Walking Among Us*, David Jacobs states that "neural control" (he previously called it "mindscan") is central to the abduction phenomenon. The close gaze of the "doctor" likely allows the passage of thoughts directly into the subconscious mind of the Experiencer through the neural connections between the eye and the brain. The thoughts transmitted through neural engagement are rarely remembered by the Experiencer. Other times the Experiencer is shown realistic videos of future events and told that this is our future if we do not change. Some have even been part of presentations where groups of Experiencers are shown images or receive messages they cannot readily remember. These methods of thought transfer are common, but their purpose is almost never explained to the Experiencer by the aliens.

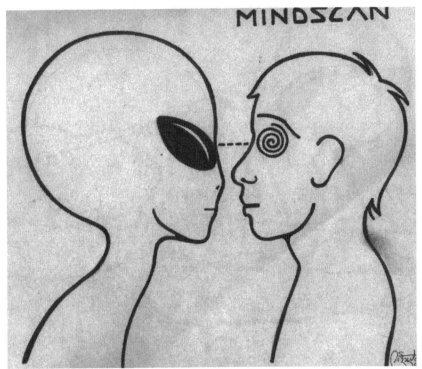

Artist Marcus Pizzuti

Last October, David Jacobs spoke at a CERO International event on the changes in the alien agenda. He sees a real change in the direction of the hybrid program. It is ending and the late stage hybrids are beginning to live among us. He sees this as ominous and that Abductees are often unconsciously helping them assimilate. Under David's hypothesis, the recent "urgency" could relate to the alien hybrid program changes and new roles for abductees.

Mary Rodwell, Barbara Lamb, and the FREE Survey findings of most Experiencers that participated each believe they are here to help us. Upgrades, hybrids, new humans, indigo children and other positive efforts are being made to help us survive and ascend. They see the alien program as benevolent and helping us reach a higher level of existence and prevent destruction of the planet.

Mary Rodwell from Australia also spoke last October for CERO International. Her latest book "The New Humans" details how children are born that exhibit extraordinary abilities and claim to work with aliens. They claim to have been "upgraded" and are here to advance humanity. Quite startling information from 4 to 12-year-old children. Their parents profess amazement at their intellectual abilities and are baffled by their explanations of the source of their knowledge. These "upgrades" are needed to help the planet and the human race avoid catastrophe. This camp sees earth changes approaching during the lifetimes of these children. Either they succeed or humanity does not progress. Like other theories of Experiencers and researchers, Experiencers are to play a significant role in the coming changes.

Suzanne Hansen, a New Zealand researcher and experiencer, has just written a book, *The Dual Soul Connection,* who explains that she was part of a program that began around 2011 to educate people, through their subconscious in large groups, for roles they will play in their lifetimes. This is the same time that I started seeing similar patterns of urgency in my clients. She claims the roles Experiencers will play are varied from disaster recovery, alien disclosure issues, exposing the secrets of world leadership groups, and educating post planetary changes leadership.

According to Suzanne, the roles also varied by age group with those born in the 1980s and 1990s mostly chosen for roles in post-earth change governance. She sees ominous things occurring in our near future such as wars, environmental disasters and natural disasters on an unprecedented scale. She also sees the creation of "Star Children" or "New Humans" chronicled in Mary Rodwell's new book as helping us develop innovative technology to deal with our problems.

Suzanne Hansen states:

> Yes, as both a long-time researcher and an experiencer, I am aware of a massive preparatory stage taking place with ETs and humans. I have actually been speaking about this in lectures since 2007, when I had certain experiences leading me to believe things were 'ramping up', and this became even more evident in 2010-2012. Much of this info is not in my book as there was just not enough space, and so I had to select events that illustrated an overall picture. (Hansen, *The Dual Soul Connection*, New Zealand. Skylight Books (2016).)

I believe this recent trend has great meaning and shows a change in the program and/or purpose behind Abductee/Experiencer alien interactions. The changes may not apply to all abductions or to all alien groups that are interacting with us. However, it shows that there is more to this phenomenon than just a hybrid-breeding program. The people who appear to have insight into the intentions believe that there are events unfolding that will include direct participation by Experiencers.

These "upgrades" are needed to help the planet and the human race avoid catastrophe. Earth changes are approaching during the lifetimes of these children. Either they succeed or the human race does not progress. Like other theories of Experiencers and researchers. Experiencers are to play a central role in the coming changes.

Regardless of who is right, we are wrong to ignore the messages from Experiencers. They are the ones who interact directly with aliens. Regardless of alien motives, the science is as clear as science ever gets. We are witnessing planetary changes daily. Many Experiencers state they have viewed the home planet of the Grays and it is a barren, desolate place. On our current path, we are likely to share the same fate. The pace of political change; the intensifying weather patterns and the degree to which power continues to be consolidated in the hands of the privileged few lend credence to the warning calls of Experiencers.

One of the main reasons that the voices of Experiencers are largely silent is the way our government has treated them. Since the coming of the Flying Saucers, official government policy has been to marginalize the voices of Witnesses/Experiencers. One of CERO's missions is to give a voice to Experiencers and support their unique perspective.

We must pay attention to what these people are saying. No longer can we allow Experiencers to be silenced. From what I have heard in working directly with Experiencers, I am convinced that "Disclosure" will not happen through our government, but from the masses of people who will start coming forward...people from all walks of life.

CHAPTER 10: **John: Revisited**

"John" is the subject of Part One, Chapter Three. He was also part of the mass abduction in my book, *Coronado*. After working with John for over twenty years, John called me in early April. He told me he had some childhood memories come up that have been bothering him for the last two months and feels he needs to undergo hypnotic regression.

John arrived at my office on Sunday, April 9th. He was confused about the fact that these latest memories bubbled up to the surface after so many years of regression. He thought he was done.

> YS: Ok, John, when you said you remember something happening in the 7th grade, I don't remember you ever mentioning this.
> J: Never mentioned it. You know I have had enough stuff to go through and some things take a bit. I don't remember the last time when I came to look at something. I think it was when I took a trip with Phil and Artie. So yeah, I was in the 7th grade and we were going to Camp Schweitzer up in Angeles Crest. I was going to Burbank Middle School which is off of Figueroa. It wasn't summer time but it wasn't really super cold, so I believe it was just before summer. So, they had a thing where they offered people to go for the weekend, for two days for camping, but they have structures, bunks, kitchen.
> YS: So this is for kids?
> J: Any kid who wants to pay the thirty bucks. It was camp counselors. It wasn't no teachers. So it was separate from school. I wasn't going to go until the last minute I decided to go.
> YS: Did you have other school friends go as well?
> J: I had nobody that I knew that was going, I kind of knew one girl that was going, she was a friend of my sister. My sister was still in grammar school.
> YS: And it was over a weekend?
> J: Over a weekend...two days. So when we got there, Friday, and then settled in and whatever. So Saturday was the day they decided we were going to go on a hike after lunch, I believe, but I'm not sure about that.
> YS: So you had breakfast.

J: We had breakfast for sure and then I don't remember having lunch, I remember having breakfast. Then we left and we were supposed to come back, I think for lunch or dinner, I didn't know the itinerary. So we left, it was still light and we went on a hike.

YS: Was it boys and girls or just boys?

J: It was a boys and girls combination and of course, we didn't go that far. This place is down below so it was a hike up. So, we left and for some reason, I thought it was peculiar we left when we did, I'm not sure it was before lunch or after lunch, I don't remember that part exactly. But all I do remember is coming back and it was dark and I know that wasn't part of the deal. Because the counselors didn't have flashlights.

YS: Yeah, because if you went before lunch, that was a long time.

J: I'm positive, I don't remember having lunch, just breakfast. So, I don't know if we were going to skip lunch and we went or what.

YS: Ok, so you said nobody had flashlights from what you remember.

J: Nobody had flashlights coming back.

YS: And when you came back were you still with the group?

J: I was still with the group. The only thing I remember was walking down the hill towards the area where we were staying. And I was sort of in the middle, there were some kids behind me and kids in front of me. I remember one of the counselors in the back of the line and she came up to me and she passed, I don't know, five, six, seven kids. She came up to me, I was in the middle and she said, "Are you ok?" And I said, "Yeah." Then she walked ahead of me and then there were a bunch of kids and she didn't ask any of them if they were alright. So, I remember her coming from the back, kind of scurrying real fast and didn't ask anybody behind me if they were alright. And then she came up to me and definitely, I remember this. She goes, "Are you alright?"

YS: And that's all she said?

J: Yeah. And she walked ahead.

YS: And you don't remember her asking other kids.

J: Oh, I know for a fact she didn't ask anybody else if they were alright. Then we got back and it was after dinner so the kitchen was closed and the counselors didn't do the kitchen detail, you know they had people to do that. You know they would give us a little carton of milk and orange juice and breakfast and whatever. The counselors just watched the kids. So, they had a nurse and a cafeteria staff. So, I remember coming back and we didn't eat and it was dark and I don't remember eating lunch or dinner and they just scurried us into our places.

YS: And you don't remember any conversation.

J: There was absolutely no conversation, it was kind of eerie, no conversation.

YS: Ok, so when you came back, you just remember...

J: They put us in our rooms...our dorms. And then I remember we were starving, hungry, me and a couple of guys got up at two o'clock to raid the kitchen. And it was all locked up. And we got access to the refrigerator and got some orange juice.

YS: You did get access?

J: Yeah. I didn't think they expected any kids getting up and raiding the fridge. It was kind of dangerous leaving the fridge, it was a big walk-in fridge.

YS: Oh. But that was a long time for anybody to go without food.

J: I think that's why we got hungry. And we woke up and it was two and messed around a little bit in the kitchen.

YS: How many of you?

J: I think there was three of us, three or four of us. Because we all woke up for whatever reason and then woke the others up, but the other boys stayed. Then we went.

YS: Especially for young kids in the 7th grade. You had breakfast and then came back after dinner time and the kitchen was closed, that's a long time.

J: And I think that's why we woke up and raided the fridge.

YS: Now do you remember, talking to any of your...

J: Of course the age I was, nobody said anything and I don't know if the kids even knew to say anything. The one counselor, only the lady, she seemed to be the one that was aware of something.

YS: Do you remember her name?

J: No, of course not. I just remember she was thin, last, kind of tall. Camping type person, young not even twenty-five, probably something like that. The odd thing that I remember is she scurried in the middle and bent over and asked me, "are you alright?" And I don't know what answer she wanted.

YS: When you were coming back and she was asking you, it was already dark, you said.

J: It was definitely dark and they were concerned. Of course, they had been that way before, but it was dark coming down the trail and it was hard walking because it was dark. Why they decided to leave when we did, maybe we weren't going to have lunch anyway.

YS: Or at least take lunch...right? And stop along the way.

J: I don't remember reaching a destination or a final point, kind of, but not really. And at that point, you know the stuff that happened to me before then, I wasn't aware of the gravity of the total situation. Because when I was eight it happened before, when I was gone in the kitchen and that happened before this incident and I never put two and two together because I didn't remember anything that happened when I was in the kitchen and my mom's like screaming, "Where were you?" Because I don't remember anything before that and they (*family*) all go, "Where were you?" I never did give them an answer, I thought I was under the sink, but I couldn't have been 'cause there's always so much shit under there.

YS: Ok, so John with this one, when did you start thinking about it, or how did it come to you?

J: About two months ago, I would say. It started, I would say, bothering me, not to the point like my sessions before, you know, it's just to the point where, wow, maybe there's something to this.

YS: Do you remember what came to you first? When you said two months ago when you started thinking about it, was this a memory that popped in?

J: Yes, it was a memory that popped in. Because I always felt I had done everything I need to do.

YS: Right, I remember you saying that after we did Coronado sessions.

184

J: Then I did the one with Phil which I didn't need to, but I just wanted to anyway, it wasn't bothering me, but yeah it was. It was just like this one. I have always known something happened because of this lady. We came back when it's dark, I know we weren't supposed to come back in the dark because it's unsafe, they have done the hike before, and when she passed all of these kids behind me, I recall her not saying anything to anybody, but then she came directly to me and asked me and then scurried ahead.

YS: And she was the only counselor that...

J: The other two were in the front, she was coming up the rear. And maybe she got spooked, like "I don't want to be in the rear" or I just think she was being really nice and wanted to know was I OK. She was concerned. That's the thing that bothers me. "Why are you concerned about me?" And there's all of these other kids and I vaguely remember she scurried to the front with the other counselors, I think there was one other lady and one guy.

YS: Do you think she was the only counselor in the back?

J: She was the only one in the back. There was three counselors. There was a fourth one, but it was a main one that stayed behind, you know an older one, you know to watch the younger ones. So that's the reason why for the last couple of months...it's not that it's going to change anything, it might, but not that I really have to know because I know plenty already. I have seen you go through a lot of people I'm sure. There's a few probably I would say had the amount of experiences that I have. Of course, not everybody divulges everything. But I can remember a handful plus people really had the amount of activity that I've had. Like you said with Kat, you wished her a Happy Birthday, I'm sure she's had a lifetime of them, you know, Steve, there's probably at least a half dozen.

YS: You know some people will come for some sessions, but they need to absorb the information that has come forward so they take breaks in-between. But other people will come to me and want to know as much as they can, they just keep coming back. Everyone's different, some people need to take time.

J: Yeah and they won't come for a while. When I first started seeing you in '93, I came quite a bit, I came often. Of course, since you were right there. (*chuckles*)

YS: Yes, which was great. I remember.

J: And I was working at the time. I was doing construction, I think I had quit roofing and I was on my own. I didn't start tile until '95. It was a good time, that's the other thing, I was in-between gigs, I wasn't having to show up to work every day, so I was having a lull between careers which was nice. Yeah, it was just a weird circumstance and I remember those details and they seem to be kind of strange.

YS: Ok, so after you raided the refrigerator, do you remember going back to bed?

J: Yeah, we went back to bed.

YS: And do you remember the next morning?

J: Uh, not so much, no. Yeah, I remember when we were in the kitchen, the one guy wanted to make people breathe really quick in and out so they pass out. Stupid things like that.

YS: He wanted to do that while you guys were getting something to eat?

J: Yeah, we didn't really get food, just some juice. Yeah, we were messing around. It was stupid kid stuff.

YS: Yeah, I don't understand that, what kids are doing now is they are choking each other and passing out.

J: Choking?

YS: Yes, choking each other! Like the choking game. Some kids have died, my God. Yes, you say stupid things, kids are dying. Ok, so John, do you want to do a session on this memory?

J: Yes, if you don't mind.

YS: (*Laughing*) No I don't mind. I just want to make sure you want to do this because you said you want to know, but...

J: I want to know, but I don't care what I do find out, it doesn't matter to me. But there's always the thing about, "Am I making it up?"

YS: I'm laughing because I can't tell you how many times I have heard that from people.

J: (*Laughing*) And I'm still saying the same thing!

YS: Like you said, it's not going to change anything, but, when those memories come up, I feel, it's what your subconscious wants you to remember.

186

J: Yeah, I think I need to get it out whether there is something there or not. I believe I need to do it. This is probably, oh I always say that (laughing) this is the last one.

YS: (*Laughing*) Never say never!

J: I know, 'cause then there's...you know, the other stuff was major, it was big time stuff. And it was easy pickings, whatever and they were big events. This one seems to be, now, an issue with me.

YS: You know, people try to shove these memories aside and say, "I don't want to do this right now."

J: That's exactly what I'm doing. I've been waiting for two months and I say, "Oh, I'll do it" and then, I say, "Yvonne's busy, I'm busy."

YS: Yes, it is so easy to shove it aside. But then the memories begin to percolate up to the surface.

J: That's what this is doing, it's percolating up and I can say it's not going to change anything, but it possibly could for me. You know the more that I get out and figure out...well, I know what's going on, but...

YS: Now have you had dreams of this?

J: No, I haven't had dreams.

YS: Have you had more than one flashback?

J: None, it's just a conscious memory that something happened. It's not a flashback or dreams, nothing like that, just a circumstance of a few weird events. I think they might have left at a marginal time, where they had just so much time and because it was on a Saturday. So, Sunday of course we are leaving, they are not going to take...you know I think it was an impromptu, "Let's do this."

YS: Like, "Take the kids for a short hike."

J: Yeah, sure and probably the counselors wanted to take a little break and do what they needed to do.

YS: This is significant to John because I've known you for twenty-five years and we have done a lot of work together and for you not to ever mention this and then these memories started coming up for you just recently. You never before brought it up.

J: And I could have brought it up, I could have if I wanted to, but you're right I never brought it up. I could have mentioned it if I really wanted to, but I didn't feel there was a need to.

YS: And like you said, you had those other events that were significant and you needed to go through. Ok, I am to take some notes...so you said you were in the 7th grade, so you were, how old would that have been? That's junior high, right?

J: Yeah, junior high, so about 12-13 years old.

YS: Ok, I will put down 12, not that it matters, your mind will go there.

J: I think I was 10, I was held back in grammar school and when I graduated I was 16.

YS: Ok, so you joined the group for camping, what was the name of the group?

J: It was just like up the 2 freeway so it was "Sweitzer?"

YS: Yeah, I've heard of it.

J: There are a couple of campgrounds, but it's pretty much "Sweitzer."

YS: Ok, you went to Sweitzer campground. Ok, so you arrived. Oh, what time of year was it?

J: It wasn't cold, at night we'd wear a jacket or beanie. So it wasn't summer time, it was like springtime. And now it gets dark at seven, we just had the time change a couple of weeks ago. It was springtime for sure.

YS: How did you get to the campground?

J: We took a bus, we met up at school and we took a school bus.

YS: You arrived on Friday.

J: Friday afternoon. It really isn't that far, a couple of hours.

YS: Ok, you arrived Friday afternoon and you said there were bungalows, girls section and boys. Ok, so what we'll do is I'll take you back to your school when you are getting on the bus. Is Luther Burbank still there?

J: Yeah, it's still there.

YS: Ok, we'll have you on the bus and arriving at the campground. And as you always do, just verbalize everything and we'll see what comes up. I didn't bring your file because you have a very thick file (*laughs*). What's your favorite place, John?

J: Oh, I think it's probably in the mountains. I bought a book and DVD on self-hypnosis and it goes through the history and it's interesting, but I haven't tried it.

YS: Well it's good for relaxation, but I tell people I do not recommend doing self-hypnosis for this.

J: I wouldn't suggest it (*laughing*).

YS: I tell them that something may come up that you don't expect and you are by yourself. I could increase my practice and make more money if I did something like Skype, which I have been asked many times to do, but I feel I have to be there with my client, there's just too much liability.

J: Like you said, it's ok for relaxing, but not this.

YS: Ok, John, go ahead and get yourself comfortable on the couch.

Induction Begins…

YS: Ok, John, we are going to be leaving your mountains for just a little while, knowing that they are always there waiting for you, but for now you're going to allow yourself to take a trip back in time to a very significant experience or memory that you have had for a very long time. So we're going to be leaving April 9, 2017, and begin now to go back in time, back to when you were about ten years old, going to Luther Burbank, just go to Luther Burbank and during this time in your life you are preparing to go on a camping trip, the bus is picking you up, just feel yourself there at the school. All of your surroundings are coming in very sharp and very clear, you can look down and feel and see the clothes that you are wearing, everything is very clear to you now. And when you're ready, just describe where you are at the school and what you are doing.

J: (*Breathes deeply*) I remember, it's clearer now that we did leave from the school on the school bus, medium size and we were waiting in the bus for kids to show up, about half hour or so before we left. I remember leaving from there and going north getting on the freeway up the 210 and getting off on Angeles Crest Hwy. And going up that way and reaching the top where the Sweitzer campground is off to the right, but we went to the left and went down that road to the left to an area I have never been, this was a private area.

We started going down into this little area and traveling down quite a bit towards the bottom and an area opened up where there were some cabins and where the boys were staying was towards the back, the girls cabin was a little above us and the cafeteria area was pretty good size off to the left. So, we arrived and it was still daylight and settled in and met the counselors, there were four of them. One seemed to be in charge. We put our bags away and they showed us around. We still had two or three hours of daylight. We sat at some picnic tables and they brought us out some juice or milk.

Then we went to an area where there was a fire pit with benches around, they were explaining things to us what we would be doing and how long we were going to be there. Introduced us to all the kids, which I knew most of them anyway. There were a few I didn't know. There wasn't a lot of kids, maybe eight to ten guys and five or six girls, so maybe seventeen to twenty kids. And they showed us different areas, they walked down where there was supposed to be a creek but there wasn't any, we stayed pretty close and we went back. They gave us something for dinner, a little snack, a sandwich and some chips, really small little bag of chips and milk and some fruit.

That was in the cafeteria, then we sat at the fire pit, they had a little fire and the counselors were doing something to entertain us, they were telling some stories, they asked everybody to participate. They had stories about camping stuff like that and I don't think too many people contributed in telling camping stories. It started getting dark and they told us we had a big day the next day so they took us to our areas where we're going to sleep. They let us pick where we're going to stay, there are bunk beds, there is plenty of room so we could pretty much pick where we wanted to stay. I remember waking up in the morning and we had pancakes for breakfast, sausage, juice and milk, it's pretty good actually. Then after that, we did some activities there at the camp.

YS: Do you remember what they were?

J: Uh, some kind of little crafts thing and it wasn't really that big of a deal, it was some paper and glue, stuff like that, probably to keep us occupied. Then we went down to the fire pit again and the counselors were talking about stuff, how to behave, what we needed to do because they wanted to make sure everybody was ok. And that's where they told us we were going to go on a hike and asked us to go back and get our stuff ready, bring our jacket or beanie or whatever.

YS: And what do you take?

J: I took a little coat and a beanie and I had a little backpack thing. It took a while to organize. I don't remember having lunch. I don't know how long the trip was supposed to be or when we're supposed to be back later and have lunch.

YS: And do you know about what time it is? Do you see a clock anywhere?

J: Um, there's no clocks, but I think it's, I'm not really sure. Mainly because we had a big breakfast, they weren't going to give us lunch but I think it was two or three, something like that. We have plenty of time to be back for dinner before dark because we are way in this valley. It started to get dark at six. So, it might have been springtime. So we left at two or three. I think the counselors brought some fruit and small candy bars with them and that was it. We were going to have lunch on top of the hill after we went hiking. After all that was arranged, we left. And the hiking, it was all uphill.

YS: Ok, now, take a deep breath. I'm going to touch your forehead and when I do just drift down deeper, just relax. Your mind is sharp and clear. Now just start describing as you're beginning your hike, that little afternoon trip. Just describe everything that you are doing.

J: Well, we started hiking and we started going uphill, it's kind of dusty. They had water for us and it was getting warm. Some kids are getting a little sore and we had to stay in a group of course. Counselors are saying "stay in a group", there were two in front, one in the back. The lady in the back and the guy and other lady up front. So we just started going up and up and then we reached this one area, a clearing with some picnic tables and we sat down and they cut up some apples and candy bars and water. So, we were sitting there in this little clearing area and having kind of a late lunch. And we sat around there for a while. I don't remember anyone mentioning they were going to go back. I think we had some kind of activity there in the open area with the tables. The counselors were talking and telling us about stuff, about the trees and bushes, the animals that were there in the area. And so I remember sitting there, it might have been about four.

YS: And as you're sitting there, John, just look around where you are and describe your surroundings. What does it look like?

J: Uh, it's a clearing area, there's some tables and a little knoll and they are just describing the area, the plants and animals.

YS: Do you see any animals while you are up there?

J: Um, I don't see any animals, but it feels strange for some reason (*speaking slowly*).

YS: Ok, now get in touch with that emotion of "feeling strange," describe that feeling. Why does it feel strange to you?

J: (*Breathes deeply*) The counselors seem concerned and making sure everybody is alright. They did a head count and everybody was there.

YS: Now why are the counselors concerned? What are they saying? What are they doing? How are they reacting?

J: They're asking us to stay together in this one area because there are three tables and the kids are kind of spread out. They want us to get together and there's a noise that they are concerned about.

YS: Ok, do you hear the noise, can you describe the noise?

J: Yeah, well I heard the noise. It's not like a humming noise, but lower, more like a drone noise. And the counselors are looking around to see where this noise is coming from. Seems to be a droning noise and it gets louder.

YS: Do you see the source of this droning noise?

J: No, I don't (*voice quivers*).

YS: Take a deep breath and continue describing everything.

J: One of the counselors…she screams.

YS: Now which counselor screams?

J: The lady that is super nice.

YS: The one that's behind the group?

J: Yeah.

YS: Now, what happens as she is screaming. Just describe what she is doing.

J: She screams, "Oh God!"

192

YS: Do you know why she is screaming?

J: She sees something because we're focused on the counselors and I guess she sees something because she's looking past us and above the hill and um she screams, "Oh God!" or "Oh no! What's that?"

YS: Now do the other counselors see something as she is screaming...are they reacting?

J: They're all looking behind us and up and they're not saying anything. They don't look bothered or worried about what she is screaming about. They just seem to be standing there.

YS: Now what is she doing as she is screaming? Do all of the kids look at her? Can you tell what the kids are doing?

J: Everybody is wondering what's going on and she tells the kids to get over where she is, near her. And she is still looking up past us. And so we all kind of move towards her and I look back at what she's looking at. (Slowly speaking) And it's a round object, I see part of it, with the trees and everything, I just see part of it. Maybe a third or quarter of it. And the noise is still there, the droning, low droning noise. And so, we gather around her and the other two counselors seem to stand there, they don't have any emotion, they just seem to be kind of just standing there, paralyzed or not moving. They're just standing there. She just screams out, "Oh my God! What the f...," what's that?" She told everybody not to worry, they're going. And I walk away from where all of the kids are, I walk toward the object.

YS: And are you walking toward the counselor?

J: No, away from her now. Kids are gathered around her. And then I see this round thing and I don't feel concerned. Everybody else is afraid and not knowing what to do.

YS: Now from where you are, do you have a better view of it?

J: Yeah, everybody sees it, there's a few kids just cry. They look at it and they are just crying and huddling. The two counselors are just standing there and the lady counselor is crying. After a few minutes, I seen it for a minute or so, I walk away from them and towards the ship.

YS: Can you tell how high it is?

J: It's above the tree line. And we are in the middle of nowhere pretty much. So, I'm thinking that why are they afraid and um, I didn't want to be part of that...being afraid and cowering and crying. I wanted to go, I don't know if I'm being told to walk closer to the ship or I just do, but I start walking and then this counselor screams. And for whatever reason, I start running toward the ship. And then I don't look back to see what's going on with the people. I just know I'm supposed to go over there, underneath.

YS: Is it still in the same position?

J: Still sitting there. It's only about 50 yards from where the group is. And I start running up the hill towards where the ship is and the lady screaming, "No...come back!"

YS: And are you afraid, John, as you are running toward the ship?

J: (*Voice quivering*) No, I'm not afraid. I know I'm supposed to go to the meeting place.

YS: Now continue describing as you are approaching it. Just describe everything that is happening.

J: I'm running up this hill and getting closer and closer to it. And then I hear a voice saying, "We're over here."

YS: And which way do you go?

J: I go off to the right a little bit and the voice says, "We're over here...we're waiting for you." Actually, more than one voice.

YS: Now as you hear the voices calling to you, do they sound familiar?

J: Yes, they do sound familiar. Same voices when they were teaching me stuff, showing me games and asking me to play games. The same voices from before when I was at the house when they took me from there. They said, "We're waiting...hurry." Then I see three of them there, they are hiding behind the trees. Then they said, "Oh good...we're glad to see you." (*voice quivering*)

YS: And how many are there?

J: Three.

YS: Can you describe what they look like?

J: The same ones that were in my bedroom when I was eight. The only thing is in my bedroom, they were floating around and telling me they wanted to go play. These are hiding behind a tree, it's the same ones...gray

194

with the eyes. They are happy to see me, they told me that, "We're happy to see you, we're waiting for you...you'll be ok, we'll be back." They said they have some stuff to show me. Stuff they wanted me to do and now is a good time. So, when I got closer to them, they circled around me and held their arms around each other. I don't remember seeing a light this time, we're pulling into the ship, no light this time like before. We're in the ship and they said, "We have to leave this place for now so nobody sees us and then we'll be back." "Don't worry about them, they'll be ok."

YS: So now you are inside the ship?

J: Inside the ship. They first came out from behind the trees and circled around me and we went up to the ship and that's when they told me we have to go.

YS: Now where you are in the ship, can you describe your surroundings?

J: It's the same as before, it's round and these three beings kind of disperse, it seems they go in different directions. And another one comes out, same kind. So that one is with me, the other three left in different directions. So, the one comes out and said something like, "we don't have a lot of time and this won't take much time" and "we have some information for you to remember". They seem to be in a hurry, they said they don't have a lot of time. I wasn't afraid of them, they didn't seem threatening at all, they are familiar, so it wasn't something that I was upset about. So at that point they weren't doing things to me other than give me information. So again, he says, "We don't have a lot of time."

YS: So where does he take you, can you describe as you are going with him?

J: We are in the same room, only there's a chair and um, it's over near some switches, lights and a screen. There's this thing that comes down and goes over me, it has some ear buds on it and um, he said "sit here, we're going to put this on you, you are going to listen to this and you will remember...you're supposed to remember this for later."

YS: Now can you describe what you are listening to?

J: Sort of like a tutorial sort of thing that the last time I was there and um, that I was afraid after a while and afraid of being away from home. My parents would be upset, they said, "You don't have to worry about that because they don't know." And they told me about the previous time that I panicked, I was afraid. They said, "You don't have to be afraid, this is for you and for us so we can be together." And he said, "As you can see, you don't have to be afraid, you're not afraid." Only one was there, he wanted me to answer and I said, "No, I'm not afraid." He said "good, you have nothing to be afraid of, you're helping us." He said something about working together, but he said, "We don't have a lot of time." And then he told me about some things in the future that these things will keep happening to me and there's nothing to be afraid of. And he said this happens only to certain people to do this, to be with us and help us with what we are doing, of course, never any specifics.

YS: Is there anything on the screen?

J: There's nothing on the screen and it's just him coming through the ear buds just having a conversation with me without speaking. So, I don't know if this device is just to make me comfortable to accommodate our conversation so it doesn't seem so weird. So that's what he said that we're communicating like this and later we will do it a different way. Right now, we need to tell you this is part of your life and we assure you to not be afraid. We always bring you back. He tells me that everything will fall into place for you later, "You'll know, as I'm telling you now, you'll know, this is part of what we are doing together and we need to work together on this." And he asked me if that's ok. I tell him "As long as you say you're going to bring me back," and I say "Yeah, ok, if this is what we're doing, yeah, of course." And after that they showed me around different things, they took the thing off my ears and my head and I got out of the chair.

YS: John, describe as he is showing you things, you are going to remember everything enough to draw what he is showing you.

J: He shows me another room with a table and he says, "This is for later." It's not lit up like it usually is. A stainless table.

YS: So this is now in a different room?

J: Yeah, he shows me a different room. We don't really walk in the room, but from the doorway, we look

in. And he says something like "We're just going to do
some medical examinations on you and this is no big
deal." He said this helps and you are going to be ok.
He said, "When we have more time, this is for later."
He said, "We have to spend time together to be
comfortable with each other so you can get to know us,
and the medical stuff comes later." "Screenings," he
says, "Screenings." I said, "Alright, so we're done?"
And apprehensively, he said, "We're done." I said that
I didn't know how long I've been gone, they are all
panicked, screaming and crying. And he said, "Don't
worry about that, that's their response, because you
know there's nothing to be afraid of here." And I said,
"OK." And then I remember they put me back where I
was, kind of a little closer to the group.

YS: Is it the same three that brought you back?

J: No, they just put me back with the light. One counselor
and the kids didn't even know I was gone. Seems to be
getting dark already, it's almost a few minutes from getting
dark. They told me not to say anything to anybody, they
said, "You won't remember anyway, but don't say anything
if you do." "They are going to be afraid and concerned, but
they won't ask." So I just came back in the light, I can see a
little ways from the group. The counselor is screaming.

YS: Is the object still there as she is screaming?

J: No, it left, I think she was scared for me and saw the
thing leave, because I heard it leave. She's screaming at
me, "Why did you do that?" "Why did you walk away
from the group?" She says, "You shouldn't have done
that." And she said that we have to get out of here before
"it" comes back.

YS: And what are the other kids and counselors doing?

J: They are all agreeing that we have to get out of there. She
had to kind of nudge the other two counselors and they kind
of came to. Like they don't know what went on. It was
getting dark and we started heading down the trail, the two
counselors in the front and the lady who was screaming in the
back, she was talking to herself loud, "I can't believe what
happened," "We need to get back, everybody stay together."
All of the kids were in shock and were quiet, really quiet.
There was one girl that was weeping. And they told her
to stop, that everything is OK. They told everyone to be

careful because we were walking downhill. And part of the way, I guess the lady counselor felt bad for me or concerned and she came from the back of the line, I was in the middle and she just asked me if I was ok. And I said "Yeah, I'm alright," then she went to the front of the line because we were back by that time. It was dark and they scurried everyone in their huts.

YS: So everything is dark at the campsite now?

J: Yeah, everything is off, no one is there. The cafeteria people are gone and they said that the kitchen is closed. And they put us all in our rooms and they told the guys, "Don't go anywhere and don't get into any trouble, you guys just stay in here." I don't know what they told the girls. And that was it, they shut the door and we didn't see them until the next morning. We had something light like cereal the next morning and stayed until twelve, and we took off after that, the bus came and took us home.

YS: Now John, I am going to touch your forehead, I want you to take a deep breath. Are you ready to stop here for now?

J: Uh-huh.

YS: Ok, take deep breaths, everything that you remembered from this experience you are going to go on remembering and remember more consciously. So we will leave that time for now and come back to the present time of April 9, 2017.

Session Ends

On Thursday, May 10th, John and I had a long phone conversation about his feelings of "Urgency."

> J: Yes, I have been feeling this for years. I remember in 1962, I was about six or seven years old, we had the Cuban Missile Crisis, then there was Russia. Then with the year 2000 coming, everyone was worried about the computers. And how many times do we hear about asteroids flying close to Earth and we are not told about it. And Planet X...the tenth planet? I don't know whether I believe it or not.
>
> The last four to five years, my feelings have become stronger and I'm preparing. I have a fifty-gallon barrel of water and saving cans of tuna. I don't feel this has

anything to do with aliens. I feel what is about to happen nobody knows about it. When it happens, it will start a chain of events…maybe with an economic collapse which will start a war. We can speculate, but I don't know and I can't give a timeline.

Yvonne, you always told us if someone tells you they know for sure what is about to happen and gives exact dates or tells you exactly what the alien agenda is all about…RUN! (*laughing*)

I have accepted the reality that something big will happen, just like we all know that the "big one" (*earthquake*) will happen.

John's recent change in behavior is common among Experiencers. Many are taking precautions without being able to explain the root cause behind their new behavior. He humorously refers to the many past warnings that something "big" is going to happen. As John remarks, predictions are almost never accurate. Yet, his newly found concern is strong enough to affect his daily habits.

John is an example of the many Experiencers who have felt the "urgency" to change behavior in the last few years. He has been an Experiencer his entire life and his progression fits into this new pattern of grave concern for our well-being and the condition of the planet.

CHAPTER 11: **Debbie Archer**

A. Debbie Reconnects With Yvonne

Debbie grew up in Levittown, Pennsylvania, with her twin sister (Denise) and Paige, her younger sister. Little brother David came along later. Her mother was Catholic and, according to Debbie, a guilty Catholic. Her father was protestant. She grew up in a strict household.

I met Debbie in 1992 when she booked an appointment with me to explore some partial memories that were disturbing to her. Even though she only had one session with me back then, she became a regular member of my support group, CERO. In 1994, I was invited along with other A-List UFO researchers and several of my CERO members to *Walt Disney World* in Orlando, Florida to test their new ride in *Tomorrowland, ExtraTERRORestrial Alien Encounter*. Media from all over the United States were invited to interview us and test the new ride. We held individual lectures and I moderated the panel of Abductees who bravely shared their experiences. The entire event lasted one week and it is a week I will never forget.

In 1995, the documentary, *Alien Encounters From New Tomorrowland* was produced by Thomas & Friends Productions, Inc. in association with The Walt Disney Company, hosted by Robert Urich, with an introduction by Disney's CEO, Michael Eisner. Several CERO members were featured in this film sharing their lifelong encounters, Debbie was one of the members featured.

Well, life happens and we lost touch, but about mid-2015, I was pleasantly surprised to receive an email from Debbie after 20 years!

This is what Debbie told me…

> So, I got this communication from this disembodied being that I should get in contact with you. And so, I thought, "Who the hell are you to tell me what to do?" (chuckles). First, it's been so long I don't even know if she's alive. He didn't actually say your name, but used my memory and brought up a face of you. He said, "Find her." Ok, so I knew what it was because I communicated

with it for years. So, I said, before I make an ass out of myself, I tell it, "You need to give me some proof."

So, I get a phone call from Paige a few days later and she asked me if the military ever came to our door? I went, well, what do you remember, Paige? And she explained what she remembers which corresponds with mine and I told Paige, "I have memories like that too." "OK," she said, "I just thought I was crazy." And I said, "No crazier than I am." So, then I acknowledged "him" and I said, "OK, Paige and I never talked about this stuff…I'll accept it." That's a clue. So then, I said, "Not good enough." A week later, I get a call from my twin sister asking me the same damn question. So then…I just got a chill right up my arm…then when I got off the phone with Denise, I said "OK," I'll go this far, I will see if CERO and Yvonne Smith exist on the internet. If they do, I'll contact them. I did and you were there and I contacted you!

During a phone conversation, Debbie revealed the fact that she does not drive long distances on Southern California freeways. She was ready to explore an incident that occurred in 1995, so I agreed to make a "house call". During her interview, this is what she told me…

D: Driving home from my friend Brad's house in Burbank, an hour's drive, I left at 2:00 a.m. Just before reaching the underpass at the I-5 truck route interchange to the I-14 a very, very large truck that appeared to be decorated in red, green and yellow lights pulled up beside me on my right; I was in a Ford Thunderbird. As I looked out the passenger window of my car I saw that the truck's left front tire was huge, way taller than my car, I could only see the bottom half of its left front tire. There was a sensation of being drawn into the truck, like standing close to a passing vehicle. I felt fearful like I was losing control of my car because of the feeling of being sucked in or pulled over to the truck so I held tightly to the steering wheel, looked straight ahead and concentrated staying in my lane as I remembered and repeated my mother's driving education words when I was 17, "Your car will go in the direction your eyes are looking."

I saw the overpass coming up, at that point the truck veered off to the truck route. I felt relief as I thought, 'That guy's ready for Christmas and it's only May.' Then nothing looked familiar, it looked as though I was on a dirt road like there was some kind of fog or mist covering the road giving the road a dirt like appearance. Startled at the idea I was not on the freeway anymore, I felt confused and frightened. Wondering in that second what was happening I mentally looked back at the last thing I clearly remembered; seeing the underpass I would be going under and the truck veering off to the truck route.

I knew then I must be on the I-14 even though I didn't remember going under the underpass I realized I had not veered off anywhere along the way. I calmed myself down with some self-talk instructions, 'just continue going straight on this road for a bit, maybe things will start to look familiar. I looked down at my speed, 50 mi/hr. The clock showed just after 3:00 a.m. Continuing then, I noticed the Denny's restaurant, recognizing where I was I looked at the clock again, 3:10 a.m. I was relieved and calmed down to normal; I knew I would be home in about 40 minutes. I got home by 3:45 a.m. and immediately went to bed.

In the morning, I was awakened by my own crying, sobbing actually. I figured I must have been dreaming of something sad but was unable to recall it. This crying continued on and off all day and the next day Tuesday. The oddest part of it was I had no idea what about or why I was crying.

March 16, 2016...Debbie's Hypnosis Session-Missing Time on Freeway...

Yvonne: Ok, take a deep breath. You are at Brad's, put yourself there, you are leaving his house. Everything is coming in very sharp and clear. Just describe everything that you are doing.
Debbie: He's bent over looking through the window and I'm sitting in the car. I feel anxious about going home.
Yvonne: Ok, just get in touch with that feeling, that emotion of feeling anxious. Just be there with Brad, do

you know why you are feeling anxious? Your body retains memories.

Debbie: I didn't want to go home...I had to go home. Brad just kissed me good-bye...It's 2:00 a.m.

Yvonne: Ok, as you begin your drive home, just describe everything that you are doing, get the feel of your car, look all around you. Using all your senses, just verbalize everything.

Debbie: Um, I don't know the names of the streets, I just know the direction. I just turned the high beams on and had a sense of which way to the freeway, I can see the freeway, I'm stopped at a light. (*pause*) I'm on the freeway, I'm comfortable, I know right where I am.

Yvonne: Ok, just continue, just verbalize what's happening.

Debbie: Trying to find something on the radio to listen to. I can hear music but can't make out what it is. Going through the events of the day. No one on the road...just me. I'm going faster than I should, I decide to go 70. (*long pause*) Something is wrong.

Yvonne: Ok, Debbie, just take a deep breath and verbalize what you are sensing.

Debbie: (*long pause*) I don't know how to describe this. Something's wrong behind me.

Yvonne: Do you see through your rear-view mirror?

Debbie: No, I don't look.

Yvonne: Just get in touch with that feeling that something is wrong behind you and verbalize it.

Debbie: Just the feeling that something is wrong.

Yvonne: Now are you able to see in the rear-view mirror as you are driving?

Debbie: I see lights...a light. I guess it's a headlight. I'm hearing something, like a real low, loud hum, if that makes any sense. I turned the radio down cause I'm feeling that what's behind me is getting too close. And he's driving so close...why is he driving so close? He's got a whole other lane.

Yvonne: So as you are looking in the rear-view mirror, you see two headlights?

Debbie: No. I only see the one headlight.

Yvonne: And do you still hear the humming with the radio down?

Debbie: I think I'm hearing that, it feels more like he's so close, I can feel the vibration from him. And that's what's making the noise, I'm afraid I'm going to be sucked in...he's so close...so close! (*becoming agitated*) I'm trying to figure out why I don't see the truck, if it's a truck, why am I not seeing a truck, I'm just seeing a big wheel!

Yvonne: Where do you see the wheel?

Debbie: Next to my passenger door.

Yvonne: Do you have your window up?

Debbie: Up...yeah.

Yvonne: Just describe as you're looking at the wheel.

Debbie: I have to hold the steering wheel real tight because the air is pulling me in. And I'm afraid I'm going to smash into it! And I'm angry because he's so close, he should move away. And that wheel is so big. And all you see is the wheel, front wheel, his front left. Like it would be a really big, huge tractor, but it's not a tractor. And it's going 60-70 miles an hour, it caught up with me and driving right with me. It feels like he's coming to get me!

Yvonne: What makes you feel that he's coming to get you?

Debbie: Because he came up so fast and so close. Now I see lights that look like, doesn't make sense, along the wheel well, along the step.

Yvonne: Ok, try not to analyze it, what color are the lights?

Debbie: Different colors...blue, green, red and yellow. Like he's ready for Christmas.

Yvonne: So you're not looking at the wheel anymore, you're looking at another part?

Debbie: Yeah, it looks like a door. Because he pulled away, this doesn't make any sense at all.

Yvonne: Try not to analyze or question. Just continue, are you still seeing his lights?

Debbie: I'm looking at the door it's almost as if there's nobody there, but there has to be somebody there because it's driving.

Yvonne: What color is the truck?

Debbie: I think maroon, but it's too dark to see. As he was coming up to me and I felt I was being pulled, it felt like there's somebody there, but then I see the door, there's nobody there. I get this feeling that it's empty.

Yvonne: Are you still holding onto the steering wheel tightly?

Debbie: Uh-huh, until he veers off, then I could relax. The bridge overhead. I see the lights going in that direction, but I don't actually see a truck, I know it has to be a truck...he's on the freeway.

Yvonne: So just describe what those lights look like as you are looking at it now. Are they steady lights?

Debbie: Yeah, solidly lit. It doesn't make any sense. I didn't notice the lights until he was next to me, until he pulled away or veered off. That was really rude. What was the purpose of doing that? Just to scare me?

Yvonne: Do you see any other cars on the freeway?

Debbie: No, not on my side, not on the other side...I'm just totally alone. All by myself (*takes deep breath*) I don't remember going under the bridge.

Yvonne: Ok, Debbie, I'm going to come over and touch your forehead and when I do, take a breath and drift down deeper. We're going to back up just a little bit in this memory to where you are driving along the freeway and you first notice the headlight behind you. Using all of your senses, your mind is clear, your body retains memories, begin describing as you first see the light behind you.

Debbie: It's just one white light. He's off to my right so I assume that it was a truck because it was only one headlight. It would have to be a really big truck.

Yvonne: Ok, just continue describing what's happening.

Debbie: I feel a sense of something is wrong... this under current that something is wrong and as the truck get closer, I feel fear that I'm going to get sucked in.

Yvonne: Is it getting closer now?

Debbie: It goes from back there and right next to me, he pulls up really fast like it's deliberate. The weird thing is he was just there in my rear-view mirror.

Yvonne: Now as you look toward your right at the truck, are you able to see the driver.

Debbie: No.

Yvonne: Are you able to see inside the truck?

Debbie: No, that's what does not make any sense. The tire is so big, I'm seeing half the tire and the other half is way above my car, so that would mean the cab would have to be way high up. But when he moves away, I can see the door and I can see the window like it's normal size, but when I see the door, it feels like nobody is in there.

Yvonne: Just feel all around you, do you sense any sound around you?

Debbie: The sound of the truck, it's real, real loud. It's like a low-pitched rumbling, real loud, where you feel it in the back of your head rather than in your ears. There's pressure in my ears, a sucking pressure.

Yvonne: Which ear?

Debbie: In both my ears and in the car. (*pause*) The air pressure changed.

Yvonne: Just continue describing what you are feeling, sensing or seeing. Can You still see the tire?

Debbie: Yeah.

Yvonne: Are you still feeling the pressure in your ears?

Debbie: I'm feeling more of fear not being able to control the car. Feeling unreal, I'm not able to control the car and not believing this is happening but it's happening and I have to control the car otherwise, I'd be sucked in!

Yvonne: Ok, take a deep breath...just continue describing what is happening.

Debbie: I actually had to pull the steering wheel to stay on my side of the road, because that's how strong the suction was and it wasn't easy. It was pulling me in, that's what scared me. (*long pause*) I feel "spongy" right now...he drove off and I'm feeling "spongy."

Yvonne: Ok, I'm going to touch your forehead, allow yourself to go deeper, take a deep breath and just relax. We're going to back up just a little bit as your mind is very sharp and clear, your body retains memories. Just describe now, the moment you began to feel "spongy," just get in touch with your body and describe how everything feels.

Debbie: Adrenaline going through me. Like I can feel the blood rushing through me. Feeling of disbelief. (*long pause, breathing deeply*) I had to go under the bridge...I don't remember going under the bridge. When I get to the other side of the bridge, I feel like I was asleep. Everything is blurry, like I'm in a fog, and it was like I am on a road...a dirt road.

Yvonne: OK, Debbie, just take a deep breath and get a sense of being on the dirt road, get a sense of your body and your car. Are you still driving?

Debbie: Yeah, I'm still driving. And I start to slow down a little bit because I don't know where I am. What happened? I don't know where I am!

Yvonne: Do you see any signs around you?

Debbie: No, I'm only looking at the road, want to make sure I'm still on the road. I look back and remember seeing the truck go under the bridge and that's the last thing I remember. So, I'll just continue on this road for a few minutes. Maybe things will look familiar...I'm a little scared.

Yvonne: Ok, Debbie, take a deep breath and allow yourself to bring everything forward as we're backing up in this memory. You are able to see the truck with his lights as you felt the pressure in your ears. Everything is slowing down...just describe everything now.

Debbie: Ok...I see the light, it's just a white light, I'm assuming it's a headlight, in the mirror and I feel like there's something...it came out of nowhere. And the sound gets louder and he's right next to me, like he sped up. (Long pause) Ok, I keep having this thought...where's my car?

Yvonne: Do you feel you're not in your car?

Debbie: I know I'm in my car...but where's my car?! It feels like something is dissected. There's something wrong! If I think, "Where did I go?" I can't think those thoughts because it doesn't make any sense!

Yvonne: Don't analyze, just describe.

Debbie: Ok...I have a far away feeling...I don't know how to describe this. Everything I have been saying is still there but, within me now, there's this far away feeling, this can't be, where's my car?

Yvonne: Ok, Debbie, what can't be?

Debbie: (*becoming upset*) I feel like I'm floating...like I'm floating in my car! This isn't possible!

Yvonne: Don't analyze, don't question, allow it to come forward. Describe what's happening.

Debbie: It's this peaceful feeling like I'm just sitting behind the wheel... floating, totally peaceful...nothing's wrong, everything's ok. I'm in something...It's all dark.

Yvonne: Just get a sense of your surroundings.

Debbie: I'm not hearing the truck, or the engine of my car. I'm just in my car. Feeling calm, relaxed and I have a sense that something is surrounding me and my car. It's like this dome-like blackness, but my headlights are hitting a boundary and I see that there is still some light in the car. I sense it is all "domish." (*long pause*) I'm sensing somebody looking at me.

Yvonne: Try to describe who is looking at you.

Debbie: I see it on my side, in my windshield. Like looking in at me, one of those little gray things…and there's two others and they're telling me something.

Yvonne: Describe the communication.

Debbie: The one that's on my side has me locked into a feeling that everything's ok, it's not really mine, it's his, like he's spraying me with "it's OK." And the other two are giving me the information. And I know them from before and I know exactly the incident where they came from.

Yvonne: What is the information that you are receiving from them?

Debbie: (*long pause*) Kind of like it's about to happen or this is the beginning or this is the start. Like a confirmation of what I was told back in the 80s.

Yvonne: And what is that information?

Debbie: When they first came in the 80s, I couldn't remember everything that they had told me, but whatever it was…was really sad. (*pause*) OK, let me see if I can…I think they're making reference to…"About to begin"…that they will be leaving.

Yvonne: Do you understand what they mean by that?

Debbie: Something, not a permanent thing, like there's a sense that they'll be going, but it's not permanent. It's almost like they're saying, "We are going to be leaving you now so you can accomplish what you came here to do and until then." That's what it feels like.

Yvonne: Are they communicating anything else to you?

Debbie: I'm trying to understand it, it's like you need to feel the feeling and allow your mind to interpret that feeling. There's two of them standing there, but only the one that's absorbing his thoughts in me (*don't like to call it communicating*).

We ended the session at this point. Before I brought Debbie out of hypnosis, I gave her suggestions that she will once again be able to get in her car with great confidence and drive long distances on the freeway once again.

B. Debriefing, 3/16/16 Session

Debbie: Does this mean that my car was taken off the road?
Yvonne: Yes, I have hundreds of cases about
people being taken while in their car.

Debbie was in disbelief about what she was experiencing during her regression...her reaction is very typical. The communication she received was quite curious and like many others, Debbie is still processing this information.

On March 18, 2016, I received an email from Debbie at 5:01 AM, *"Subject: Guess What!"* Of course, I was curious!

> *Hi Yvonne,*
> *I've ordered my GPS. Should be here in 5-8 business days. Would you be so kind as to send me the address for our Burbank CERO meeting so I can program it in?*
>
> *Then...*
> *I've had this paradigm shift about an hour or so after our session resulting in no longer fretting over, worrying over, or chastising myself about what is "real" and what is not. I can't wait to share it with you!*
> *Thank you so much for being you and doing what you do.*
> *Debbie*

Then on April 10, 2016 at 9:29 PM, I received another email from Debbie, *"Subject: Test Drive:"*

> *Hi Yvonne,*
> *I did it!! Took a test drive with my GPS today.*
> *Justyn and I went down to 150 Angeleno today. So, we will be seeing you next Sunday!*
> *Debbie*

Of course, I was so happy for Debbie. Whenever I receive feedback from my clients, it brings tears to my eyes! I immediately responded back to Debbie...

Hi Debbie,
I am sooo proud of you! News like this just confirms
that I am doing the work that I am meant to do! I am
looking forward to seeing you next Sunday.
Blessings,
Yvonne

I interviewed Debbie on March 15, 2017…the first memory we discussed went all the way back to July/Aug of 1958…

D: My little sister, Paige came along when we were five. The house only had two bedrooms, the upstairs wasn't finished, so my parents had one bedroom and we had the other bedroom. Paige's crib was in our room. I woke up one night and saw two skinny little gray things looking into Paige's crib. I have a memory of looking through the slats of Paige's crib, but only seeing a hand and I thought that it was my hand. I think I gave you that picture.

In the last two weeks, I realized that memory always bothered me. Because I'm seeing the hand, but what I realized the other day… my mother had the two of us twins in one crib. So, the hand I was seeing was Paige's and I'm viewing it through the slats. I see Paige's little hand go up and reach for these little gray things. Up until two weeks ago, I didn't understand what was wrong with that memory. Now I understand what it was. It was the second time they came around, I was able to go and watch what they were watching, Paige. At one point, one of them looked up at me, but their interest was Paige.

1959...

This memory I have and always had full conscious recall of was of it. I was walking into the bedroom, as I got to the doorway I saw two little gray beings come out of a closet, walk across the room and walk right into the wall disappearing into the wall. I felt excited, wanted to play. I went over to the wall and saw it was covered with all these tiny grey dots. I didn't realize it was wallpaper design. Thinking they left the grey dots when they went through the wall I found a diaper pin and started digging into the wall. I got caught and punished before I could dig to the other side to join them. When I explained to my parents what I saw go into the wall my father took me outside to show me that what I was seeing was just a shadow. That didn't quite settle in me right because what he was showing me was on the ground, what I saw walked across the room and there were two. From then on, I called them "little shadow men."

About 1960, a knock came on the door and it was these two men in green dress uniforms. So Denise and I scurried to the door right behind my mother, and I see a green pant leg and I follow it up and I see this one guy's left shoulder lapel. I see all the ribbons that are on it, somewhere along the line, I had drawn what those ribbons were and then I went and looked them up and they were real ribbons. But now I don't know where they are and can't remember what the ribbons were. But, there was something shiny on his chest and that was the first time I ever saw gold. So it stuck in my head forever wondering what that was on his lapel.

It was something round, like a medal...it was a pin. Then in 1994-1995, I thought, wow, maybe there's books where I can find out what this pin is I kept in my mind all of these years. So, I went over to the library and I got books about insignia pins. And this one book was just drawings, I found the drawings that was closest to what it could possibly be of what I saw in real time. I went ok...that's what it is. But now, I had to look further back in the book to find out what that pin was. The pictures were in one place, description in another. It turned out to be the pin of the 111th Regiment of the Pennsylvania National Guard. I was living in Pennsylvania when I saw it. So now in 1994-1995, I know that the National Guard came to our door.

I remember they just stayed outside and as I look back on that, it's like, I could feel my mother's fear…I could sense that there's familiarity between them. And all this man said was, "I don't care what you have to do, shut these kids up!" We were forbidden to talk about "them."

There are two other times similar to this but I can't place them in a specific year. I was in the front yard and a really nice-looking man came up to me. He had on a white shirt with short sleeves, black pants. On his shirt shoulders, was a black rectangle with a bar and a star on it, and he had a gold braid on his hat. He came over to me and asked if I would help my mommy and daddy for him. And I said yeah and he said to stop talking about "those things." Basically, he said to stop talking but didn't say what "it" was, he knew I knew. I remember that I said "OK." Then he said, "You could go play," and I ran off and didn't know what happened after that.

I had the feeling that he came with somebody else. You know as an adult, this was the only part of the memory that was important to me. But there was always a sense that someone else walked in the house. It was summer because he was wearing a white short sleeve shirt and I was wearing a dress.

The third visit is where the knock came on the door and my mother answered the door and it was real somber and you could feel the fear. I was probably about nine at this point, going into fourth grade. My Mom looked scared. She told us to go to our room, so that's when we were upstairs. I remember the man was wearing black or navy blue, chances are it was a navy blue long coat. Never found out what that was all about. No one was talking.

It was in 1962, we were on the way to my grandmother's. We lived in Levittown, Pennsylvania, she lived in Line Lexington which was about a 45-minute drive. Paige was four and Denise and I were nine. It was one of the times we were going to see the house before she bought it. So I have three memories of going to my grandmother's…three different times. One time you see there are drawings of sitting in a car, my mother and father's head is there against the window and you see through the windshield.

Fall of 1962 on way to grandmother's house. We got lost in a detour. Parents in front seat.

That was one of the times. I remember seeing an arm reaching through the car door, so it's materializing through the car door and it's taking Paige out of our laps and I'm screaming to keep Paige from being taken and I look up and see my mother and father's heads to the side.

After that incident, I began having the same dream over and over. Me, Denise, Paige and my parents are traveling over the Burlington Bristol Bridge from Pennsylvania to New Jersey. In the dream, the door came off and Paige fell out into the water and all I saw was her head bobbing in the water. I'm screaming and screaming at my parents in the car but it was as though I was saying nothing. It took years and years before I could cross over a bridge with water under it without feeling incredible fear. I would flashback on the dream.

When a person has a *"recurring dream,"* as Debbie experienced, it is an indication that there is an unresolved issue in the subconscious mind that must be addressed. In Debbie's case, it was the abduction involving her family. She continued:

There are others like that on the way to my grandmother's that same year. Another time when we stopped at a gas station and my father went to get out of the car and my mother said, "Duane, don't." I saw through the windshield some little gray creature and the man that was at the gas station was really, really creepy, I didn't see him, I could just feel him. It just felt really creepy and that's all I remember there. And then there was two other times where we were lost in a corn field.

I had hypnosis with my therapist years ago to look into the first time we were lost in a corn field, I wanted to know what happened. We were transported. We got in the cornfield and there was a ship and I felt really excited to see a real spaceship. I don't remember my father driving off the road, I just remember ending up in a corn field. Even my father didn't know how we ended up in the cornfield.

They came and transported us out to the ship...me, Denise, Paige and my parents. When we were taken into the ship, we were separated. In the regression, I just basically remember an examination but I don't remember probing or prodding.

Very often, when family members become concerned for each other, the alien beings will give them a telepathic message that their loved ones are doing well as in the case of brothers John and Jesse Long.

Well that time when we finally arrived at my grandmother's, she asked us "Where have you been?" Remember, the drive was only forty-five minutes. We had no idea that we were two hours late and my father said "there was a detour and we got lost." My father had a sense of direction, like the birds, you know.

Another time, I remember my father having to take a detour, he became very agitated and complained about it out loud. He worked construction and part of the work he did was road construction on Interstate 95. We had to go through the same detour and it had already been another month, he felt the work on the road should have been done already. I remember that part and then I remember the corn field and that's it.

Now Paige, before we stopped communicating after my father's death, about six months before that, Paige called and asked me if I remember getting lost in the corn field. I was shocked because I kept all of this to myself. I wouldn't even talk to my twin about it because I didn't want to contaminate anyone else's memories with my memories, what good would her memories be then, she'd still have doubts?

Paige was about four or five when, one night, she started screaming, "they're coming...they're coming." When my parents realized what she was saying in her terror they panicked because now Paige is starting to see "them," so I knew my parents knew. Paige, as an adult remembers her screaming and waking up, and screaming that "they're coming." It seemed to be months before she grew out of it. Well, you want to know how she grew out of it? When she would scream one of my parents would come to her bed and spank her for waking everyone up.

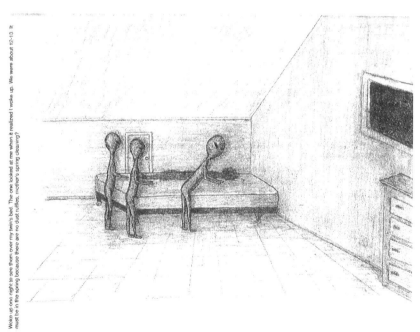

Neither my mother or father would ever own up to UFOs and our family experiences specifically, only in generalities. For example, if you brought up the subject of UFOs…like, "daddy, I remember this or remember that," he'd say, "You know, when I was working for McShane Construction, we were over at Fort Dix doing some building and I looked in one of the hangars and I saw this spaceship in a hangar and this army guy walked by me and said, "You didn't see anything." He would always bring that up. Of course, he'd say he didn't know if it was the army, the navy or whatever at Fort Dix, he didn't know if it was man made or it was something else. But whatever it was, he saw it! I spoke to him about this incident again on my birthday in 2016. My mom would admit to ghosts but nothing more.

During that "house call," Debbie shared a conscious memory with me…

D: OK, there's another thing that I remember. It feels like and I can only say "feels like" because in the memory there's motion, OK? I'm getting a tour of the ship. One of the things I saw was, it was like a round room with windows on the top, it was like windows. Um, I could even say that they were actually video screens. And they weren't seen in real time like looking out the glass, but the video screen had hookups so you can see out and it projected on the screen.

So anyway, I'm in this room with this…it wasn't one of the gray things, it was a "human" one and he's showing me this thing. It's probably about 8 feet in diameter. It's on a pedestal and inside there's a glass-like substance, ok? It's not the kind of glass we know. For years I used to call it plexiglass, but I don't know what it was. And he showed me what he was doing with the earth. And that he could touch the screen or touch this glass and bring up an actual segment of the earth all the way down to be able to see a person. It's like on your cell phone…like Google maps…but this was back in the 60s!

Artist Jason Friend

Oh, there's another thing. I feel I'm with someone although I don't see who it is to my right. But I'm looking at a group of individuals that look human, they all have blonde hair. They are all dressed in white one-piece pantsuits with a belt with this silver thing. They sit down at this table and the belts connect up with something and whatever is in the belt that connects to the table, brings a crystal that comes up in the center of the table, it's almost like a laser that hits the table.

Once everyone in the "council" is seated, there is some kind of protection so that they can communicate and no one can infiltrate. It's almost like a laser that hits the table.

I think that this is the second memory I have where I feel like I'm being given a tour. And whoever was with me...was male.

On March 24, 2017, Debbie decided to explore what she remembered consciously being given a tour of the ship to see if there is more information hidden deep within her subconscious.

Yvonne: Ok, now take a deep breath and allow yourself to go back to the memory or experience when you recall

217

being given a tour on a ship as you recalled the "GPS" unit. Just describe everything that comes forward.

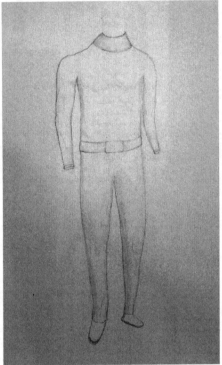

Artist Jason Friend

Debbie: Seems like I'm standing 8 feet away from it and there's a guy, he's dressed in white…he's got blond hair.
Yvonne: Describe the white clothing that he's wearing.
Debbie: Long sleeves, pants, it's like a one piece. Um, some kind of belt? But there's definitely a separation between the top and the bottom, like a sewn in waistband. I feel like there's someone standing on my right, like I'm not alone. I'm curious about what he is looking at and there's windows…I can't really say they're windows. Like looking at a screen at the same time (chuckles) that doesn't make any sense. Or it could be…like you can see outside, but you're not seeing outside.
Yvonne: Can you describe what you can see out of the windows?

Debbie: Well, I'm still quite a distance from him, so I'm just seeing blue, like a blue sky in the atmosphere of Earth, but there's no clouds. But it doesn't feel like I'm looking out a window, it feels like a projection or it's a light source. The reason I think it's windows is because there's light coming in from it. Like if you had a screen in a dark room and you projected the sky on it, the illumination from that is coming back in the room. Because I don't feel like I'm looking outside.

Yvonne: Now as you feel yourself across the room, just describe your surroundings.

Debbie: There's the windows, it's a roundish room and what I thought was windows, they come halfway down and below that is just white… everything is white.

Yvonne: And like the GPS unit you described, is there anything else in that room?

Debbie: Not that I can see, I'm just focused on what that thing is, I feel this curiosity. And he invites me over. It's a feeling of "come on over." Permission…it's a feeling of permission. And I'm really curious as to what that is. I get the understanding on how they can locate us. Like a touch screen like we have now. It's a "touchscreen." And he touches it and opens it up and shows me a piece of geography. And it can get smaller, you can actually see a person and bring them up. I don't know if what I was seeing was in real time as it was happening or it was like a time delay like on Google Earth, I don't know what Google Earth's time delay is. It could have been something underneath for us to see but it was close to real life. Like if they showed me a person standing on the ground, was I really seeing that person standing on the ground or was I seeing a picture of that person standing on the ground moments later. I don't know if that was explained to me.

Yvonne: So you don't sense any communication with him?

Debbie: No, just that he is showing me how they observe us. But I wasn't allowed to touch.

Yvonne: Now is the other one still behind you?

Debbie: I'm not aware of him at all. I have questions, how did I get up here? He showed me.

Yvonne: Is he familiar to you?

Debbie: No, I'm familiar to him.

Yvonne: Does he tell you that?

Debbie: No. It's not like he knows me, but he knows of me. Familiar with me because I've been seen before, but he is also aware that I am a child and he is not.

Yvonne: How old are you?

Debbie: Let's see, I have breasts, so I'm 12.

Yvonne: Now take a look at what you are wearing, look down at yourself if you can.

Debbie: I don't feel exposed like I'm naked or anything. I can't tell, I know my legs and my arms are covered.

Yvonne: Do you feel like you're wearing pants?

Debbie: (*Takes deep breath*) I'm only aware of my waist up.

Yvonne: Do you get a sense that you are wearing your own clothing?

Debbie: No…it feels cleaner, crisper. Like I strip you of what you are wearing and put you in sterile stuff.

Yvonne: Just continue verbalizing about what is happening there.

Debbie: Ok, so I can understand that he can locate, this thing is used to locate. It reminded me of times I felt I was being watched and as I'm standing there with him, I'm remembering that incident of being watched. And realizing this is how I am being watched. Hum, I have a question, "How do you know where to find me?" And it wasn't answered, like that question is too…like as if someone from our government tells me it's classified, so this is "classified." Kind of like that kind of answer, like "too complicated for your age." That kind of response.

Yvonne: When you sense his communication, is he looking at you?

Debbie: Yeah.

Yvonne: What does his face look like?

Debbie: Well, it's friendly, he has blue eyes, light hair, no hair on his face, no whiskers.

Yvonne: Do you feel he looks human?

Debbie: Yeah, definitely looks human. And I don't think in my mind is he human or not, it's not a concern.

Yvonne: Describe what else is happening.

Debbie: (*After a long pause*) I'm feeling some kind of confusion. Like as I'm standing there, it's like there's some kind of memory that's trying to surface and there's resistance and there's a sense of I started to remember and more resistance and confusion. The other one is still in the room because they are communicating with each other.

Yvonne: Do you sense that the other one also looks human?

Debbie: Yeah, nothing alarming, I don't feel alarmed at all, I feel curious. (*pause*) You know I just got... I don't believe any of this...just go to sleep.

We ended the hypnosis session at this point.

C. Debriefing

Yvonne: How did you feel about this session?

Debbie: I understood. When I said I remember when I was down the street and I felt like I was being observed, well as he is showing me what that thing is, I'm remembering that there were times in my childhood that I felt I was being observed and now I have the evidence that I was being observed.

Yvonne: And when you asked him how it worked, he wouldn't explain it to you?

Debbie: Yeah, I wouldn't even understand now because my knowledge is very limited as far as technology goes.

Yvonne: And when you were describing what the being looked like, back in the 90s we used to call them the Nordics. They were described as almost perfect, hair, skin. Now after so many years, we are thinking these are the perfected hybrids. Travis Walton saw them as well while he was on board the craft. So, you came to your age, you said you were twelve. Now when you were looking at the GPS, do you think it was around the same time as your other experiences?

Debbie: Yeah, it could have been the same tour because it feels like it. Remember when I said Sherry, Paige and I had the same dream? We all saw the beings sitting around the table that I described in my regression.

This dream was very telling for me. People do not have the same dream unless they have the identical "life script" in their subconscious mind...which is impossible. This looks like a "multiple witness" abduction which needs further investigation.

Debbie continued sharing her conscious memories...

So now let's take me up to 1973-1974. I didn't know what was happening to me all my life, I just knew something was and I needed to figure it out. During that search, I came across the book, Dianetics, read it and thought, Wow, could this be what's happening to me! I had just graduated nursing school and I thought, I could help my patients with this information too. I went to the back of the book to see if there were any churches and I found one in New York. I wrote them a letter, they answered inviting me to come up. And I had a session and that's when I got involved...finally some hope. I then found an organization in Ardmore, Pennsylvania and I started taking some classes.

I started with the communications course, in what they called the *"Hubbard Qualified Scientologist Course"* and then the *"Dianetics"* course on how to do *Dianetics*. Because I had been "in and out" of my body throughout my childhood, I knew there were "out of body experiences". L. Ron Hubbard, not only acknowledged the existence of the experience or state but he gave it another name. I knew Robert Monroe called it an "out of body experience" I could identify with that. When I was twelve years old I came across and read his book during my earlier attempts to figure out what was wrong with me. But here was a whole organization that not only acknowledges "out of body experiences," but gives it a name... "Exteriorization." I remember sitting in class thinking that's what I have been experiencing! All of these weird experiences, that had been on *"suppress,"* were now on *"release"* and started manifesting. I was able to leave my body at will. I joined staff after less than a year. This is when it was a mission, it was great, everybody was wonderful, the *"Sea Org"* wasn't involved in the whole thing. My twin sister, Denise and I would go home with some other staff members and we'd play this game. And the game was...I'd stand in the kitchen, someone would take an item and hide it. When the item was hidden they let me know and I would leave my body to locate it. Our military calls it *"Remote Viewing"*.

No one on staff at the time could do it. But here I am unleashed! "I'm allowed to talk about it, I'm allowed to feel it, I'm allowed to do it!" Yay! So, I started doing it. Well, not too long I got a clamp down. I was told, by the ethics officer, I was not allowed to do it anymore. He called me into his office and he told me, "I understand you have been playing with some of your abilities." Well this is actually discussing "case." ("case" is the information that is stored in your "reactive mind," anything bad that ever happens to you is "in your reactive mind" and if you discuss it with anyone you're discussing your "case"). In *Scientology,* there is no discussion of *"case"* outside of a therapy session, what they call *"auditing."* Apparently one of the staff felt slighted because they couldn't do what I was doing and reported how it made them feel. It triggered or in *Scientology* terms, "re-stimulated" their *"case."*

I was shut down until I'm on staff for about a year there and then in 1977 I go into the *"Sea Org."* I went to the *Sea Org* in New York. Now there's the *"Flag Land Base"* which is in Clearwater, Florida, *Scientology's "Mecca."* At one time, they were on a ship at sea but established a base on land. There were organizations linked to Flag called *"Flag Operations Liaison Office"* – *"FOLO"* for short...one on the east coast and one on the west coast. So, Denise and I were at *FOLO East* in New York. One day it happened that some higher Officers came in from *Flag* and of course you have to treat them like they're royalty. And one of them lost their purse, so my sister, Denise, heard this and she came running to me and she says, "Debbie, I know you don't like to do this, but this Sea Org member lost her purse, can you find it for her?" Denise takes me to the ethics office where the Officer was because she had to report it to the ethics office that her purse was missing. Ok, so Denise explains to this girl that I can leave my body and find it. She asked me to do it...I do. I tell the Officer, "I don't know if you came in on an airplane, but it's under a chair at the airport." She goes, "Oh, I remember sitting on a chair." I never knew if they ever found the purse or not. The next thing I know is I'm being accused of stealing her purse!

Another time I had just had some auditing on a Friday. I went down to Pennsylvania to visit my parents for the weekend. So, I'm coming back on a Sunday night and all of a sudden, I lose my eyesight...half of my eyesight, it was like looking without my glasses or contacts on. If anything, physically goes wrong or you have some kind of emotional meltdown within a certain amount of time after auditing, you are what's called "*red tagged.*" In other words, something went wrong in the auditing and they put a red tag on your folder, they have to get you into a session to correct it within seventy-two hours of the red tag being on your folder. Once I got back I reported what happened to what's called an "examiner." It's done on the e-meter, you hold on to the cans connected to the meter and I say this is what's happening, it's called an "*origination.*" So I "originated" that my eyesight decreased all of a sudden. He asked when was the last time I had a session and I told him on Friday, at that point he indicated to me that I was "*red tagged.*" On Tuesday, I was taken into session, into someone's sleeping quarters because all the regular auditing rooms were filled and I was an "emergency case." Now the meter has a board covering it so you can't see the meter. I'm sitting there and he's asking me questions which makes the meter needle move and he will look up and ask me about that question. It could be questions like "are you upset with someone" or "during your session were you looking at one thing and all of a sudden you were looking at something else?" But they are very specific questions. So, we're doing this and all of a sudden, I look at the door and the door is not there, I watch this guy walk right by and I smile because I knew who it was. Mind you, we are in a room with the door shut, but I'm looking at the door seeing him walk by. Then I look over at the auditor and I see the e-meter and the needle is doing what they call "*floating*" which is a good indicator. It basically means whatever was bothering you is now released. I'm seeing the needle float, and he looks up at me and he says, "Is there anything you would like to say?" And I say "Yep, I see my needle floating!" There's a piece of board there, right? And he gets up out of his seat and looks around just to be sure that the board is still there and says, "You can see the needle floating?" "How are you doing that?" I said, "I don't know." Then I look at a dresser and see clothing in it and mention the color of the clothing, he turns and only sees the drawers. He lets me know my needle is floating and ends the session. I went from impaired vision to seeing through solid objects. I was pleased with my recovered eyesight.

The next thing I know my folders are up at the *"Guardian's Office."* The Guardian's office is like *Scientology's* CIA! Well, these are abilities that are supposed to be achieved by those who are "clear" and above, I'm not even "clear" and I'm manifesting this shit! Ok? Shortly after that, I'm being declared a *"Suppressive Person."*

In 1975, I was in Bryn Mawr, Pennsylvania, living in a house with a group of us that were on staff and there was no heat. One of the guys had a kerosene heater and he went to visit his Mom's for the weekend so I got to use the heater. I woke up and I found two little beings looking into the kerosene heater! I then rented a room in Havertown Pennsylvania and was "floated" out of the window in my room. Then I went to live with my twin in Devonshire and they followed me there. I was moving often to avoid them and I had night jobs for years because I didn't want to go to sleep.

In 1980, I moved to Los Angeles *Scientology*. I thought I was safe at the *"Celebrity Center"* in Hollywood because I was on the third floor! They showed up outside the window! I started getting audited again but I never brought any of the abduction stuff up in session because I didn't know how to articulate it. And because as a child, I was told I was having *"hallucinations."* And if you're having hallucinations, you are psychotic and if you're psychotic you don't have a right to Scientology!

So besides the fact that I didn't know what to call these things or what they were, *Scientology* never addressed anything like that and I never brought up the subject. But I kept on hoping. I kept hoping until 1983. I began making statements in session that apparently were in *Scientology's* *"upper confidential levels"* and was accused of having gotten a hold of confidential material and was eventually declared again. Never mind the person who was auditing me had done those levels, so I was probably just getting the information from her on some psychic level. At that same time, there was a big break-up in the church, the church was in such an upheaval that a bunch of us left. I resigned and never looked back.

On March 18, 2017 at 4:46 PM, Debbie sent me the following email…

Hi Yvonne,
    Here's an experience I finally figured out.
    My twin and I were in Harrisburg, Pennsylvania in the summer of 1967, but according to my sister it was 1968. I always thought it was 1967, it's been a disagreement for many, many years. Anyway, when we visited our Aunt Carrie and Uncle Ray, they had 2 children at home. Mark who was under 2 and Deena, who was about 2 months old.
    After a day or two while there, Carrie and Ray took us to a barbecue. It was outside starting in the afternoon and went way past dark. The adults would ask us to get them paper cups of beer and we'd take a sip. I ended up drinking, in all, about 8 oz. over a few hours. It made me slow and dizzy. There were guys there and they took us for a drive to get away from the adults. One of them dirtied his hands and put them on Dawn's white shirt. They did the same thing on my white shorts. Then they took us back to the barbecue. I remember standing in the house waiting to use the bathroom and coming out of the bathroom but then my memory goes blank.
    The next thing I remember is coming into consciousness, hearing my name being called. I yelled out "I'm here," then some guy came toward me to help me down out of the tree. I was sitting in the "V" between two large main branches of a tree. When he asked me how I got there I had no answer, I didn't know but I thought "they" left me there. As he helped me down I realized I had lost one of my contact lenses. Knowing I was going to get a beating when my parents found out I started crying. By this time Denise and some others came over asking where I was, stating everyone was looking for me. I had no answer. The guys chalked it up to the beer I drank. Everyone went back to the barbecue, alerting everyone I was found. I went and laid in the grass in fear, crying because of what I knew I'd get when I got back to Levittown. Maybe about 45 minutes later we left and Carrie took me over, probably Denise too, to the church to give confession. After all, I had been missing and had

hand prints on my pants. The priest asked me if I had sexual intercourse. When I asked, "What's that?" He said, "Never mind, you didn't." We went back to Carrie and Ray's and went to bed.

It was about lunchtime when Carrie's next-door neighbor came over in an excited state claiming there was a report of a UFO over Harrisburg (we were in the suburbs). She wanted to leave her baby with Carrie to baby sit so she could go into the city to see what she could see or find out. She also said it was on the news, we should turn on the TV. I wanted to see it on the news so I asked to turn on the TV but Carrie said "No, your parents don't want you watching or talking about that stuff." It was then I knew she had talked to my parents about our "craziness." The neighbor would not speak to us about it when she came back, referencing what Carrie stated.

Okay so this morning, 18 Mar, I decided to solve this mystery once and for all. I remembered that I had my optometry records from when I was a little girl. But after searching all over I couldn't find the records. Damn! The replacement of that lost contact lens would have been documented in those records giving the year it was replaced. Damn, dead end!

Out of curiosity I then went to the Internet and searched for UFO sightings over Harrisburg in 1967. Look at this...

Date: June 11, 1967
Location: Harrisburg, PA
Time: 11:15 p.m. EDT.

"A woman saw a bright cigar-shaped object with a red light. The object hovered, accelerated straight up and disappeared. The red light turned green when the object ascended (color/motion correlation). (NICAP report form.)" http://www.thinkaboutitdocs.com/1967-june-ufo-alien-sightings/ *[scroll about 1/2 way down the page]*

Excited now to narrow down the year for sure, I then remembered I had Carrie and Ray's family in my genealogy. So off to Ancestry.com to look up Deena's birth date. Wouldn't you know it, I didn't have that date info in the tree. I began searching Ancestry's records.

227

Found the birth and death dates for Carrie, Ray and their 2 boys.

My tree had Deena's married name so after some searching, using her married name, I finally found a public record listing Deena's birth date, apparently, she's still alive. Her birth date was April 1967. That confirms my recollection of Deena being about 2 months old and corresponds to the above sighting in June and the next-door neighbor's claim. Mystery solved!!! We were there in June of 1967.

It only took me 50 years to bring this all together and solve the mystery! Whatcha think, I missed my calling? Instead of nursing I should have been a detective? Maybe even a cold case detective? LOL.
Debbie

D. Debbie And Her Recent Concerns About Our Future

Debbie followed up recently with an email that reaffirmed her role in the latest "urgency" group. She reached out to me again to talk about her intensifying concern following the same trend of intensified feelings and concern about our near-term future shared by so many others. She is just an example of the many long-term Experiencers that are feeling the recent shift in her own feelings about humanity's fate.

As for my feelings of *"impending something"* that causes a feeling of urgency to prepare. I've experienced it on and off most of my life. Up until recently it would be like a breeze blew by, I noticed it, wondered what it was all about and then it would be gone. The last few years they would last a little longer so I would purchase some extra water when they would happen. But about May of this year (2016) I noticed it was stronger and continuous. It continued to intensify to the point I had to do something to prepare for it, whatever "it" is. September (2016) I purchased a pressure canner and learned how to use it. It seemed somehow to have a connection to the elections this time. That's a whole other thing.

Because I have been told by some Experiencers about feeling anxious about the elections, I asked Debbie about what she meant about the urgency having a connection to the recent elections.

Debbie: I'll give you an example of what I mean. Our country is divided right now. Setting aside the racial aspect of the division, what I am referring to here is between the Democrats and Republicans; more specifically the demonstrations and protests. I would say most of these people, the demonstrators, are decent people who have their views and preferences and want to make them known, they are acting out their anger and disappointment by demonstrating. Then there are the protestors who didn't vote either way, are bussed in and paid to protest, make plans to and/or instigate and commit the violence we are seeing and are proud and arrogant about it. These are the ones who are in allegiance with the evil source albeit indirectly. They are being paid by an individual(s) closer to the *"evil source."*

As for the "*evil source*" being within our government. Not directly, there isn't really an individual one could point at and say, that's it or that's him or her. However, there are those that are in allegiance based on purpose. Some semi-knowingly and some unknowingly. This is where the contagion of emotion comes into play. The individuals who are in allegiance unknowingly really think their superiors, colleagues are doing the right things and so align themselves with those purposes. Those semi-knowingly put up a front of doing good but behind the scenes are committing crimes and/or participating in unscrupulous behaviors, they are the narcissistic sociopaths and psychopaths.

While most messages are related to some future environmental or other catastrophe, Debbie's messages are about how we govern each other. Her reactions to the feelings she has do not seem to be partisan, but relate to unseen people who control governance from behind the scenes. This message seems timelier and related to the recent unrest in our country, and many others, that appears to be on the rise.

There is much more work to do on Debbie's case. Unfortunately, I could not include the enormous amount of information in her chapter. I am encouraging Debbie to write her own book...I hope someday she will.

CHAPTER 12: The "Need To Do Something": James Lough

A. Responding To The Urgent Call

Nearing the end of 2012, I was beginning to feel uncomfortable with my sense of direction. My law practice was going very well and I was handling some of the most important work of my career. My children were flourishing as adults and, except for some family medical issues, my problems were typical first world problems faced by most of my peers.

Despite all this, I was drawn to issues involving my interactions with ETs over my lifetime and what it could mean. Most of my adult life, I had tried to put these issues in a box and ignore them. I would go through periods of reading about the subject and had attended about three lectures in thirty years, but I mostly ignored my experiences and went on with life. There were times when I struggled with it, but would eventually put the subject back in its box. However, my newfound obsession with the subject seemed to overwhelm me.

To try to answer these troubling questions, I attended a MUFON Convention in Irvine, California. It was my first UFO/ET event in over twenty years. I sat in the back and hoped nobody recognized me. I avoided eye contact with the other attendees and listened to the program with extreme interest.

After the Conference, the uneasy feeling I had intensified. I chalked it up to a mini midlife crisis and tried to go on with life. However, work, family and the usual causes were not the source of my angst. In fact, my focus on the normal work and family issues was supplanted by feelings I had a mission related to ET in some way. Almost all my free form thought time concentrated on this new focus. Work, family, and other issues took a back seat to my efforts to figure out what I was supposed to do. I still handled my day-to-day responsibilities, but my focus was elsewhere.

While the focus was ET-related, it was more about the messages that many of us have come away from after our contacts. Environmental, warfare, and basic human rights were the focus of my thoughts. Why do we want to destroy or irreparably damage ourselves by the way we relate to each other? I even started to change my retirement plans to move my retirement date up because I felt that "time was running out" and I needed to act sooner.

My reading habits became almost exclusively UFOs and subjects related to our planetary decline. That is how we treat each other and the earth that sustains us. I was reading two to four books a month on these topics. Many of my nights were taken up by stargazing. Much of the time, I thought about my previous ET experiences that, for twenty years, I had tried to put in a mental box and ignore. I also thought about how we can change our destructive habits.

During this time, I had two significant sightings. First, I was roused from reading in bed one night by a military fighter plane passing over our house with its afterburners on. I went out to see and noticed two fighter jets were flying at less than two thousand feet over my neighborhood in wide loops that crisscrossed about four miles southeast of my house. This went on for about ten minutes.

At the point where they were crossing, I noticed a bright white light rising from the ground. I assumed it was a helicopter but it made no sound. It rose about 200-300 feet off the ground. At that point, I was unsure what it was but realized it was heading towards me. My next thought was that it might be an ET craft since it made no sound and was too close to the ground to be a plane.

As the bright, silent light kept getting closer, I began to think that it might "not be from here." As it approached my house, despite my desires to meet an ET without being under their control, I began to think: "I am not ready for this". No sooner than that thought came to my head, the light blinked out. It did not turn away or change course; it just disappeared. It was the second time in my life I had seen a possible ET craft that changed course at the same time as I thought about it.

Afterwards, I was kicking myself for rejecting the possible opportunity to see if it was ET in origin and possibly on its way to my location. The next morning, I checked the papers and other local news websites to see if there were any reports of the incident. I was hoping I would find something to clear up the mystery. Possibly a crash or a military exercise. There was nothing about it in any local news source. Two fighter jets do not just "buzz" a residential area at low altitude with afterburners on for no reason.

The incident increased my anxiety. I saw it as a missed opportunity to possibly find out what role I have and why I am so fixated on "doing something". My interest in ET issues and my possible role increased. I began looking for a group or organization to join. Because of my public position representing elected officials, I decided to look in Los Angeles, rather than near my home in San Diego. Eventually, I came across the Close Encounters Research Organization ("CERO"). In April 2103, I attended one of their programs and listened to Grant Cameron speak. Not only did Mr. Cameron's program speak to me, but I felt very comfortable with the people I met at the lecture.

I had assumed that Mr. Cameron would speak about the "nuts and bolts" of UFO sightings. However, he talked about a "download" he received that focused on the metaphysical aspects of the phenomenon. He analogized to the coming "Super Bowl" of "Disclosure" where each of us will play a role. To paraphrase him, we do not know if we will be the quarterback or the waterboy, but many of us will soon learn about the role we will play. His talk energized me and made me think maybe I had a role to play in coming events. It fit with my recent feelings that I "need to do something."

I enjoyed the interactions among the members during breaks and picked up Yvonne Smith's card as I was leaving. It took me a while, but I gave her a call and set up an appointment for a hypnotherapy session. I met with Yvonne but never did a hypnotherapy session. Instead, we talked about my urge to pursue "something" but was not sure what I should do. I knew that my urges to change the course of my life were strong and they had something to do with my multiple paranormal/ET type experiences, yet it was only part of my need to act urgently. Yvonne was very understanding and said that she had been hearing the same thing from many people in her practice.

I left this first discussion session with some hope that I was on the right track. However, I was suspicious of her confirming statement that I was not alone in these thoughts. Being the lawyer that I am, I wanted confirmation that her reassurances were genuine. I did an internet search and quickly came across a six-month-old interview of Yvonne Smith in LA Weekly magazine. In it, she stated that many of her clients had been having similar urges, preparing for something that was going to happen. This was eerily like my sense of urgency to "do something". Like me, they felt time was running out.

This was the link I needed. Soon thereafter, I began working with Yvonne and her organization, CERO. My individual sessions with her were helpful. They calmed down my internal anxiety and let me see things more clearly. I did not have any major breakthroughs in the hypnotherapy sessions but our discussions helped me better able to see inside of myself.

Just as important were my interactions with the CERO members at support group meetings. I instantly felt at home in a non-judgmental environment discussing similar experiences with others. It was like finding a family I never knew I had. The theories behind why this is happening were broader than I could have imagined. While we do not agree many times on the "why," "how," or even the "who," we agree on the reality and similarities in our experiences. Most members of the group have similar feelings of being part of a plan and all who had these feelings felt that they were picking up in intensity.

The support I received in these groups settings helped me see myself with more clarity. Prior to joining the CERO group, I was an example of someone who has refused to discuss the subject openly and most of my

232

closest friends and confidants have been unaware of my experiences. As an attorney who primarily represents government, my credibility with public officials, judges, law enforcement and the public is necessary for me to earn a living. As my career winds down, I have begun disclosing these experiences.

In fact, there are very few people, until the last four years, that I have even mentioned that I have a passing interest in the subject. I have gone to extreme lengths to cover up my interest including not carrying books I read on the subject in public. When I purchase books on the subject, I have traditionally bought other reading material at the same time and sandwiched the UFO stuff in the middle to avoid conversations on the subject. I go to these lengths because there are no topics that can subject a person to ridicule quicker than "flying saucers." It is one of the last topics where ridicule is a societal norm.

In addition to adding my voice to those who are asking our government to admit to the truth, a closely related reason is that I am aware from my everyday experience that there are others who have the identical problem. If more of them would come forward, it would be another step towards society's acceptance of our interactions with the phenomenon.

Even though I was enjoying attending CERO functions, I was still unsure of myself. After all, many of us have concerns about our sense of purpose. Why should mine be any different? I continued to sit on my front patio most nights and gaze at the stars. We live in a remote area where the sky is breathtaking. Satellites, meteors, commercial and military flights are all part of the show.

One night I was particularly disturbed about things. I had been attending regression sessions, which did help me understand my own situation, but I had doubts filter into my thoughts. I went outside and consciously asked for a sign to help guide me. After a few minutes of stargazing, I saw a large, circular, bright light to the northeast. It was about one quarter the size of a full moon and appeared to be very close.

It was a cloudless sky and I had an unobstructed view. I did not see it arrive. I just turned around and it was there. Based on the terrain, it had to be within a mile of me. It was soundless; did not move; and was much brighter than the moon. As I watched it for a minute or two, it suddenly began to shrink in a uniform manner. After about twenty seconds, it disappeared completely. I had gotten my sign.

From that point forward, I decided to start putting down my thoughts. I felt I should be writing about something and began drafts of various ideas. Some about me; some about how we can fix our earthly problems; and scattered research about legal issues that might relate to the phenomenon (i.e. government and societal efforts to stifle discussion).

233

About this time, I decided to start talking to my friends about my experiences and my feelings of urgency. The first person I talked to was my meditation teacher. She is also a dear friend of the family and often takes vacations with us. As a lawyer, I am used to organizing my arguments, but everything I said to her was a jumble of unconnected thoughts. This first attempt was unsuccessful and made me think that I really had no clear idea of what I wanted to do or say to others.

I kept attending CERO support groups; doing research; and attempted to write in my spare time. In February 2014, I attended the International UFO Congress in the Scottsdale area with other CERO members. Attending helped my focus. I began to feel I was heading in the right direction. I attended the Conference's Experiencer Sessions and listened to people from all over Canada and the U.S. who were going through the same feelings and felt the same type of urgency. While experiences vary, the most common element shared by about 70% of the Experiencers was the feeling of a need to "do something" with time running out.

Through Yvonne Smith, I met Reinerio Hernandez who was setting up the FREE Foundation. This is a group using surveys and scientific methods to research the phenomenon. I began to help this group. Rey is a recent Experiencer and was as excited as a revival tent preacher about his message. He talked about starting up an annual Experiencer Day every October 1st to try to provide a forum to allow people with experiences to come forward.

At the same conference, I met Pat Frascogna, a practicing attorney from Mississippi. He was representing two of the retired Air Force enlisted men who were part of the Rendlesham Forest Incident. They were seeking medical records from the Veteran's Administration to help with physical problems that are possibly connected with their proximity to UFO's in 1980. Without legal authority, the records were classified. This conversation with Pat was a firsthand confirmation that the federal government was still willing to violate the civil rights of military veterans to keep secrets about ET contacts.

Neither of the ex-Air Force men were ever part of a classified program. Only personnel who were part of a classified program or signed a waiver allowing the classification of their medical records could have their records withheld. The Air Force and VA were violating their civil rights to cover up the 1980 UFO/ET experience. Mr. Frascogna later announced at the Conference that he had reached a compromise with the VA to allow his client's doctors access to the classified medical records. However, the records remain classified for all other purposes. Pat had achieved remarkable success in helping his clients gain access. However, the underlying larger issue of the reasons why the military and VA fought so hard for many years demonstrated that secrecy was more important than the rights of our veterans.

Attending the Conference helped me to focus my attention. First, I was not alone in my feelings. The support I got from the CERO group meetings was helpful. Hearing people from around the country with similar experiences and feelings of urgency made me realize I was not alone and on the right track. Second, the FREE Experiencer Day idea struck a chord with me. I wanted to work with CERO and FREE to start a new tradition. One day, once a year, where Experiencers could share their interactions in a safe and supportive environment. This venue could help others realize they are not alone in having these experiences. Third, I realized that my legal experience handling First Amendment and Civil Rights issues could be applied to help break down societal and governmental impediments faced by Experiencers.

Since the February 2014 Conference, I have been working on these issues with renewed enthusiasm. Since the Experiencer Day did not happen in 2014 or 2015, I worked with CERO to get it off the ground in October 2016. We could live stream it and had many important speakers. I gave a small presentation on the background of the public policy beginnings of the truth embargo on the ET presence.

When Yvonne Smith asked me to do a presentation on civil rights, I did not think it would be as easy for me as it was to undertake. However, my disjointed research materials I had been gathering fell into place much easier than I expected. My short program focused on the civil rights aspects of a 1953 government report that recommended spying on persons who believed that ET had arrived.

While it has taken four years, I now feel comfortable about what my role is. It is to educate those around me about how the rights of people who have had experiences are violated by a government that denigrates Experiencers and is willing to violate their rights to keep ET secret. I have started disclosing my ET Experiences to friends. I am helping several organizations with my business and legal skills who support Experiencers. I am writing a book on issues surrounding the civil rights of Experiencers. It is not a UFO book per se. It deals with the illegal methods used to keep the public from knowing the truth about what is happening to Experiencers.

While my urgency has not gone away, it now has some direction. The latest change in presidential administrations leads me to believe that the federal government is going to squeeze tighter to hold on to its secrets. In Washington, it appears there is only one person who is working to shed light on these issues. I very much admire the work of Steven Bassett to get the federal government to disclose what is buried from the public.

However, I believe the new White House occupant will make our work harder. This means our work is more important than ever.

I am still practicing law. I still represent local government. I am still disclosing my experiences to an ever-widening group of friends. I am trying to write a book in my spare time. Because of these conflicting priorities, I get discouraged occasionally.

One thing that keeps me going are synchronistic events that seem to come when I need them most. They are too numerous to mention but seem to happen whenever I doubt what I am doing. Sometimes as simple as finding a coin when I am thinking I should stop this obsession and just play golf. One week, I was particularly down and, within 24 hours, found a pile of coins next to the driver's door of my car in two different parking lots. One time I was reading a book in bed called "Owls and Synchronicity." My wife asks me to explain its premise. As I was explaining, we heard owls hooting back and forth from two ends of our house for about five minutes. It had never happened before or since. License plates, bumper stickers, and clocks all have given me messages when I seem to need it most. I "know" I am supposed to "do" something. I think I am "doing" it or beginning to "do" it. However, it feels both necessary and urgently needed.

B. Past Firsthand Experiences

By way of background, let me share a few of my more significant experiences. Each has shaped my view of the larger reality. While I have had other experiences, these three experiences are illustrative of my journey and, while I kept each experience to myself, or only shared with my wife and one close friend, they helped put me on my current path.

At the age of five (1958), I was staying at a cabin that my parents, aunt and uncle were building on the site of previous family homes. The family had homesteaded the property before the Civil War. The previous one had burned down around 1950. The family was building a vacation home with modest amenities.

The property was the last twenty acres of a land grant given to the family in the 1820-1830s. It sat on a hill about five miles outside of the now abandoned town of Moselle, Missouri on a gravel road. Just across the road was an artificial pond and a vacation home. The next closest residence was over a mile away.

We were outside on a summer evening, after the family had been working on the interior of the cabin. The family was sitting around a large fire. It was a clear, moonless night. Away from the city lights, we could see a multitude of stars. To keep me occupied, the adults had me looking for Sputnik. I cannot remember if I saw Sputnik, but I vividly remember seeing what the adults later told me was a "comet" to the northwest of our location.

It was about four times as large as a full moon. An intense, white circular light appeared to be very close. It lit up the ground around us. I could not judge the distance, having no point of reference. My best estimate, based on looking at the adjoining pasture, was that it was about five hundred feet away at its closest point. It was so bright that it was hard to view directly. I remember being transfixed. It had sparks shooting off it and looked like it was dripping, white-hot metal. The best I can recall was that it was at about a thirty-degree angle up in the sky from our reference point.

I do not recall how it came to be in its location. My memory was that it just appeared over the adjoining pasture and moved closer. It did not change direction while we watched it and I do not recall it moving away. It was just this large, intensely bright light that discharged sparks like a sparkler around its top and sides. The bottom part did not spark but seemed to drip metal, but no fire could be seen on the ground underneath it. Beneath was a dry, summer pasture that would have caught fire if sparks hit the ground. Yet, there was no ground fire.

It seemed to be in view for at least several minutes and the adults remarked about its brightness and other characteristics. It never changed shape or moved towards or away from us after its initial approach. When I looked up at the adults and my older cousins, its light reflected off their faces. After the event, I do not remember going to bed. The next thing I remember was waking up the next morning.

There are few memories that stick with you from such a young age. However, this memory is as vivid as my first day at school a month later. In fact, the next morning, when the adults were outside drinking coffee around the fire pit, the talk was all about the "comet" we had all seen the night before.

After that Sunday morning, I do not recall any other discussions about it with my family for several years. Later, when I brought it up, neither of my parents could remember the incident, which I found strange. My memory was that my father was there but not my mother. She had recently given birth to my brother and probably was not present. My family never explained the event except for the morning after discussion about the "comet." I never talked to my Uncle's family about it after that morning. My family quietly forgot it, but I retained a vivid memory of that night to this day. I did not think I saw a Flying Saucer. I thought I saw a comet.

Later, we moved to San Dimas, California. As a teenager, I learned that a comet would appear and I got excited because of my previous experience. By that time, my parents did not remember the incident when I brought it up so I dropped the subject. I did look forward to the comet's appearance with these memories of a spectacular sighting firmly implanted. However, my memory did not match what I had learned in school about comets and I wanted to see one while I was older and compare what I learned in school to my "comet" memory. The two versions of a "comet" did not match.

When I saw a real comet, I was very disappointed. It was so small in comparison to the object I had seen long ago. It made me question what I had seen. It would have been awkward to discuss something that my parents did not remember and would write off as a dream or my imagination. However, my experience as a five-year-old and the realization that whatever I saw was not a "comet," made me question what I really saw that night.

After we had moved to California, my father started showing an interest in UFOs. He would bring home books on the subject and I would read them and wonder. However, I never connected the dots with my experience as a five-year-old until college.

About the same time, I had an experience that is more difficult to ignore. It was a spring evening while I was a junior in high school. I had walked over to a friend's house to play basketball on a lighted half court in his backyard.

After playing for a couple hours, I started walking home. While it was a cool evening, I was very hot and sweaty from physical activity. Instead of heading directly home, I took a small detour to a new park, Lone Hill Park, with newly planted grass, to lay down and cool off. I had never done this before but I just did not feel like going home quite yet.

Lying on the ground, I watched the stars on a clear, moonless night. Out of my peripheral vision, I noticed something moving across the sky to the southeast. It was moving westward almost parallel to me at about five miles, judging from the surrounding terrain. It was about ten to fifteen degrees above a row of streetlights across the street. The line of streetlights was about two hundred feet from me.

I had seen it cross about a third of the horizon at a constant speed. Since it had no running lights, it caught my attention. It was much darker than the surrounding sky so I could make out its shape. It was lenticular and did not appear to have any appendages. It had no lights so I thought it might be a military helicopter. However, I could not hear any noise. It moved too fast to be a blimp. Once it got to about my two o'clock position, I thought to myself, it might be a UFO. I had no sooner had that thought when it performed a ninety-degree plus turn and headed straight for me. It did not bank, it just started heading my direction. In other words, it made an acute 120% turn without slowing down. As it approached, it seemed to be descending towards me, but I could not determine its speed.

238

I was struck by this maneuver because, until that point, I was trying to figure out if it was an airplane or helicopter. It went from an airplane without running lights to something I could not explain. The fact that it changed directions at the same point I had the thought it was something unknown, made me concentrate harder on the flight path. When I first saw it, it was more of a casual look at something that just happened to catch my eye after I had adjusted to sitting in the darkness and looking at the stars.

After it made its abrupt turn, I stood up to see it better. While getting to my feet I momentarily lost it. Once standing, I quickly reacquired it and began to get worried. However, my curiosity outweighed my fear and I wanted it to fly over me so I could get a better look. I continued to try to figure out other explanations for the object, but, the closer it came, the less likely I could come up with a conventional explanation.

As it approached, I tried to listen for any engine noise but it continued its silent course in my direction. It was a quiet night, about nine o'clock with no traffic in the neighborhood. The first time I saw it, it appeared to be over a small airport (Brackett Field) about seven miles away. For this reason, I kept asking if I would start to hear noise from an engine that would explain this strange occurrence. It never made a sound for the two minutes I watched it.

The indistinct object continued heading towards me on a straight line, descending and appeared to be maintaining a constant speed. Later, I realized it was slowing down but, since it was heading straight for me, I did not realize it was slowing. As it got closer, its configuration became clearer. It was a dark circular object that did not reflect the streetlights across the street. It took about 30-40 seconds, after it started heading towards me, to reach my location from about five miles away.

It did not look like a dark object, but more like a hole in the sky that was slowing down and descending towards me. I could tell it was circular as it got closer when I could see it from underneath. I bent down while I watched and found a rock, never taking my eyes off the object. I stood up as the object slowly passed over me. If it was eighty or ninety feet above me (two telephone poles high), the circular hole in the sky would have been approximately thirty feet across if my estimate of the height were accurate. Because of the lack of features, I could not definitively tell how high it was.

To see how close, I threw the rock at it with a pretty accurate throw that probably was less than seventy-five feet high. I threw it right where the object was at the peak of the trajectory of the rock but did not hear it hit the object.

When I was directly underneath the object, I could tell that it was circular and did not make a sound. I could feel no turbulence, as it seemed to glide effortlessly along its straight path. It continued to the northeast, passing over a water tank in the neighboring City of Glendora, towards the San Gabriel Mountains.

The entire sighting lasted about a minute and a half to two minutes. First, it went west. Second, the object came towards me from five to ten miles rather quickly. Third, it seemed to slow and pass over me at a lower altitude. After it passed over me, it accelerated and gained altitude as it headed towards the mountains. As it quickly approached the mountains, about eight to ten miles away, it was above the ridgeline that was approximately six to eight thousand feet.

I never told anyone about this experience for twenty years. Even though both of my parents were very open to the possibility of UFOs and supportive about the subject, I did not feel comfortable talking to them about it. I walked home, never telling anyone about it for the next twenty years.

Forty-five years later, I returned to the spot of my sighting. I surveyed the area, which had not changed much except for the maturing landscape and added playground equipment. I stood at the spot and looked out over the area. While I was standing there, I noticed a rock on the ground. It was scarred from being hit by a lawnmower in several places, but it fit my hand like the rock I threw at the craft as it passed over my head forty-five years earlier. It was strange to see a rock on top of thick turf that had replaced the patchy newly planted grass all those years ago. I pocketed the rock and continued surveying the area.

Later, I used an online mapping system to determine distances to area landmarks. The object must have covered about fifteen to twenty miles while in my range of vision. My ability to see over the one-story homes across the street was the same and I could track the approach of the object in my mind's eye while standing and looking to the south. Its transit towards the west and abrupt turn to the northeast were easy to track from where I stood those years later. However, when I turned around, to simulate how the object went over my head and disappeared over the San Gabriel Mountains, I could not follow the object the way I remembered it. Since I was a little self-conscious standing in a park in broad daylight pointing and turning around and round looking in the sky, I left with most of my memories verified to my own satisfaction.

About a month later, I returned and stood at the same spot. I tried to simulate turning around to follow the craft as it passed over me and accelerated over the mountains. My memory was that it passed me in a straight line and traveled over a reservoir in the foothills. However, the reservoir was located to the northwest and not the northeast as I remembered it. Either my memory of the direction after it passed me was faulty: turning around caused a disorientation; or the object suddenly changed directions and I did not notice it. All my other memories are consistent with my memory of the event as I stood there.

While I have had numerous 'paranormal" events in adulthood, one other event stands out. I was living in Fresno, California. It was October 1998 and I returned from a City Council meeting close to midnight. I changed in a walk-in closet so as not to disturb my wife or our two dogs and went straight to bed.

Somewhere in the middle of the night, I awoke to find myself standing on the walkway between the sidewalk and our front porch. Only in my underwear and facing the front door about fifteen feet away. I was surrounded by an intense white light from above that did not seem to cast its light beyond a narrow area close to where I stood.

Once I became aware of my surroundings, I said aloud: "So that's what they look like." My next thought was that I needed to concentrate on my surroundings so that I would remember everything I could. First, I felt the cold concrete on my bare feet. There was a slight breeze from the north that moved the hairs on my bare legs and gave me a chill. I noticed that there were two lawn chairs on the porch that moved from backyard poolside to the front porch depending on circumstances. There was no welcome mat out. As I stepped up to the concrete porch and grasped the brass door handle which opened, to my relief.

Never once did I think of looking up at the light. I felt very happy and my only intention was to get in bed. Once I hit the pillow, I went right to sleep.

The next morning was a different matter. As I awoke, my field of vision was extremely blurred. It was like the entire range of vision would shift from left to right and then return to the left. It was not spinning like normal dizziness. The movement was so violent that I began throwing up and could not stop. As I lay down, if I twitched a finger, the nausea would start up and would not subside. After about an hour in which I must have thrown up at least a couple of hundred times, my wife put me in the car and drove to our family doctor's office.

He saw me and said that I had either suffered a blow to the head or developed a virus. At the time, I told no one about what happened the night before. The Doctor gave me prescriptions for anti-nausea and steroids, to shrink my inner ear. He sent me home to ride it out. It took two weeks before I could drive or see straight. After the "spinning" stopped, I had blurred vision for those two weeks and could not drive.

When my vision settled down, I noticed two roughly parallel scars from my scalp to my left eyebrow. I had never had scars in this location. It was quite perplexing. I had no accident that would account for two four inch scars on my head. Pictures of me taken before the sudden illness did not show the scars.

I did not share the ET experience that I consciously remember with anyone except my wife until recently. In my CERO support group, no one had a similar experience. I attempted regressions with Yvonne to try to recover memories of the incident. While some information came forward, the sessions did not add more than fragmentary glimpses of the event. In the regression, my third on this incident, I finally had some recall of what happened that early morning back in October 1998. Suddenly my body was paralyzed and my head was numb. My eyes were shut but I could make out shapes and movement through my closed eyelids because the "room" I was in was very bright without a discernible light source. The lighting was very bright, but was not emanating from any direction. After my head was numbed, I saw a boomerang-shaped object sweeping in front of the left side of my face in what appeared to be circular motions. Soon thereafter, a large almond-shaped black eye appeared in front of my face very close to my eye. I could make out the top half of the head that was hovering over me. It was a large headed Grey-type alien.

Yvonne had me draw what I thought it looked like. I drew a traditional Grey, but it did not "feel" right. Large black, featureless eyes, large head, no discernible ears, slit mouth and nose with a pear-shaped, rounded chin. While I was proud that, despite my lack of artistic abilities, it seemed close but not right.

I started to look at "alien" drawings on the internet but nothing stood out. Finally, I came across a Grey-type with a pointed chin and I visibly shuddered. Since I had been to several UFO Conferences recently, I thought back to different presentations that showed "alien" drawings. Each time, they would show a set of drawings, I would watch without reaction until they would show a Grey with large, black eyes and a pointed chin. Invariably, I would wince or shudder each time a drawing of this type of Grey would flash across the screen. While this may not be evidence to a skeptic, it was an emotional confirmation for me.

In addition to the regression memories, my conscious recall was clear and direct. There was no doubt to me that I had experienced direct interaction with an otherworldly craft and its occupants.

Within a month of my last regression, I had further personal confirmation of the October 1998 incident. I was sitting around the house looking for a new book to read. I had just finished a book and did not have the next book lined up. I went into a spare bedroom to go through some of my older UFO books to see what might be interesting. I came across a book with a bookmark in it and decided to start reading from the point I left off. The bookmark was a receipt showing I had bought the book in 1997, about a year before my incident. It was the Communion Letters by Whitley Strieber. The book shares many of the personal letters written to Whitley after his pioneering book Communion. I started reading from that point and finished the chapter I had started about 19 years ago before going to bed.

The next morning, I started a new chapter at breakfast. The first incident in this new chapter talked about a man who had an abduction and was placed on a table. The taller Grey brought out a boomerang shaped object and started waving over the abductee. It opened his forehead area above his eye. Once opened, the Grey placed some objects inside the head of the abductee between his flesh and his skull. Using the opposite motion, the Grey closed the wound.

This process was remarkably like what happened to me. The same circular motion with a boomerang-shaped object. In my case, it left a scar I did not have before. It also left me with severe vertigo for two weeks. It is more than coincidental that I stopped reading the book that I had bought in 1997 at the chapter before the one with this similar incident. I picked up the book a month after my third regression on this incident where I recovered fragmentary memories about the incident. I have never heard of a similar incident as the one described in Whitley's book.

C. Assistance From Someone/Somewhere

After I had become convinced that I had a role to play and began acting on my feelings, things started happening to me that seemed more than coincidence. As I began to realize that the "calling" to act was real, I began having other strange occurrences. I noticed that these incidents almost always occurred at synchronistic times. 12:34, 1:11, 2:22, 3:33, 1:23, etc. meant that something was about to happen. After my first brush with these happenings, I had trouble being around electronic devices. I would set off ATMs with my fingers three inches away. Any touchscreen pad would react before I touched it. Even when there was no static electricity in the air, I would get a shock. Such as a four-inch spark between me and a wooden door at a point more than a foot from any metal parts. This lasted for about a month.

It reminded me of when I lived in Fresno, around the time of the incident discussed earlier, I would take walks at night for exercise around 9:00 to 10:00 P.M. As I would walk under street lights, they would go off while I passed. It would not happen every night, but it is unnerving to have this happen on a regular basis. It lasted for about a year.

Two recent incidents stand out. On January 22, 2016, my wife and I checked into a hotel in Paris for our 40th Anniversary. We used a ton of hotel points to stay on the Champs Elysees. The hotel gave us a welcome package of confections and champagne, not my normal evening snack. We went to bed and I woke up and looked at the clock. It was 1:11 A.M. I felt a little dizzy, but who wouldn't after champagne and cookies. The next day, I deserted my wife for the day, while she shopped, I took the train to London to watch a soccer match. At the match, even with my eyeglasses, my vision was blurred and I could not make out the players names or numbers. Since I had been to this stadium several times before (Craven Cottage), I was surprised by my vision problem. I had always been able to see the pitch (field) from the stands. I felt a little hung over and had trouble with my balance. Once the second half began, I decided to take off my prescription glasses since I could not see anyway. To my amazement, my eyes could see the pitch and each player's name and number. I had never been able to do this before in my visits back to 2007.

While my long-distance vision has degraded somewhat, I still have an overall improvement. The one element of my vision that has remained strong is the distance of about three feet. This distance was always a problem for me. With my glasses, I could read things close, but had trouble reading from a podium while speaking at a meeting or in court. Now, I can do it without switching back and forth with my glasses. I am now back to reading at a distance without glasses that allows me to speak at a podium. With the advent of PowerPoint presentations, I was having trouble with the distance between the materials on a podium. Now, I don't. This told me that I should do more than write, but speak about my issues.

My latest episode occurred at the February 2017 International UFO Conference in Scottsdale, Arizona. I was now a regular at this annual conference. The 2017 conference was a little different as Yvonne Smith asked me to speak on the civil rights issue. I had spoken about it at the October 2016 CERO conference. I spoke after Yvonne for twenty minutes on the first day of the Conference. In addition, I attended the Experiencer Support Group meetings that Yvonne facilitated. At each session, she asked if anyone had any experiences at the conference. Each day, only one or two hands would go up out of the one hundred plus attendees at each session for the first two days. On Friday morning, Yvonne's question got a different response. At least six or seven people that I could see raised their hands, including four of the seven or so CERO members in the audience. I was one of those who raised my hand.

The previous evening, I had joined a small group outside of the conference center for drinks after dinner. I was tired and let the evening get to me and had several drinks, just enough to worry about how I would feel the next morning. I went to bed after ten and slept soundly until about 4:30A.M. As is appropriate for my age, I had to go to the bathroom. Because I felt a little "off balance," I turned on a light to see my way to the bathroom. Once I got up and started moving, I felt better and was happy that I did not feel "hung over."

I returned to bed and, rather than follow my normal routine of reading until I got sleepy again, I turned out the light, just laid down on my back and shut my eyes. I immediately had a view of something I had never seen before. With my eyes closed, I could see a three-dimensional object in the middle of my field of vision. It was metallic silver and was shaped like a domino. Engraved on the top one-third was a classic flying saucer. The middle third had a darkly etched line that began at the bottom of the saucer and went down to an object that enveloped the bottom third of the rectangular-shaped object. At the bottom was some script that wrapped tightly around the object. It was shaped like a ring made up of interlocking symbols that resembled a Keltic design like bracelets and pendants I had purchased in Ireland for my wife.

I stared intently at the object trying to memorize what it looked like. It stayed in my "eyes closed" field of vision for about a minute. After about thirty seconds of that time, another square, three-dimensional object appeared just below it. The second object had substance, but every time I concentrated on the one above, I forgot what the square object looked like, except that it was square. Eventually, they both faded away but I only retained a memory of the upper object.

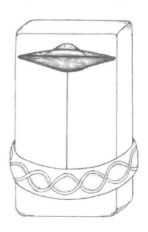

Artist Sharon Tittle

After the Friday morning session, I compared notes with the other three CERO members who had their own experiences. All of us had highly symbolic experiences, each within an hour of the others. All four of us were staying within a quarter mile. Each incident was hard to

245

explain. They were not typical experiences for us. I was wide awake for mine and it took me about a half hour to get back to sleep as I struggled to put the incident in perspective.

About three weeks later, I had Yvonne regress me to see if I could learn more about the incident. Under hypnosis, I was very relaxed. However, I could not recover any memories besides what I could consciously recall. As the session wore on, I began to feel pain in the right side of my head. Later, it turned into a full-blown tension headache that stayed with me for about thirty-six hours. My interpretation is that there is something that I am supposed to remember, but not now. As I have heard from numerous Experiencers, an ET tells them that, "When the right time comes, you will remember."

Overall, I believe I have had a lifetime of interactions. I am not unique in that many people have had similar experiences. I wonder how many have had these experiences but have no conscious memories of them. I have several significant events that make it undeniable to me, but may not convince most people. However, I am the only person that I need to convince and I have.

These experiences make me believe that ETs are real and interact in our lives. However, what we do with our planet is entirely up to us. I firmly believe I have free will to decide what course I should take and how I need to help my kind grow up and manage our affairs before it is too late. Most of our problems boil down to two issues: our fear and our self-interest. The primitive part of our brain dominates much of our thought and generates unnecessary fear.

Sherry Wilde, a fellow experiencer, has written a wonderful book, *The Forgotten Promise*. She has conscious memories of many of her interactions with ET. She has passed on some valuable lessons in her book including one that resonates with me. She was counseled by an ET to "monitor her thoughts." Since we react out of fear so often in our daily lives, taking this simple step can help us stop reacting out of fear and start acting in a positive manner.

I cannot speak for all people's experiences. While mine were often quite scary, I believe that the ETs that interact with me are not here to take over the planet. I am not playing a role in a big budget Hollywood alien invasion movie. Instead, I am following bread crumbs to play a small role in helping us and our planet survive and hopefully thrive. We live in a world that scientists have only explained about four percent of the makeup of the Universe. I believe that I am dealing with part of the other ninety-six percent that ET can seamlessly occupy. Perhaps someday, we will too.

CHAPTER 13:
Conclusion: A New Emphasis By Et?
(Yvonne and James)

Since the pioneering work of Budd Hopkins and Dr. David Jacobs in the 1980-90s, the existence of a "Hybrid Program" has been a part of ET research. The "Hybrid Program" uses both human and ET DNA to create Hybrids that are part ET and part human. This discovery has changed much of UFO research from being only a "nuts and bolts" review of the physical aspects of ET craft to one where the UFO occupants are the central focus. Experiencers have been a part of the Hybrid Program, according to Dr. Jacobs, since the 1890s. The program is primarily carried out by ET entities referred to as the "Greys," but other ET species appear to participate. It has been the dominant purpose for Human-ET interaction over the last several decades.

Since 2010, there appears to be another facet to the ET (Grey) plan. The recent surge of Experiencers who believe they are receiving messages that indicate "time is running out." As discussed in Part Two, the "messages" received by Experiencers talk about near-future catastrophes. Whether this new emphasis is taking the place of the "Hybrid Program" or merely complimenting it, remains to be seen.

Dr. Jacobs, in his recent book[18], believes that the "Hybrid Program" is winding down. Other researchers believe the "Hybrid Program" is also winding down but do not believe in Jacob's sinister reasons. Many believe that the hybrids now consist of humans who are being "upgraded" with DNA adjustments to help with our ascension to a higher level of consciousness.[19]

Whatever the reason, the ET program has a new element. Yvonne's research demonstrates a new trend of messages received by Experiencers. For many, it appears to be the primary reason for their ET interaction. Part Two has chronicled this shift among both new and long-term Experiencers. The predominant theme is not the Hybrid Program, but a renewed emphasis on the warnings from ET about the way we treat each other and our planet.

---

[18] Jacobs, *"Walking Among Us: The Alien Plan to Control Humanity"*, (2015) Disinformation Books, San Francisco.

[19] Rodwell, *"The New Human: Awakening to our Cosmic Heritage"*, (2016) New Mind Publishers, Australia; Lamb and Mendonica, *"Meet the Hybrids: The Lives and Missions of ET Ambassadors on Earth"*, (2015) Wordpress.com.

The beginning of this trend is hard to pinpoint. By 2011, Yvonne was convinced something was going on with many new people seeking her out with these feelings of urgency. Also, many long-term Experiencers were having the same anxiety. However, the messages were like those she had been hearing since the early 1990s. It was the increased frequency and specific detail of many Experiencers that made Yvonne take notice of this trend.[20]

This "urgency" issue has been hard for Yvonne to address. While many researchers voice their opinions about the meaning and purpose behind the ET Agenda, Yvonne has tried to leave these issues to the Experiencers themselves. Her main purpose is helping them deal with the trauma from their experiences rather than imposing her own judgment on the nature of their experiences. She published *Chosen* and *Coronado* to mainly focus on the "how's" of the phenomenon rather than the "why's" behind it. In fact, while debate rages in the researcher community about the purpose of ET's intervention in human lives, many CERO members, including James, have called Yvonne "Switzerland" for her ability to keep neutral on the issues such as "Good ET/Bad ET." Up until this point, Yvonne has been a "nuts and bolts" chronicler of the Experiencer and their ET interactions rather than an interpreter.

After so many have come forward, most preferring to remain anonymous, she could no longer keep silent. Ignoring the change of emphasis or only discussing it with small Experiencer audiences would do a disservice to those who have come forward. Each feels an anxiety that they must "do something" to get their message out. These Experiencers want their message told but would prefer to stay out of the spotlight. This trend sets it apart from previous waves of people with "messages" from ETs. In the 1950s, "Contactees" brought messages of peace and love to the world. These messages came from people claiming to be the representatives of mankind chosen by our "Space Brothers." Self-promotion seemed to be at the heart of many of these 1950s claims.

Today, none of those who came forward claimed that they are the earth-bound ET representatives. Instead, they are confused, worried and seek answers rather than make pronouncements. They talk about their experiences out of concern for our future rather than to seek fame and fortune.

In the first edition of *Chosen*, Alfonso Martinez, in 2007, talked to Yvonne about his feelings of impending earth changes and the role he

---

[20] Alimurung, Gendy: *"A Hypnotherapist Built a Career on Alien Abductions, and Her Experiences May Unnerve You"* LA Weekly Magazine (December 5, 2013).

needs to play.[21] His disclosures were consistent with others but not yet part of a noticeable larger pattern. By 2011, there were enough Experiencers with similar messages to indicate a new pattern emerging.

The emerging messages include Experiencers with whom Yvonne has had a long-history. John and Debbie have been part of CERO, off and on, for thirty years. Each has had the typical long-term concern about our future, but both are now stocking up on supplies and feeling that events are accelerating. Neither brought out these concerns during previous periods (*i.e.* Y2K or 2012) so their concerns are today being part of this newly emerging pattern. Their concerns come from "intuition" that so many long-term Experiencers exhibit. Yet, they have also had these concerns planted in them through other methods while aboard ships or at ET facilities.

In general, these messages are conveyed by three methods. First, on viewing screens used on ET craft to give the Experiencer visual messages. These viewing screens have amazing detail that give the appearance that the viewer is present at the events being shown. There also appears to be a subconscious element that conveys ideas through the visual display.

Second, there is eye to eye conveyance of information from a tall Grey to both the conscious and subconscious mind. It is usually done by the "doctor" or "leader" that controls the interactions with the Experiencer. This "neural" engagement, like viewing screens, has been a frequent element of a typical abduction experience. The Experiencer might remember a portion of the message immediately but usually memories of the message are repressed to emerge later through hypnosis or conscious recall. Without hypnotherapy, the memory does not surface until it is intended to be remembered by the ET that placed it in the Experiencer's subconscious.

Third, sometimes there is the placement of symbols or messages remotely into the mind of the Experiencer. This appears to be a recent method of conveying information. James is one example when he recently had symbols placed in his field of vision while alone in his hotel room. He received this "message" in the early morning of February 17, 2017. Within an hour before and after his "vision," several other CERO members had similar ET-related paranormal events. Most were staying at the same hotel and some were camping at a nearby campsite. It is the only time James has had anything like this happen.

Overall, the messages received by those discussed in this book are about potential future events. Most are distressing. Looking at these messages and taking them at face value is difficult. Many are

---

[21] *See*: Chapter Four, Part C (Alfonso's Personal Progress Report).

contradictory and even the Experiencer is not confident whether the message they have received will happen. For example, Linda Napolitano has received disturbing messages that indicate a possible incident in 2017. She saw three possible scenarios. As explained in Chapter 9, Linda is extremely concerned but could not determine with certainty which scenario will occur, if any. She leans towards a "false flag" alien invasion threat used to distract the public from other problems. Considering the turmoil in Washington D.C. as this book goes to print, the scenario has a little more potential than one might have thought when she brought the issue to Yvonne's attention in 2016.

If we look at these predictions with an eye on past pronouncements, they are likely not to occur. Over the years, so many dates have come and gone where people have made predictions of events that did not occur. As far as predicting detailed events, the "messages" of Experiencers are probably no more reliable than other forecasts.

What are we to make of these people who are coming forward with these apocalyptic visions or messages? None, save Suzy Hansen and, perhaps, Sherry Wilde, seem to indicate they have or want any leadership role. In fact, most have no clear idea what they are supposed to do with this information. As opposed to the Contactee Movement of the 1950s, these Experiencers, interviewed or regressed by Yvonne, are not claiming any mantle of leadership or special connection with ET. They are mostly typical Experiencers. The difference is that the information bleeds through into their daily thoughts. Messages of environmental stewardship or the need to divert mankind from its fear-based decision-making have been around as long as the phenomenon. However, past messages seemed more generalized and do not have the element of urgency currently expressed by the current group of Experiencers.

The messages of environmental concern have always been part of the ET discussions with most, if not all, Experiencers. The "urgency" many now feel is echoed today in the headlines. Hurricanes like *Katrina* and *Sandy* show how fragile our modern world is to the increasing wrath of Mother Nature. As this book goes to print, President Trump has begun the steps to withdraw the United States for the *Paris Treaty* to combat climate change. The U.S. finds itself in the company of Nicaragua (who refused to sign because the *Paris Accord* was not strong enough) and Syria. What this action means for the future climate that the accelerating concern about our future remains to be seen.

Of the Experiencers chronicled, Linda Napolitano has had the most visible role in the past. She was the main player in the ET "staged" abduction in New York City for the primary benefit of the Secretary

General of the United Nations.[22]   However, as she explained, she is uncertain about what her "messages" mean or what she should do about them. Ms. Napolitano shares a common trait with the others in the new category of "Urgency Experiencers." She fervently believes that the events she sees in her messages or something similar will occur soon. This differentiates her and the others from previous Experiencer messages, conveyed either via viewing screens or by eye to eye neural engagement with the "leader" ET on board a craft. Past messages were conveyed mostly to the subconscious to be revealed at an unknown later date. The current messages, for the most part, are being consciously remembered now, not later.

The conveyance of these messages in the 1980-2005 period were often couched in longer term language. "If humans do not change their path, terrible things" will happen at an unknown future date. Now, while the specific message differs, the language or impression conveyed to the Experiencer in the last several years portends events to occur within the lifetimes of Experiencers, even those 50 or older. Suzy Hansen talks about being one of those who are training people for the upcoming events. In her book, she talks about specific time lines within the same timeframe that Yvonne has noticed in the Experiencers who have come forward to discuss the same or similar concerns. 2010 seems to be a common starting point for most of the warnings.

When looking at the specifics of the messages, they appear to be conflicting and all cannot occur. There are several possible reasons to view the overall trend as something of grave concern, but each Experiencer's "vision" is probably not predictive of specific future events. Many, such as James, have no specific events that they see. Rather, they have an overwhelming need to alert others to the fact that "time is running out," yet they do not know what they are supposed to do.

First, over the years, the messages from ET talk about, if man continues on its present course, these catastrophic events will occur. In other words, Experiencers have been given the impression that there was still time to change the trajectory towards an unfortunate end. The more current messages may not have an offramp if we change our behavior. The messages are now geared towards "damage control," rather than changing our outcome.

The accuracy of the specifics of any message, especially those conveyed via channeled or indirect contacts, seem to be difficult to be used as predictive of future events. Research on channeled information has shown that there is

---

[22] Hopkins, Budd: *"Witnessed: The True Story of the Brooklyn Bridge UFO Abductions"* (1996) Pocket Books, New York.

a significant possibility of misinterpretation. In a recent study, the person who channeled information from a remote or unknown source had no brain activity in the areas of the brain that would be active if the information were coming from the subject themselves.[23]   In other words, the areas of the brain that should be active, have no brain activity while a channeled message is being conveyed. It is as if the person's brain activity "stands down" to allow the channeled message to come through unfiltered. If the person's brain activity is still active when the "message is received," there is a likelihood that the person receiving the message will apply their own filter and alter the content.

In James's opinion, the possibility of distortion means that, while the general nature of the warnings should be taken seriously, it is likely that the specific timing and outcomes mentioned by the Experiencer are not an accurate predictor of future events. We should be looking at the overall trend of these messages rather than the accuracy of a specific prediction. The number of Experiencers having these "messages" alone should be enough for people to take them seriously.

Should we take them seriously? Yes. First, they are the people who have direct contact with entities that appear to be able to travel great distances, travel between dimensions or both.   They apparently can manipulate time, at least on a local level. ETs with these abilities are likely to have some ability to accurately forecast the future, even if the future is not fixed. In fact, the messages, past and present, indicate that they do not control our future but respect our autonomy. We, therefore, have control over our future. Experiencers have been called upon to help change the human trajectory towards destruction. These warnings indicate that we have the ability to change and the free will to make our own choices. In other words, ETs are not here to take control of our situation, but to plant ideas that will allow us to see the folly of our present course. This "help" allows us to understand that we should change our course to either prevent or mitigate the future catastrophic events. Taking these messages at face value indicates that ETs are not here to take over our planet for their purposes or to make us their "welfare recipients." It is up to us.

Second, those that are coming forward to discuss these issues with Yvonne, as stated earlier, are not different from the typical Experiencer. In the past, their experiences followed the same pattern as others caught up in this new reality. Now, they are not used for purposes of the hybrid program, but seem to have been re-tasked to warn humanity of its imminent peril. It is not like these messages are unique to Experiencers.

---

[23] Betty, Stanford, *"When did you ever become less by dying?"* (2016) Whitecrow Books, United Kingdom; citing research by Dr. Andrew Newberg on brain activity changes during channeling.

These warnings mirror the physical/scientific evidence that is mounting of a planet in peril. Many are shaken out of comfortable lives by concerns about the future of our civilization.

Changes in perspective among Experiencers is not a new phenomenon. Like people who have had Near Death Experiences, Experiencers find themselves changed from their contacts with ET. According to the Experiencer Survey conducted by the Dr. Edgar Mitchell Foundation for Research into Extraterrestrial Encounters ("FREE"), most feel that their contacts have changed their perspective in a "positive" way. Of 794 persons who answered this question, only 13.35% had a negative change. The rest saw positive changes coming out of their ET interactions. Overall, the survey notes increased awareness of environmental, social justice and positive, as opposed fear-based, changes have come about in the Experiencer's life because of their interactions with the phenomenon. They feel more intuitive and connected to other life on Earth. Most, according to the FREE Surveys, believe they are now part of a plan to lift humanity.

The negative aspects of this current trend are borne out in the FREE surveys. They show the increased anxiety over planetary issues. Of 1685 that answered, 60.42% have seen catastrophic events portrayed. Barren or desolate landscapes have been shown to 37.66% of those surveyed. This trend mirrors the increased catastrophic visions given to the Experiencers that visit Yvonne in the last several years. The correlation is during the survey period of the FREE research.

Third, if we have free will to decide our own fate, how could we be influenced to make the right kind of choices? This argument assumes that overt interference is not an option for ET. The authors have no special knowledge about ET-Government Contacts, if any. We do not know whether our world leaders have been given any special knowledge from ET about our fate. Regardless of whom ET has contacted, it is logical to assume that Experiencers would be prime candidates to receive these messages of concern about the future of our planet. Whether the reasons for ET concern are altruistic or meaning meant to "protect their investment" in our DNA, they already have connections, both physical and non-physical, with Experiencers. As discussed earlier, the FREE survey finds that most of this group have heightened connections beyond the physical with the ETs with whom they interact. Regardless of any other subtle efforts being made, Experiencers are a logical choice to carry warnings to the grass roots of humanity.

Absent *Klaatu* coming down to meet with the world's scientists to discuss our crisis as in *"The Day the Earth Stood Still,"* species that are advanced enough to be here would likely not want to make a public declaration without some long-term preparation. We would likely see them as a threat, which is the normal first reaction of mankind to anything different, let alone otherworldly. Also, our first response, after threatening them, would be to ask for their help to get us out of this mess. This would likely have two consequences. First, we would lose our free will to determine our own destiny. Second, we would become dependent on outside forces and that dependency would impede our growth as an independent civilization. If ETs wanted to turn us into a slave or welfare planet, they would have done so long ago.

The fact that ETs have chosen a relatively small group of people (*Experiencers*) to pass along these messages does not mean they are mankind's only hope. The authors do not assume that Experiencers are the only ones being contacted on these issues. For instance, while the scientific community has largely ignored UFO-ET issues, they have sounded the alarm on issues, like climate change, that fall within their expertise (i.e. matters of the observable physical environment). They speak with near unanimity of the issues that are related to the messages of "urgency" received by most Experiencers.

In fact, Suzy Hansen discusses in her book (*The Dual Soul Connection*) that ETs are planting the same kind of "thoughts" in non-Experiencers on a global basis. They have "thought seeds" placed in their subconscious that will spring into their conscious thoughts at a time when they will need them. While this concept may sound far-fetched to many, it is the same method used to plant the "urgency" in Experiencers that is the premise of this book. It is likely that the same "thought seeds" are being implanted in scientists, opinion makers and leaders around the world.

However, the Experiencers chronicled here are not the only Experiencers receiving messages. Others, as discussed earlier, are receiving differing, but consistent, messages from ET. UFO Historian Grant Cameron calls them "downloads" but many are receiving them and they convey varying, but consistent themes. As discussed above Suzy Hansen and Sherry Wilde fit in this scenario. Both seem to have a special relationship with ETs and their unique perspectives should be viewed as indicators in this new trend. Both have multiple contacts that can be recalled. Each has changed their life path to discuss their experiences that are mission-based rather than just another cog in the Hybrid Program.

Both have written recent books to get a similar message out. These books have been published in the last three years and the timing they received their messages mirrors those received by the Experiencers that approached Yvonne.

Sherry Wilde, in her book *The Forgotten Promise*, details very similar messages she has received very close in time to the recent recipients of the "urgency" messages. She has had a lifetime of interactions with an ET that, as a child, she started calling "Da." Da, appearing to be a Grey, would share insights with her over her lifetime. In 2009, she had a vision that mirrors the messages discussed in this book. In her book, she wrote about it as follows:

> "We, the human race, were like a parasite on the planet, destroying and infecting our home. She, the Earth, is a living organism, and she has reached her limit. Humanity's time is about up. Either we wake up and realize what we are doing to each other and the planet, or we pay the consequences." (*The Forgotten Promise*, pp. 193-194.)

This is the same message as has been received by many for decades. The difference with Sherry Wilde's messages is that she receives more spiritual messages that are aimed at making us more caring of each other and less aggressive. She has more direct interactions with a single ET, both conscious and unconscious, than the typical Experiencer. While she has had more active interaction since 2010, they are directed at the spiritual side of humanity.

Sherry's messages corroborate those received by New Zealand's Suzy Hansen. In her recent book, "*The Dual Soul Connection,*" (2014) Hansen has been given multiple tasks to prepare us for near-term catastrophic Earth changes. Like many Experiencers, she states that she is given information in an auditorium, likely in an underground facility. In February 2010, the visits started that had her playing a role in preparing people, some skeptics, to play a role in mitigating future earth changes. In addition to Experiencers, she writes that ETs are able to scan cities around the globe to find suitable persons that can help in a crisis. Since the events are likely to overwhelm typical disaster response resources, these people are given subconscious information that will help them with quick, intuitive decision making when responding to a disaster. For those that have seen the movie "Sully", it is the difference between having foreknowledge about an emergency (*which allows a person to react more quickly*) and being faced with an unprecedented situation where one naturally hesitates before choosing between feasible alternative actions.

Whitley Strieber, Author and Experiencer, received similar messages but in an unusual circumstance. While on a 1998 book tour, he was sleeping in a Toronto hotel when awakened by what he thought was room service. It turned out to be a "man" with whom he engaged in the most unusual discussion. It is the subject of his book, *"The Key: A True Encounter."* ((2011) Penguin, New York.) This "man" engaged him in a lengthy discussion about our future, including a broad range of subjects such as the nature of man, future technological breakthroughs (*some of which have come to pass*) and our upcoming troubled times. When discussing our near-term future, the revelations were eerily like what CERO Experiencers have been talking about. An example, the "man," Whitley calls the *"Master of the Key,"* stated about our rampant consumerism:

> After the suffering you are about to endure, mankind will never again lust after material wealth. You are about to suffocate in your own garbage. (*The Key: A True Encounter*, p. 114.)

Throughout the book, the conversation talks about struggles humanity must face for us to progress and reach our potential. The conversation also discussed a future where ET will be more visible, but will leave our fate to our own devices.

> There will come a time when your planet is dying, and you will see these aliens all around you. They will not help you, no matter how hard you beg, and you will beg, believe me. Their inaction, however, is their help. As agonizing as it is for them to see you suffer, they do it out of compassion, for without it you will not succeed in the mission of this age, which is to open the elemental body to ecstasy. (*The Key: A True Encounter*, pp. 82-83.)

Overall, the consistency between the "messages" received by those who have turned to Yvonne and simultaneously published books by Experiencers who tell unique stories, one in Wisconsin, U.S.A. and the other in New Zealand. Each of these books are not the typical "abduction" scenario as chronicled in Part One. They tell of experiences that do not fit into the normal trend of the *"Hybrid Program."* They speak of a more participatory process where ET appears to be grooming people to play various roles in the near-term future. They are providing clandestine help, but appear to otherwise leave the problems for us to solve. Based on our preliminary review of this trend, more Experiencers are likely to come forward with similar experiences.

Whitley Strieber's "conversation" with the *Master of the Key* had many parallels to the "messages" brought forward by Experiencers from around the world. This book primarily focuses on those CERO members that appear to be touched by the same concerning visions of our near-term future.

We expect to see this trend accelerate. The Experiencer Messages should be cataloged and compared on a worldwide basis. The FREE Survey is a helpful step in the right direction. FREE is moving forward with a more detailed surveying of smaller samples of Experiencers. This work may help document this trend. More research is needed into the "whys" of the ET Agenda rather than just measuring physical evidence of contact. While both efforts are important, the images witnessed by the Experiencers discussed herein demand attention. Further corroboration is necessary to see the extent of this new ET emphasis. Specific Messages with dates and times of action should be followed to determine accuracy. People need to listen to these unique people. They provide an insight no others can. How to interpret their interactions with ET and the messages they convey is important.

Finally, we would like to revisit why ET would use this clandestine method to try to influence humanity to deal with its ultimate crisis. For the purposes of discussion, let us assume that at least one government has obtained technology from ET through an exchange with a visiting race or through recovery of a crashed vehicle. Obviously, the "news" is still a carefully guarded secret. If true, there are two scenarios: The secrets are being kept for military purposes and/or specially chosen companies are provided the information for commercial application. Under the first possibility, we have shown ET that our governments cannot be trusted to use advanced technology for the benefit of mankind. The secrets are kept for selfish purposes to gain advantage over other humans. Hardly an altruistic purpose.

If a government supplies or "seeds" this technology to private companies, the choice of "how" and to "whom" will also show that we cannot be trusted to make the right choice for the benefit of all. First, the choice of the company to receive the information for its purely commercial purposes is not a benefit to all of humanity. Those receiving this special benefit have not shared it. Their loyalty is to the shareholders to protect its "investment." So, if ET technology is already in the hands of humanity, it has been shielded from universal application for either one selfish purpose or another. To date, we have failed the ET ethics examination. Based on past practice, why would ET share technology that would help us respond to a crisis when it will only be used to benefit a small segment of the world's population?

The "messages" received by Experiencers, likely since 2010, are focused on some near-term crises that humanity will need to deal with themselves. Before we can ask for technical help from ET, we need to show that we are morally or ethically up to the task to govern our own planet. In "The Forgotten Promise," Sherry Wilde writes about three rules that she was taught by her ET mentor. These are:

1. We are One with Our Creator.
2. We are Multi-Dimensional Beings on Multiple Levels.
3. Monitor your thoughts.

The first rule shows that all living things are connected. This rule can be read as a spiritual lesson or a moral imperative. What we do to other living things, we do to ourselves. From the ET perspective, perhaps we should follow the "Golden Rule" towards the living beings on our planet. We cannot ask for help as an equal until we start acting that way.

The second rule talks about how we all are part of many realities. The consequences of our actions extend beyond this reality. Experiencers have a glimpse of this during their interactions with ETs. These glimpses make them a more likely messenger than others. It is no coincidence that the UFO phenomenon took center stage after we started exploding nuclear weapons. If we are part of a larger reality than our three-dimensional world, we are likely creating problems with our new weapons on a multidimensional level. Experiencers have been part of other realities not seen by our physical world-based scientists. Perhaps they should be listened to by others.

Finally, the third rule (*monitor your thoughts*) seems to be at the heart of humanity's problem. We react from a place of fear first when dealing with others. We have dividing lines on the ground. We have dividing lines based on religion, skin color, and in so many other ways.

We are destroying our planet and will not be bailed out by ETs. We seem to have retained our free will, even if it means we will destroy ourselves. Our Nationalism (*tribalism*) is our biggest weakness and will be our downfall. ETs will not help as we fight each other.

These messages indicate we are close to the brink and need to change. Experiencers are the messengers that are being ignored by mankind. They need to be listened to before it is too late. When you look at the moral and ethical implications of this new wave of Experiencers, it is easy to see why ETs are focused on these "messages." We need to get our act together before we ask for help or qualify to join a greater community. Experiencers are but one voice in the chorus of voices asking that we treat each other with respect. We need to look to the needs of others first since we "are all one." Perhaps the Experiencers discussed in this book are pointing out that we are getting what we truly need from ET at a time when we need it most. Before we need technology, we need a moral compass.

About the Authors

Yvonne Smith

Upon graduating from the California Hypnosis Motivation Institute in 1991 as a Certified Hypnotherapist, she immediately began to work with Post Traumatic Stress Disorder (*PTSD*) victims. She observed through hypnotherapy what many of her subjects described as a pattern of Alien Abduction or other Close Encounter experiences.

Since she felt group therapy would assist in their trauma recovery, Yvonne founded Close Encounter Research Organization (*CERO*) in 1992 which conducts monthly meetings to this day.

In addition to maintaining personal contact with her clients, she has traveled extensively, lecturing about the recollections of her subjects' close encounters described during hypnotherapy at M.I.T. and other American universities and conferences as well as several international conferences from Europe to South America.

During the 1990s, Yvonne traveled extensively with her abduction research colleagues Budd Hopkins, David Jacobs, Ph.D., John Carpenter, MSW, LCSW and the late John Mack, M.D. as a participant in a lecture series.

Comfortable in front of cameras, Yvonne's many television appearances have included programs such as *The Joan Rivers Show*, *Montel Williams Show*, *History Channel*, *MSNBC*, *The Discovery Channel*, *Encounters*, *Sightings*, *Roseanne Barr* and *The Leeza Show*. In addition, well known radio hosts, Art Bell, Paul Harvey, Dr. David Viscott, George Noory, Jerry Pippen, Joe Montaldo and Sweep/Radio Ireland have all had Yvonne as their special guest.

Yvonne has frequently been a consultant to producers, directors and actors for film and television programs.

In "*CHOSEN*," Yvonne has taken the time to reveal explicit and dramatic transcripts of clients' descriptions during hypnotherapy, their recollections of alien encounters and abductions.

James P. Lough

James attended California State University, Fullerton where he earned a Bachelor of Arts in Political Science. In 1979, he earned his Juris Doctor degree from Southwestern University School of Law in Los Angeles where he was a Member of the Law Review and a national semi-finalist on the Phillip Jessup International Law Moot Court team. In 1980, he received his Master of Laws (LL.M) in Urban Studies from Washington University School of Law in St. Louis, Missouri. Mr. Lough is a member of the California State Bar. He is also admitted to practice

before all the Federal District Courts in California and the Ninth Circuit Court of Appeals.

Mr. Lough has published numerous articles for various legal publications, including *Duquesne Law Review*, *California Public Law Journal* and *Western Cities Magazine*. He is also a co-editor of the 2001 edition of the *Municipal Law Handbook*, published by the League of California Cities.

Since 1980, he has specialized in municipal law, election law and constitutional law. James has served as a City Attorney, County Counsel and Special Counsel for a variety of local governments throughout California. He lives in rural San Diego County with his wife of forty-one years, Martha, and his mother, Donna. Martha and Jim have two adult children.

Made in the USA
Columbia, SC
16 May 2024

35404273R00154